Blood, Sweat & Gears

The Story of the Gray Ghost and the Junkyard Firebird

by

David G. Barnes

TELEMACHUS PRESS

This book is a work of historical fiction. But for the main characters and historically accurate places and events, the names, characters, places and incidents are either the product of the author's imagination or are used fictitiously. Any resemblance to other actual persons, living or dead, or to other actual events or locales is entirely coincidental.

BLOOD, SWEAT & GEARS

The publisher does not have any control over and does not assume any responsibility for author or third-party websites or their content.

Cover designed by Telemachus Press, LLC

Cover photos by Theodore Roc Lambiris

Cover art:
Copyright © iStockphoto/13018042_fcknimages

Published by Telemachus Press, LLC
http://www.telemachuspress.com

ISBN: 978-1-941536-45-2 (eBook)
ISBN: 978-1-941536-46-9 (Paperback)

Version 2014.10.15

Printed in the United States of America

10 9 8 7 6 5 4 3 2 1

Acknowledgements

Blood, Sweat & Gears

Thank you to each of the following people; without your contributions and/or support this book would not have been written or published:

- Heidi Barnes
- Herb Adams
- M. Joan Barnes
- Emma Barnes
- Colin Barnes
- Al Rucka
- Sandi Adams
- Bob Tullius
- Milt Minter
- Joe Brady
- Tom Nell
- Ted Lambiris
- Harry Quackenboss
- Jonathan Brelsford
- Susanne Fox
- Lori Stone-Handelman, PhD of Clear Voice Editing
- Mike Miletic, MD
- Kevin Rushton
- Gail Wambsgans

- Steve Jackson of Telemachus Press
- Karen Lieberman, PhD of Telemachus Press
- Susan Adams, of Susan Adams Photography

This book is a fictional account of actual historical events. It's based on a true story but is not purely factual. Memories of the people who lived this story have faded since the early 1970s. Over 40 years had passed at the point this book was published. Also, this book does not purport to be a scholarly, historical publication with footnotes, annotations and sources. Rather, it contains creative elements. The dialogue is largely fictitious and some events have been changed or excluded. For example, the description of one race in 1971 has not been included here because, while at least one historical document indicated that the Trans-Action team raced there, Herb Adams has no recollection of it. Also, one of the characters in this book (Jim) is fictitious; he did not participate as a team member in 1971 and 1972, but he is loosely based on a young man who was, in fact, a member of the team during their brief 1973 NASCAR season. His real name has been lost to history (so far).

Dedication

To my wife Heidi, our children Emma and Colin and my parents Joan and Gordon.

"Don't talk to me about aesthetics or tradition ... what the American people like, is to think the underdog still has a chance."

–George Steinbrenner

Blood, Sweat & Gears

Chapter 1

MILT MINTER WINCED at the earsplitting blast echoing from below him on the bridge abutment. "Jesus *Christ*," he shouted, recoiling. For a moment he thought the overpass would collapse and he white-knuckled the railing. Minter stared incredulously at the smoking wreck below as if it were a fleeting vision from a nightmare.

The shock wave from the massive collision rolled through him and across the racetrack like a thunderclap. The sounds of the crash, an alien reverberation of squealing rubber and crunching metal, hung in the pure, still Wisconsin air. Broken glass, tinkling onto the warm asphalt, punctuated the smoking silence. An indifferent raven flew overhead. Minter glanced wide-eyed at it before regaining his senses and running off the bridge to the aid of his fellow driver. The ring of distant church bells wafted absently over the abruptly silent track.

The Firebird racing pit crew, like everyone in the vicinity of the racetrack, heard the crash. They *felt* it. They knew who it was. Their car was the only one on the racetrack; their driver was practicing. The racetrack's emergency crew immediately swung into action, racing toward the crash site at the bridge abutment, sirens blaring. Moments later the crew extricated the bloodied, unconscious driver from the remnants of his Firebird and rushed him to the hospital.

A few days later the driver died.

Several minutes before the crash, the Firebird driver had pulled slowly out of the pit and driven his team's blue and white Pontiac Firebird onto the Road America racetrack in Elkhart Lake, Wisconsin. Road America was built in the mid-1950s to meet the demands of amateur drivers in Chicago who, in the 1940s and early 1950s, drove up to Elkhart Lake on the week-ends to race on the old highways circling it. It was a good-sized track, four miles around with plenty of 90-degree turns, running clockwise in an L-shape. The start-finish line was halfway up the main straightaway. The first official race on the Road America track was held in 1955. By the summer of 1970, fifteen years later, five bridges spanned the track in various places, allowing pedestrian and vehicle access to the infield and paddocks. Some of these bridges were built with reinforced concrete.

On that warm July day, another Trans-Am driver, Milt Minter, had just spoken to the Firebird driver about the upcoming race. The driver was no stranger to Trans-Am racing, having won the series driver's championship a few years earlier. Minutes later, Minter stood on one of the bridges watching him drive—sizing up his competition. As the Firebird racing team looked on from pit road, its driver took the powerful Pontiac Firebird skillfully around the course, cutting the apexes, smoothly braking, upshifting, downshifting, and accelerating at all the right places on the track. He was a professional driver and it clearly showed, thought Minter.

But then something went terribly wrong.

The driver hit the brakes hard, spewing blue-black smoke and a wicked screech from its big slicks. A split second later it collided head-on with a concrete bridge abutment at high speed. No spectator experienced the thundering crash and vibration more immediately and personally than Milt Minter on the overpass above.

Chapter 2

PONTIAC MOTOR DIVISION product engineer Herb Adams sat in his suburban Detroit living room after work, watching a small black and white television flicker to life as he settled on his couch with a can of cheap, cold beer. The voices of his small children reverberated throughout his modest home. Still in his thirties, he stood a trim five feet ten inches with neatly cut brown hair and sparkling brown eyes to match. Adams ran Pontiac's Special Projects Group, which meant that his part-time responsibility was to provide engineering support to Pontiac's racing efforts in an effort to bolster GM's sales.

On the evening news, the announcer reported a confrontation between the Black Panthers and police in Philadelphia. With simultaneous raids on three locations, fifteen Panthers were arrested, one policeman was killed, and seven were severely wounded. He went on to note that the trial of singer Jim Morrison, charged with lewd and lascivious behavior, continued in Florida. Adams shook his head slowly at the little TV.

The memory of their driver haunted Pontiac's Special Projects engineers, and they threw themselves into their work in an attempt to move on from their grief and to avoid the problems absorbing America—the war, the fallout from the Kent State shootings, and the increasingly aggressive, anti-war hippies. The national news provided a constant and uncomfortable distraction that propped open the heavy, creaking door they so desperately wanted to slam shut and deadbolt.

As if the national news were not bad enough, Pontiac's engineers heard rumors at work that hit them in the gut: the UAW was talking about a strike against General Motors in September. The thought of 240,000 unionized GM workers walking off their factory jobs was difficult to fathom for Adams and his engineers. Vehicle manufacturing at the world's largest corporation would immediately grind to a halt. But GM's engineers—salaried, non-union employees—would keep working.

Morale in the Special Projects Group was clearly low, but Adams was upbeat. He had a plan.

~~~~

Herb Adams knew Pontiac's history. He'd worked there nearly a decade as a product engineer. General Motors created the Pontiac Motor Division in the mid-1920s, taking its name from the town of Pontiac, Michigan, about 30 miles northwest of Detroit, which itself was named for an Indian chief. In fact, it was Chief Pontiac who inspired the division's original Indian head logo. By 1929, Pontiac was selling more than 200,000 cars a year, but then came the stock market crash and the Great Depression. Although GM suffered greatly, it fared better during the Depression than many of its numerous competitors. In 1931, GM managed to sell more cars than any other company in the world, including Ford. This success was largely due to one man, GM's elixir: Alfred P. Sloan, Jr. Even then, Sloan was becoming widely acknowledged as a business genius. When Sloan took GM's operational helm as president in the 1920s, tiny GM was one of more than 100 carmakers in the United States. When he retired from the company in 1956 at the age of 81, GM was not only the largest carmaker in the world, it was the biggest industrial organization the world had ever seen.

GM had been incorporated by the colorful William Crapo Durant in September 1908. Well-funded financially and emotionally after GM's early success, Durant went on a business buying spree. Luckily, one of Durant's many business acquisitions for GM brought Al Sloan, Jr., who worked for one of the acquired companies. Sloan wasted little time in demonstrating his leadership prowess at the small but rapidly growing GM. Sloan was rewarded commensurately, in the form of raises and rapid promotions. As

GM's president, Sloan's most formidable competitor was the Ford Motor Company, which operated under the iron fist of its famed founder, Henry. When Henry clung to Model T production for too long during the 1920s, Sloan exploited the mistake with the introduction of new GM models and raced ahead of Ford in market share. Ford finally introduced the Model A in the late 1920s, but it was too late to catch Sloan's roaring GM.

Sloan created his corporate goliath in large part by decentralizing all but the financial operations of the company. With some notable exceptions, each of the main GM divisions were largely responsible for their own manufacturing, engineering, purchasing and other business activities, except finance; Sloan himself kept responsibility for the numbers.

GM's Pontiac Motor Division was part of Sloan's legacy. Sloan recognized a basic manufacturing problem at GM: Pontiac and Chevrolet were working too hard at the wrong things and wasting resources as a result of independently engineering and manufacturing their respective cars. Sloan's solution was to order his Chevrolet and Pontiac factories to share each other's automobile components, and on the sales side of GM's business, Sloan ordered Buick, Oldsmobile, and Pontiac dealerships to combine. In 1934, Sloan organized GM into three basic car divisions: Cadillac, Chevrolet, and Buick-Olds-Pontiac.

In the midst of these commercial changes, Pontiac continued to focus on product engineering and introduced a car called the Pontiac Eight, engineered by Benjamin Anibal—and well-styled by Frank Hershy, both of whom worked for Ford refugee William S. "Big Bill" Knudsen at Pontiac. Anibal's engineering team designed a powerful straight eight engine and a new, smooth riding, independent front suspension they called "knee-action." The car became a hit. Thanks to the Pontiac Eight, by 1937 the Division's sales were back to more than 200,000 units, establishing Pontiac as a major carmaker.

By the late 1950s, Pontiacs with names like Star Chief and Chieftain were relatively low-slung, wide, and powerful cars. And Pontiac was becoming known as a performance car maker. This image was reinforced by the introduction of the 1961 Pontiac Tempest, which Herb Adams had helped design; the Tempest had a transaxle and good performance from its four-cylinder engine.

Sloan's incredibly successful corporate setup eventually led GM to a 50 percent share of the American automobile market in the US in the early 1970s. This attracted the attention of the anti-trust people in Washington, DC, not to mention GM's competitors, many of whom advocated the breakup of GM in the interest of the American consumer. GM was simply too big, they said. GM could dictate new car prices, they argued. The solution to GM's market dominance, some advocated, was to separate the largest GM division—Chevrolet—from GM itself. Chevy should be a standalone car company. It was already vertically integrated to a large extent anyway.

For Pontiac's product engineers in the late 1960s and early 1970s, competition among and between GM divisions found no better avenue for expression than on the racetrack. At Pontiac, Herb Adams' engineers in the Special Projects group wanted to beat their siblings at Chevy and everyone else on the racetracks—particularly the Trans-Am racetracks, road courses that tested the true measure of a car. Not just acceleration, but handling. Racing is at least as much about engineering as driving, maybe more. And what better way to test their engineering skills than with a race car of their own design on a road track under harsh, real world racing conditions?

Three major types of American racing existed in 1970: NASCAR stock car racing on big ovals, USAC open wheeled racing, and Trans-Am road racing, which was a showcase for carmakers. Small, affordable, high-powered coupes—the Ford Mustang, Chevy Camaro, Pontiac Firebird, Plymouth Barracuda, Dodge Challenger, American Motors Javelin, and the Mercury Cougar—had become so popular that manufacturers were willing to sponsor professional racing teams to showcase the cars in hopes that the fans would shell out the money to buy one for themselves. The Trans-Am series began in March 1966 at Florida's Sebring racetrack and ran through the summer at tracks across the U.S. and later expanded to Canadian tracks. The factories supported the racing series with their own engineers and big budgets. As a result, Trans-Am attracted big crowds and some of the biggest names in racing.

The Pontiac engineers knew that racing was, and remains, largely a test of applied engineering. They yearned to shuck the binding shell of GM's corporate culture by building fast cars and competing with them on race tracks. They wanted to *win*. Racing has a very clear goal—you either win or you don't. That's it. This black and white measurement appealed to the engineers. Success on the racetrack didn't depend on how you parted your hair or laughed at the boss's jokes in the office or factory. Rather, success was measured by plotting lines and calculating numbers, then bending metal and twisting wrenches accordingly. It was a test of their engineering brains, judgment, and sweat. It was pure, it was competitive, and man, it was *fun*.

Chapter 3

SANDI ADAMS, A slim and attractive brunette in her 30s, pulled into her suburban Detroit garage, parked, and began unloading groceries from the long, cavernous trunk of her old faded Pontiac Le Mans. Once upon a time it had been a nice car, but she didn't fully trust the seven- or eight- or nine- or whatever-year-old thing, especially with so many miles on it. It made funny noises occasionally, creaks and groans, and it seemed the rust on the body was spreading every day, leaving brown crumbs and flakes on the garage floor. One day Herb would finally relent and agree to buy her a nice new one; he'd better, anyway. Even a used one would be an improvement over this rattletrap. She just hoped it happened before the Le Mans broke down on the highway somewhere.

Herb Adams was thinking, too, as he drove home from work. He'd pitched an idea: With a hopped-up factory Firebird, Pontiac could win the 1971 Trans-Am championship series. Citing an all but forgotten 1963 edict from headquarters banning Pontiac from any racing involvement, his boss had shot down the idea unilaterally. Adams had never been this fed up with Pontiac. If John DeLorean were still at Pontiac, they'd be racing. DeLorean appreciated performance; he was the father of the Pontiac GTO, the first muscle car. But DeLorean was gone from GM and Pontiac was more risk averse now. The product engineers were on their own.

Adams drove into his neighborhood and a neighbor's dog, running full tilt across a front lawn, began his daily routine of chasing Adams' car. It was a medium-sized, short-haired, brown mutt with pointy ears and a clear hatred of cars. The dog ran out in front of him, barking madly; Adams swerved around it, as usual, and drove on. The dog soon tired of the chase, turned and trotted home, apparently satisfied in the knowledge that he had scared off yet another four-wheeled invader. Adams pulled into his driveway and parked.

For just a moment Adams examined his house. The exterior of his home was immaculate, and he drew some satisfaction from it. Not a hint of peeling paint, stained shingles, or even oil drippings on the driveway. The shrubs were neatly pruned and every blade of closely clipped bright green fescue and bluegrass stood at attention, stoically awaiting the first snowfall. Not a weed in sight. Only a few crisp orange, red, yellow and brown leaves littered the October lawn.

Parked ahead of him in the open garage was his wife's 1964 Pontiac Le Mans sedan. Adams hauled himself out of his car and absently made his way into the garage past the Le Mans toward the house door, still thinking about the racing problem. He stopped next to his wife's car as a thought struck him so hard his head spun for a moment.

He turned, squinting at the Le Mans and cocked his head slightly.

Adams' eyes darted around the old machine ... no ... that would be *ridiculous*. His heartbeat accelerated.

The Le Mans was the luxury version of the GTO, which was built on a Tempest chassis. In fact, the GTO was the performance version of the Tempest, and was a big part of Pontiac's performance image. The GTO, *Gran Turismo Omologato*. DeLorean had known he couldn't just create a new hot rod model because it would breach GM's policy that limited engine size relative to the new model's weight. So DeLorean and his engineers devised a way around the limitation: They wouldn't create a *new model*, they'd use an *existing* car, call it an *optional version* of an existing model, and stick a monster engine in it. The new car wouldn't really be a new model; rather, it would simply be an optional version of the Tempest, a nice conservative car.

They did it. Adams remembered—he'd lived it. Pontiac's use of the GTO designation for a mere sedan enraged some automotive purists. Previously only Ferrari had used the GTO moniker. But so what? The GTO became a source of justifiable pride at Pontiac. It was a great, affordable performance car with a growing, cult-like following of enthusiasts.

Adams was sure Pontiac had homologated the GTO—certified it for racing by the Sports Car Club of America—back in 1964 or so.

With some engine and chassis modifications, Sandi's car could be made race-eligible for Trans-Am racing; he'd just need to convert it to GTO specifications. Adams knew the car. Hell, he'd *engineered* part of it. As a young design development engineer on the 1964 Tempest, Adams designed the admittedly unglamorous air conditioning system, defroster and heating duct. The job had been pure torture. In 1969, when Adams was engineering new product proposals in Pontiac's Advanced Design Department, DeLorean recognized that the competitors' muscle cars had caught up to, and even surpassed, his GTO. Sales numbers reflected the problem.

In typical GM fashion, a multi-department committee was formed to study and solve the problem. DeLorean introduced Adams to the committee at one of their early meetings. Adams sat down at the committee's table, uninvited, but with the tacit approval of the big boss. He attended subsequent meetings without waiting for a formal invitation. To his astonishment, he soon learned that Pontiac's sales and marketing people on the committee had the solution to the GTO's problem: turn the GTO into a nice luxury touring car.

Adams objected to this crazy idea. The GTO was a *performance* car, he told them. The *Le Mans* was already the luxury version. The debate raged for months, and Adams was unrelenting. Finally, the committee agreed to beef up the GTO's performance. DeLorean, who had been determined to hop-up the GTO all along, made Herb Adams the lead engineer in charge of engineering the GTO's required performance enhancements. Adams and his team soon did just that. The result was a GTO called *The Judge*; DeLorean named it himself, after Flip Wilson's character on Rowan and Martin's *Laugh-In* TV show. The Judge was an instant success. Although Adams wasn't invited to any of Pontiac's sales and marketing parties, the GTO had been saved.

~~~~

Adams smiled inwardly, staring intently at his wife's drab, dark aqua car. He ran through the specs and thought through the possibilities. The '64 Tempest had a 326-cubic inch engine with lots of blow-by and a two-speed powerglide transmission. But the engine could be bored out to 400 or so and then de-stroked to the maximum 305 displacement Trans-Am racing limit. That should put out about 450 horsepower—consistently too, if they did it right, and maybe more. A nice flat torque curve too, he'd bet. Or they could drop another engine in—a 400 or so cubic incher—and work from there. Thanks to the green light from the engine boss at work, Tom Nell and Jeff Young had already perfected a nice 303 engine for Pontiac racing that put out 460 horsepower at 8,000 rpm, just as much as Chevy or Ford, and it was legal for Trans-Am racing. Put a racing transmission in it. Tweak the chassis—he could do that himself—and put some Corvette-style brakes, a roll cage, and big gumball Goodyear or Firestone tires on it. This old goat would *move!* It would certainly compete with the smaller pony cars, and it would be relatively cheap to do.

A grin crept across Adams' face. His mind was racing now. The car wasn't worth much in its current state and Sandi would be only too happy to part with it. They had the money at the moment to buy her a new car, not a *brand* new car, but she wouldn't mind … maybe. Adams looked at the car's dingy body and noticed a rust spot. It was also a little crispy around the rocker panels—the rust could be sanded or filled in. He looked around the rest of the body quickly. And the many other rust spots could do with a bit of filling, as well.

As a racer, the old Tempest body would undoubtedly attract some attention, but so what if the body was a seven-year-old sedan? It's the guts that matter, the powertrain and chassis mostly, and Adams had just the team to create those guts. A team of some of the best automotive product engineers at the world's largest car company, a team with two years of hands-on racing engineering experience. They were heads-up guys, each a system specialist. Each had the sources, know-how, and contacts to procure all the right racing components needed to trick out the Le Mans. Not only did they know how to hop up a car, they all knew where to buy the serious racing hardware necessary to do it. They'd be an after-hours, energetic, volunteer team that would split the racing expenses and proceeds. Who needs factory sponsorship? Their ideas, which had been rejected by last year's racing team, and even Pontiac itself, could finally be put to a real world test. No more frustration; they would have complete control. They would carry the Pontiac standard against the competition even if Pontiac Motor Division wouldn't! If only the boss wouldn't stand in the way. Adams took a long look at the Le Mans, this time in a whole new light, smiled broadly, turned and entered the house.

"You look happy," said Sandi. "I like a happy husband. Good day at work?" she asked in her typically perky manner. They quickly kissed.

"Not really. In fact, it was lousy. The boss shut down the Pontiac racing program."

Sandi's brow crinkled. "What?"

"We'll still support Billy Joe, but only for the rest of the year."

"Oh, I'm sorry honey, I know you love racing. But why so happy with such bad news?"

"I'll tell you in a minute. Listen baby, I think it's time you had a new car, don't you?" Herb said somewhat eagerly.

Sandi's eyes widened in surprise, then she squinted at her husband for some sign that he was kidding. "*What?*" she asked suspiciously.

"Really," Herb said. "That old jalopy's got 75,000 miles on it by now, doesn't it?"

"80,000 plus," said Sandi rather incredulously. She hooked her thick brown hair behind an ear, listening intently now.

"And you got it used from my old man."

"Yeah," Sandi said slowly. "And you know I've been wanting—really *needing*—a new car for years now. In fact, I was just thinking about it today."

"Yep, and I think it's time you got one! I mean, maybe not a brand new one, but a car you could really rely on and you'd like," he said, smiling widely.

Sandi studied her husband. "You're lying. You must have had a real good day. Did they promote you or something?"

"I'm not lying about the lousy day at work or a new car for you or anything else. No promotion, *that's* for sure. And the chief engineer really did pull the plug on any Pontiac-sponsored racing now and in the future." Herb waved the back of his hand in disgust.

Sandi crossed her arms. "So you had a lousy day at work, yet you're happy, and you want to buy me a new car. What gives?"

"Okay, okay," said Herb, sitting down on the sofa. Sandi sat next to him, still studying his face. "Listen. Pontiac pulled the plug on the racing program, but the program was screwed up anyway, I think. Pontiac didn't give us much of a budget. The racing team didn't take all our engineering advice and their results showed it. Even the boss knows that. Maybe we are just a bunch of desk engineers, but we know what we're doing, and the boss knows that, too."

"Yes," said Sandi, "and so do I, the way you've been bellyaching about that team to me for the last 18 months."

"Yeah, well … sorry. Anyway, my guys in Special Projects went from frustration to disappointment today when I gave them the news. So I got an idea to help 'em feel better."

"What idea?"

"Promise you won't laugh or think I'm crazy?"

Sandi groaned.

"*Promise?*" asked Herb.

"Okay, I promise. What is it?"

"It's an idea that will get you a new car."

"Oh, come on—that's not crazy, it's wonderful!" Sandi said, bewildered. "Is that the idea?"

"Well, part of it."

Sandi looked sideways at her husband. "What's the other part?" she asked flatly, the smile fading quickly from her pretty face.

"The other part is about your Le Mans. It's not worth much, you know. Wouldn't really be worth it to sell it."

She paused, thinking. "You want it … *you want my Le Mans!*"

"Well, yes." Herb looked at his young wife hopefully.

"What for?" Sandi asked, leaning slightly toward her husband. "You already have a company car. Come on, spill the beans!"

Herb scratched his head.

"Oh, my *God*," Sandi said, sitting upright and looking away with an expression of astonishment slowly growing over her face. "You want to *race* it!" She looked back at her husband, wide-eyed. "You want to *race* my Le Mans?"

Herb smiled at his wife, feeling strangely grateful that he didn't have to express it.

"You can't be serious—that old bucket of bolts? It from the 1950s!" Sandi blurted.

"No, 1964 actually," said Herb, still smiling. "It's the same basic car as the GTO. It's homologated and could be easily hopped up to Trans-Am racing specs and it ..."

"Homolo *what?*" interrupted Sandi.

"Homologated. That means it's already certified as a racer."

"My Le Mans is a certified racer? Did you stop at the bar on the way home, Herb?"

"I'm very sober, Sandi. And I've got a great team of racing engineers at Pontiac who have everything it takes to turn that car into a real racing machine and mount our own campaign. We don't need factory backing. Hell, my guys would jump at the chance—no more frustration. We'd have complete control over the car. We'd make that old boat scream!"

"Hey! How dare you call my poor car an old boat!" Sandi looked out the window for a moment and then back at Herb. "So one day it's hauling groceries and the next it's zinging around a race track?" Sandi put a delicate hand over her mouth, her eyes widening again. "Who would risk driving it? Not *you!*" she said, with alarm in her voice.

"No, no, not me—we'd find a driver. A good one. A pro—you know, a guy who does it for a living. We developed a lot of contacts in racing over the past two years. Hey, what's the matter with calling it an old boat anyway? You called the Tempest a 'bucket of bolts' or something a minute ago." Herb grinned at his wife.

She didn't appear amused. "It's a *Le Mans*—not a mere Tempest. Anyway, what about money? I know you're good engineers and all, but you can't compete with the financial clout of Ford, Chevy, Dodge and American Motors. And how will you *pay* a professional driver?" Sandi asked, waving her hands about.

"Money? We don't need corporate money. What we lack in money we'll make up for in hard work and engineering. We'll all pitch in a few bucks. We won't be burdened by politics or anything either. And we'll pay the driver a percentage of our winnings. That'll be an incentive for him."

Sandi sighed. "Well, no offense sweetie, but you won't exactly get A.J. Foyt to drive a seven- or eight-year-old antique for a part of the winnings at a Trans-Am race, will you? I mean, I'm sure the car will really go lickety-split once you're finished with it, but the purse isn't very big, is it? And what about time? Where will you find time to fix up the Le Mans—the *Tempest*—and then get it to those far-flung tracks and actually race?"

"Vacation time. My guys love racing, and they love Pontiac. They'll be willing to invest some vacation time on this. And I know some drivers who'd do this. I think."

Sandi studied the wall. "Throw in a few bucks? Blow your vacation time? Skin your knuckles after-hours and on the weekends? All for the prospect of maybe winning a little prize money? I think you're *nuts*." She looked skeptically at her husband. "But if it gets me a new car and makes you happy, I guess I'm for it."

Herb kissed his wife on the forehead and hugged her.

Chapter 4

HERB ADAMS BOUNDED out of bed before the alarm clock sounded at 5:30 a.m. He quickly showered and shaved, all the while thinking of the new racing project and how he would pitch it to the guys at work. He'd tossed and turned much of the night, and his eyes were burning slightly from lack of sleep. The Tempest was the last thing he thought about before going to bed and first thing he thought about in the morning. He'd even had some kind of half-conscious dream about it, but he could only remember a blue-green behemoth with four huge, black tires.

An anti-war rock tune played on the tinny car radio as Adams drove to work, but he heard none of it. He'd decided to spring the idea on his guys immediately, just to make sure they were willing. Putting up their own money would likely be the only potential obstacle for them—or more importantly, for their wives. The wives could make or break this effort. Vacations and even some money would be willingly sacrificed by the guys for racing, especially Pontiac racing, but Adams acknowledged to himself that he had little control over the wives. None of his guys had much money, having relatively recently graduated from college or graduate school. No doubt their wives were acutely aware of this sad fact. Anyway, assuming he got the commitment from his guys, he would go to the boss and get Pontiac's blessing.

Did he really need the blessing of the Pontiac hierarchy if this were done after hours with their own money and sweat? Then again, Pontiac employed them all, and Pontiac made the Tempest. And Pontiac had really soured on racing. The safest bet would be to get the consent of his boss, the chief engineer, as well as his lieutenants. The timing was right; Adams had seen in his boss's face that he derived no pleasure in delivering the message that Pontiac had pulled out of racing, even apologizing—rare behavior for the boss.

Yes, now was the time, while the boss still perhaps felt some guilt about pulling the racing plug and terribly disappointing the Special Projects guys. The boss needed these guys for product engineering on both production and future cars, and Pontiac knew it. They were talented, smart, practical, experienced, highly educated, and not easily or quickly replaced. Without strong product engineering, you soon wither and die in the car business because your new product pipeline slows to a trickle. Chevy, Ford, Chrysler and AMC were relentless competitors, so the morale of the Special Projects guys at Pontiac was important to GM. The boss would get it. He wouldn't stand in the way of an after-hours racing effort. He couldn't stop them anyway. This was none of Pontiac's business.

~~~~

Adams strode into his little office, flicked on the bare fluorescent ceiling lights, pulled a pad of paper from the desk drawer, and began scratching out a list. Tom Nell was first on the list; he would be key. An engine and driveline specialist with tremendous energy, physical strength, brains, and creativity to boot, Adams recalled that Nell had a bachelor's degree in mechanical engineering from Penn State. Nell was young, but he was one hell of an automotive engineer. He was the hardest worker Adams had ever met, and he loved racing; the level of his involvement with the Firebird racing team made that clear. It was Nell who suggested many of the best engine and drivetrain ideas. Without him, the project might not even be worth pursuing. Adams resolved to get Nell's commitment first.

Next on the list Adams wrote the name Jeff Young, another engine and driveline guy. An internal combustion engine specialist, too. Very bright. He had a private pilot's license. B.S. in mechanical engineering from GMI—the General Motors Institute—and even better, a master's degree in mechanical engineering from MIT. But all these impressive academic credentials didn't get in the way of practical results with Jeffie; he wasn't afraid to get his hands dirty. Jeffie was young, only 26 or 27, but few people knew GM powertrains better.

Adams looked down at the paper and wrote another name: Joe Brady. A great chassis and suspension engineer. Only about 24 years old, but man, he was a real gearhead and was nuts about car racing. Very bright, talkative, intense, and ambitious. Another GMI mechanical engineering graduate. The chassis and suspension, like the engine, would require extensive work and Joe could be of great help on the Tempest. He was single, too, so there would be little competition for his time.

Dutch Scheppleman was next on the list, Pontiac's "senior experimental technician." That was the official job title, but in reality he was a very highly skilled and experienced machinist and metal fabricator. A crusty, chain smoking, hands-on shop floor type skilled tradesman, Dutch had his own machine shop at home and could perform all kinds of special fabrication work. He was a practical, salt of the earth guy who wasn't above telling his boss Herb Adams to go to hell. Trouble was, the UAW was on strike against GM at the moment, which meant *Dutch* was also on strike at the moment ... but maybe that wouldn't matter. GM wasn't behind this effort. It wasn't *work*. Hell, Dutch was probably bored out his mind by now, with nothing to do at home but putter in his shop on some pointless little jobs and chain smoke. He was a bit of a character, but he could fabricate *anything* out of metal. And Dutch, after thinking for a while—sometimes a *long* while—could convert the engineers' ideas into reality in the machine shop.

The Tempest would need significant modifications to the fuel system. Adams wrote "The Greek" on his pad of paper. Theodore Roc Lambiris was a senior layout artist in Pontiac's transmission and axle group. A born extravert who could talk his way into—or out of—anything, he had a huge network of friends and acquaintances, and could make friends faster than a hooker at a playboy convention. More importantly, the Greek knew racing. He'd won the Spring Drag Racing Nationals at Detroit Dragway in 1965, driving a '66 GTO. A natural risk-taker, Lambiris was also a paratrooper in the Army reserves. The Greek was a character, but at Pontiac, he'd proven himself as a whiz-bang fuel systems guy and good on gauges and dashboard equipment also. Maybe he could help with body rust, too; grunt work, but somebody had to do it.

They would have to get the Tempest to the races somehow. Just getting to the track was an important and sometimes challenging part of racing. "Transportation, car, and driver support," that's what the Firebird racing team called it. Maybe Tom Goad would help. Tom was Pontiac's product-planning manager. Adams would have Sandi's new car for towing … maybe. Anyway, Goad had an open flatbed trailer. The Tempest would surely fit. There were two others, Terry Satchell and Dan Hardin. Both were brilliant automotive engineers, but both were broke, fresh out of college, and still single. They were worth asking.

These were Adams' guys. Not a professional driver among them, only engineers who sat at desks for most of the day. But they were smart, hands-on guys, much more than mere pencil pushers. Adams looked at the telephone. His mind raced through the famous names of the pro drivers on the Trans-Am circuit. All were spoken for by professional, big money, or factory-sponsored outfits. No doubt they were paid well too, as Sandi reminded him last night. It wasn't like a few years earlier when Trans-Am racing was young, when little or no money was needed to race competitively. Bob Tullius had won that first Trans-Am in '66 or so when he was still working for Kodak. Won it in a Dodge Dart. He also won the Marlboro 12 Hour and the Citrus 250 in '67, all in that same Dart. Bob was racing full time now, a pro. He was one of the top ranked drivers in the SCCA and had been for years, with a great winning record in the SCCA driving Triumphs and something like four or five national championships. He was the head of a bunch of British Leyland drivers—Group 44, Inc., out of Falls Church, Virginia. Bob had a lot of contacts in racing, too.

Yes. An old buddy. Bob Tullius might drive for Adams.

~~~~

"Hey, what are you doin' here so early, Herb?" Adams immediately recognized the voice of Tom Nell, always the first guy in the office. Always boundless energy, optimism and enthusiasm, at least when it came to automotive engineering and racing.

"Oh, morning Tom. Just thinking about something."

"What's up?" asked Nell. "Something wrong? Oh, you're thinking about our driver's death. I'm sorry, Herb, I shouldn't have—"

"No, no Tom," Adams interrupted. "It's not him, it's an idea I have, an idea I think he would have liked—a racing idea."

Nell quickly looked up and down the empty hall, stepped into Adams' office, and shut the door behind him. "Well, cough it up, man."

Adams cleared his throat, summoning his courage. "Uh, well, I want to campaign a car in the Trans-Am series next year without any sponsorship from Pontiac, and I want your help to do it."

Nell paused, studying Adams' face. Adams was serious. "Whose car?"

"Mine. Actually, my wife's. It's a '64 Le Mans, you know, a fancy Tempest. We could trick it out pretty good. It'll take some money, though, and a lot of time and work."

Nell looked out the window. He wasn't laughing, nor did he appear to be incredulous or shocked either.

Adams broke the silence. "It's got some miles on it, but we could—"

Nell interrupted, "The GTO's got the same chassis as the Tempest. The '64 Tempest, it's homologated, isn't it?"

"Yes." Adams smiled.

Nell smiled back at him, his eyes sparkling. "When do we start?"

~~~~

Adams now had his wife and a key guy on board, but he and Nell couldn't do it by themselves. Adams decided to talk to Jeff Young next. Jeff was likely to be in a funk about yesterday and maybe springing the project on him would bring him out of it.

"Morning, Jeffie," Adams said to the young engineer slouched at his desk and staring down. "How you doing?"

Jeff, a thin brown-haired 30-something, looked up at his boss. "I'm for shit."

"Yeah. Well listen, I've got an idea that may cheer you up. I thought of a way to get us back into racing."

Jeff sat up in his chair. "How? There's no way Pontiac will back us. You said the boss was kind of blunt about it."

"Not Pontiac-sponsored racing, our own racing. We campaign our own car with no factory backing. No big money racing team support either, just us."

Jeff's eyes widened.

"I've got the car," said Adams. "My '64 Tempest. It's homolo—"

"Homologated!" shouted Jeff, vaulting to his feet, wide-eyed. "Right on! I'm your man, Herbie!"

~~~~

Adams recognized the slim, six-foot frame of Joe Brady at the other end of the hall near the men's room. Brady looked at Adams and slowly shook his mop of wavy brown hair in apparent disgust of yesterday's edict. "Good Morning, Joe."

"What's good about it?" muttered Brady.

They quietly watched a secretary walk past.

"Come in here," said Adams, walking into the men's room. Adams bent down and quickly walked the length of the men's room, scanning the floors under the stalls.

"What the hell, Herb?"

"Nobody else here. Listen, Joe," Adams said, straightening up. "I know you're, well, upset about yesterday."

"Upset? I'm *pissed!* We all are. What a downer, man."

"Yeah, I know. Already talked to Nell and Young this morning. But, you know, they're feeling much, *much* better now. In fact, I believe they feel absolutely great."

"What are you up to, boss?" asked Brady, cocking his head slightly and raising an eyebrow.

"Joe, what would you think about campaigning our own car in next year's Trans-Am series?"

Joe squinted, disbelieving. "You ... you mean no factory support?"

"Exactly," said Adams, studying the young engineer's face. "We could do it. We'd have complete control over the car. We'll use my car, a '64

Tempest, and we'll use my garage. We need a good chassis and suspension guy. You'd fit the bill." Adams smiled at him.

Brady smiled back. "Who is the 'we' you just mentioned? Nell and Young?"

"Yes, they're in. Feeling better now?"

Brady looked at himself smiling in the mirror. "As a matter of fact, I am." His eyes darted back at his boss. "But that old Tempest, we'd have to reinforce the frame, I'd have to plot revised camber curves for the front end …" Brady looked at the wall, thinking fast, "… bigger steering knuckles probably … lower the body a few inches … beefed up stabilizer bars and jointed links … Koni shocks maybe … Muncie transmission and heavy duty brakes … even modify the whole suspension geometry for better cornering." He looked back at his boss as someone walked into the bathroom. "Yeah, we could do this. Hell *yes*, I'm in!" Brady whispered loudly.

~~~~

More out of guilt than obligation, Adams walked back to his office to get some actual Pontiac work done. He walked with a noticeable spring in his step. The Greek, Tom Goad, Satchell, Hardin, and Dutch Scheppleman were the only guys remaining to ask. Then he'd talk to the division, and then Tullius next month at Daytona—he would likely be there. It would be better to spring this on him in person; tougher to refuse in person than over the phone.

Adams tracked down Lambiris, Goad, Scheppleman, Satchell and Hardin that afternoon. All but Satchell and Hardin agreed to join the project—money problems, they said. Adams had no reason to doubt them. Both Satchell and Hardin agreed to help the project in any other way they could.

Was this too good to be true? The Greek, Goad and Scheppleman didn't even consult their wives. And the Greek was a former Army Ranger and current military reservist paratrooper—he jumped out of airplanes once a month; that alone was a big time commitment. Perhaps, thought Adams, he didn't adequately emphasize the enormity of this undertaking. They were not doing this to embarrass themselves. To do it right would require a huge time commitment and personal sacrifice. The car had to be ready by May and it was already October; the first Trans-Am race at Lime Rock Connecticut wouldn't wait for them. At least they had some time off work between Christmas and New Year's. They'd need it.

~~~~

Later in the day, Tom Nell told Adams about another good engineer he knew in town. The guy was also a gearhead, but he wasn't employed by Pontiac—in fact, he wasn't employed by any car company. A gearhead who wasn't in the auto industry, an anomaly in Detroit. He was employed as an engineer by a little outfit in Ann Arbor. His name was Harry Quackenboss, and he had a lot of brains, Nell said. Very professional, practical, and disciplined, too. After Nell's further assurances about Harry's automobile engineering prowess, Adams gave Nell the okay to ask him to join the project. "But if he's not a good fit, I'm bootin' him," warned Adams.

Chapter 5

HERB ADAMS STUDIED Tom Nell's furrowed brow under the bright florescent lights of his office. "Something bugging you, Tom?"

Nell sat down in an aluminum chair and slowly put his fingertips together, forming a steeple. "Just thinking."

"I can tell," said Adams with a hint of sarcasm.

Nell shot his boss a mild look of disgust. "It's just, well …"

"What? Spit it out, man."

"Do we need permission from Pontiac or something to do this?"

"To race?" asked Adams.

"Yeah. I mean, we're Pontiac guys and we're going to build and race a Pontiac. Pontiac Division just pulled the plug on racing. They clearly disapprove of it. I mean, the Pontiac driver died. So, do we need the okay from them to race?"

"Hell, no," said Adams flatly. "They can't control what we do on our own time."

Nell stared out the window, unconvinced.

Adams leaned forward in his chair. "Look, man. If we play tennis or golf on our own time, it's none of Pontiac's business, right? Same with racing. It's the sport we play on our own time. They can't stop us from doing that. And nobody's going to die. You dig?"

Nell looked at his boss and a smile crept across his face. "Yeah, guess so."

"Damn right." Adams sat back in his chair. "Now we need to incorporate or something," said Adams, "and get some time and financial commitments from the guys. Tell you what; ask all the guys you see to meet at my house Friday night at seven. We'll sign a paper that gets everybody financially committed, their jobs assigned, and establishes each guy's share of the purses that we might—no, *will*—win. Then plan our strategy. No time to lose now."

Nell pumped the air with his heavily muscled forearm and large fist.

~~~~

Later that evening, empty bottles from countless six packs of cheap beer and a few half-eaten extra-large pizzas adorned the Adams' living room coffee table. Eight men sat in various places around the room holding beer cans and talking animatedly.

"Hey guys," Herb said loudly. "First, I want to thank everybody for agreeing to participate in this project and for taking the time to be here tonight. Let me assure you, it won't be the last time you sacrifice your personal time for this effort. And there won't be any beer at our future get-togethers. Well, not as much anyway ..." A few chuckles emanated from the group. "Let me introduce Harry Quackenboss over here." A tall, dark-haired man in the corner raised his hand. Adams continued, "Harry's a friend of Tom Nell, and an engineer. He's agreed to join us in this project. Please welcome him to the team." The group nodded at the newcomer. Adams went on, "It's November already, and the first Trans-Am race of the season is at Lime Rock, Connecticut, in May. We don't have much time, but with the right planning and execution—especially execution—I'm confident that we can field a very competitive car. And not just at Lime Rock, for the entire racing season. But before we start planning, we've got to get a basic understanding of who's going to do what, how much money we'll each chip in, and what our respective shares of the winnings will be."

Some of the guys grinned at each other. The winnings. Money. They hadn't fully considered that.

Adams continued, waving a piece of paper. "So, I drew up a paper here, kind of like an incorporation document, I guess. Once we agree, I want everybody here to sign it tonight. Then we can move on to planning our strategy." Adams looked around the room at the nodding heads. "Before we divvy up the assignments, let me say something about the importance of doing everything right on this project. I want us to apply only disciplined engineering methods on the Tempest, just like at work. This is no different. Both during and after the building of each system, whether it's engine, chassis, or whatever, we will go over every system in careful detail—again, and again, and again—so that nothing that we fail to anticipate comes back to bite us later. I want us to double-check each other's work. The engine guys check the chassis guys and vice versa. That's not to say I want everybody to get into everybody else's business. On the contrary, I want the engine guys to do the engine, but I want the chassis guys to help when requested and to check out the engine once it's done. We got no room for egos here. Pontiac's lost one driver this year and they're understandably smarting over it. We will not lose another."

Adams sensed the mood in the living room sobering. His point was hitting home. "Don't get me wrong, now; God only knows what caused our driver's death. Regardless, if there's going to be any accidents with the Tempest, it will *not* be the result of vehicular failure. By the way, gentlemen, if we lose a driver for *any* reason you can bet that Pontiac will shut us down faster than we can go from zero to 60—even if it's due solely to driver error or some other reason completely beyond our control."

"How can they shut us down, boss? We're independent," declared Ted Lambiris.

"Greek, believe me, they can. The division can simply say, 'shut down or you're fired' and that's it, over, lights out. You all get me?" The heads nodded. "Okay, here's what I propose. Tom and Jeff, you're the powertrain guys. You know we need a much different engine and driveline than the stock shit that's in there now. The Tempest currently has a 326 engine that's got to be bored out to 400 or so and then de-stroked to the maximum 305 displacement Trans-Am racing limit. That alone is a hell of a big job, but you've done it before. If you want to start with 400 cubic inch blocks, that's fine with me. Last year at work you two created those 303s on short deck blocks for the Firebird team. I don't know how you did it, but those things put out 460 horsepower, maybe more. If those babies had a real chance to run last season, nothing could have caught them—I mean *nothin'*. That's what we need now in the Tempest. We need a consistent 450 horsepower, minimum. And I want something with plenty of torque, too." The two engine men nodded. "And you'd better build a couple of back-up engines in case the first one blows," Adams continued.

"Then there's the transmission. It's now got a little two-speed automatic junk trannie that's got to be changed to a four speed racing stick. Maybe a Muncie would do it." Tom and Jeff nodded at each other from across the living room. "Anyway, you guys figure that out and then do it. If you two can't, nobody can."

Adams looked at Joe Brady. "Joe, you're our chassis and suspension guy. Me too. So we'll work together on it." Brady grinned. "The Tempest needs a lot of work here too," Adams continued. "Like you told me last week in the john, it'll need a lower body, beefed-up sway bars, Koni shocks, heavy duty brakes and even a modification of the suspension geometry for better cornering. That thing is going to pull over 1G ripping around Lime Rock and the other road courses, and the suspension will be critical if we don't want to embarrass ourselves."

"I won't embarrass us," said Brady softy.

"I know you won't, Joe. That's why you're on the team. You're the best suspension guy I know—besides *me*." Adams smirked.

The heads chuckled and nodded again, looking at Brady. "We need a very robust chassis to handle the high horsepower on road courses." acknowledged Brady.

Adams nodded before continuing, "Greek, I need you on fuel systems and the dash gauges." Lambiris nodded quickly at his shoes, arms crossed, cradling a beer. Ted was a trim six-foot tall. "We're allowed a maximum of 22 gallons of gas in the tank—no more. We can use as much gas as we want during the races, but SCCA rules say we can only cram 22 gallons maximum into the car. We've got to have a fuel cell made to very specific SCCA dimensions so that it can't take any more gas than that. It's your job to make the fuel cell and calculate consumption properly to ensure we don't run out of juice during the races. We'll have two gas cans to refill, 11 gallons each."

The Greek rubbed his chin, stared at the ceiling, and furrowed his brow sarcastically. "A 22-gallon tank ... that's what the *rules* say." Raised eyebrows and smirks fluttered across the room.

"And Greek, I'd like you to do something else, also. As a favor," said Adams.

Lambiris set his beer down and looked up at his boss, "Name it."

"Well, I'd like you to be the body guy. It needs a little work." Someone chuckled and the heads swiveled to gauge the Greek's reaction.

"Body? I don't know much about bodies. Not car bodies, anyway ..." He winked at the guys.

"I know, Greek, but you'll figure it out. It shouldn't take much time."

"Body ..." The Greek looked around the silent room. "Anybody got some Bondo?" The room erupted in laughter.

"Okay, okay ... thanks Ted," said a relieved Adams. "Dutch? Where's Dutch?"

"Here I am. Can't you *see?* Sonofabitch!" said Scheppleman, grinning and exhaling a blue-gray stream of cigarette smoke in the corner of the living room. At about 40, he was easily the oldest man in the room. He wore a clean white T-shirt and blue jeans. Dutch wasn't a degreed engineer, but every man in the room knew that two decades of experience on the shop floor as a skilled machinist and metal fabricator more than made up for the lack of classroom training. Dutch was their peer in every sense of the word. He was the venerable voice of experience.

"Dutch, this should come as no surprise. We're gonna need some special fabrication work. More than just *some*, actually. You're the machinist. The fabricator."

"Damn right," said the crusty tradesman through a broad smile. He dropped the butt of his cigarette hissing into his beer bottle. "I can handle it, even though *technically* I'm on *strike*. But when it comes to racin', union solidarity rides in the back seat for me." A collective chuckle rippled through the room. "Anyway," Dutch continued, "my work's better than the so-called pros—even better'n you *high falutin'* engineers."

"I have no doubt about that," agreed Adams. "We'll need real robust metal fabricating for everything from the roll bar to chassis reinforcements to Lord knows what else. We all have full confidence in you, your shop, and your skills."

"Yeah ... well ... *good*," croaked Dutch, lighting another cigarette.

"Okay, let's talk logistics. Tom, you got a flatbed trailer, right?"

"Yes sir, I do," said the tall, thin young man. "Needs a little electrical work, though. Tail light's busted."

"Will it carry the Tempest?"

"No problem. That thing'll carry a Saturn Five rocket."

"Good. We'll use my Suburban to haul it. You're the logistics guy, Tom, car and driver support, too."

"Support?"

"Yeah. It means ... miscellaneous stuff. Now, the practice rounds are usually on Fridays, qualifying is on Saturdays, and the races are generally on Sundays, in the afternoon. Except at Lime Rock. No racin' there on Sunday because of that little church by the track. The noise of our engines apparently interferes with the parishioners' prayers."

"*Hallelujah!*" said a voice from the corner.

"Anyway, Tom," Adams continued, "we can't race if we can't get to the track. I mean they ain't gonna postpone any races because we're late, you know. Logistics are important. And we're gonna have to rent a truck to carry gear, like welding torches and oxygen and acetylene tanks."

"All right," Goad grinned. "I'll do it."

"Harry, you'll be another chassis guy, with Joe and me. But we'll need your help on everything else, too. We'll all have primary systems responsibilities, but we're also all utility infielders, jack-of-all-trades auto engineers. Each one of us. Driveline, fuel system, suspension, wherever you can help, we'll take it."

"You got it," said the tall young man. "Looking forward to it."

"Okay, good. Now listen," Adams peered across the room. "I'm gonna tape a list of things to do to the car on the windshield each day. I want each of you, or in pairs, to pick out one item on the list to work on in your area of responsibility and *get it done*. When you finish, cross it out with a pencil and start on another item. Just make sure you don't work on the same thing simultaneously—*communicate* with each other. Work it out. Don't come running to me for every little thing, use your judgment, but know when to ask for help. Also, if you see anything that needs attention, add it to the list yourself. I'm not gonna be looking over shoulders all day, barking orders. I'm only going to manage the team and do a little test drive of the car …" Adams arched an eyebrow, "So *pray* for me." Another ripple of laughter rolled across the room. Adams continued, "We'll all handle the pit during the races. That's it then. We all have our jobs. Any questions?" Adams looked around the silent room.

"We got a driver yet?" someone asked.

"No, but I have a guy in mind. Since we can't afford to pay him, whoever it is, we'll have to give him a piece of the purse to make it worth his while." The guys grunted their approval. "Speaking of money, let's decide how much we each chip in for this. If we start with $1,000 a piece, that'll give us $7,000. We'll have to buy a lot of parts. That may just do it, but I think it's unlikely because of the unexpected expenses we'll hit. Keep the receipts for everything we buy so we can track our expenses. We're gonna have a budget and stick to it."

Adams glanced at Joe Brady. "Now I know $1,000 is a lot of money for some of you, but we've got to make this sacrifice if we're going to run with the big boys."

"I'll scrape it together," said Brady deliberately.

"Atta boy," someone said.

"Good. We'll split the winnings evenly, including the driver, if he's willing. Anything else about the money?" Adams looked around at the shaking heads. "All right. Each of you write me a check as soon as you can. I'll open a separate bank account. Any other housekeeping matters gentlemen?"

"How about a name?" Tom Goad asked.

"A name? What's wrong with 'The Le Mans'?" Jeff asked.

"Not the car, *us*! Our group. We need a team name. Every other group has one," Tom said in exasperation.

"Oh, yeah, I thought about that," muttered Adams.

"How about *Trans/Action*?" offered the Greek. "Ya know, with a slash or somethin' between the *Trans* and the *Action*. Maybe it's goofy, but it's the best I can come up with at the moment."

They all quickly agreed.

"One more thing," said Adams. "I think if we refer to the car as a GTO, it may give us more credibility come race time. We all know that Le Mans is just the name Pontiac used for the luxury version of the Tempest, and that's really the version we'll be starting with here. So even though we're technically dealing with a Le Mans, it's on the same chassis as the GTO and we wouldn't be stretching the truth in calling it a GTO. Right?"

The heads nodded again. It was all very clear to the engineers.

"All right," said Adams. "Remember, from now on the car's a *GTO*. Not a Le Mans. Not a Tempest. A *GTO*."

The faces beamed their approval at Adams.

"Okay!" Adams said, beaming back. "Let's all sign the paper here." Five minutes later, a smiling Adams picked up the paper and looked at the seven signatures. Trans/Action was born.

The Trans/Action team quickly began discussing their strategies for the various systems. In reality, they had already developed the basics of each system strategy in their respective minds over the previous week, many of which were based on their experience with the Firebird racing team. The remainder of the Friday evening meeting at Adams' house simply provided them with the opportunity to express the ideas. And drink more beer.

Joe Brady, the low seniority man, was dispatched to the store for more beer at 9:30. After his return, the fresh beer soon evaporated and conversations drifted away from engineering and into the future glories that Trans/Action was sure to achieve on the racetrack. Since there was no time to waste, as Herb kept reminding the team, they all left Adams' house at midnight after resolving to get started on the car at eight the next morning.

Chapter 6

THE NEXT MORNING, Sandi Adams poured herself a cup of tea in the kitchen. The faint scent of stale beer and cigarettes hung in the air. The four kids, a four-year-old girl with cute blonde hair, a six-year-old brown-haired boy, a nine-year-old boy with a blonde afro and an eleven-year-old red-headed boy, were already up and in the family room watching cartoons, so Sandi sat down at the kitchen table to read the morning paper. A loud noise from the garage broke her thought. *Must be Herb puttering again.* She went back to the paper and then heard voices coming from the garage, and another loud banging noise. Curious, Sandi walked to the door leading to the garage. She was still in her robe, but opened the door anyway. What she saw was a surprise, then a shock. Her car's tires were gone, and it was up on blocks. The hood was open and a man was leaning into it. A number of other young men with dirty hands were in the garage holding wrenches and other tools.

"Hey!" Sandi exclaimed. "What are you doing to my car?" The men looked at her, suddenly motionless. One of them dropped a screwdriver, breaking the sudden silence.

"Oh, hi honey," said Herb, walking quickly toward her from behind the Tempest. "Go ahead guys," he said to the men. "I'll be right back." Herb ushered his wife into the kitchen and quickly closed the door behind them as he said, "We're working on the car."

"I can see that, Herb. But it's not broken."

"Oh, that's not why we're ... you won't need it anyway."

"What do think I'm going to get around in?"

"Oh yeah—your new car, of course."

"Slipped your mind in all the excitement, huh?"

"Uh … no, not at all. But I did forget to tell you we'd begin work on the Tempest today, didn't I?"

"Yes, Herb, you did. Just a little detail." she said through clenched teeth. "I mean, I know you had the meeting last night, if you can call it that—more like a beer party, I think—and you never told me our garage was going to be pit stop central."

"I'm sorry sweetie. We'll get you a car soon."

"Soon? How soon?"

"Uh, today. Wait, no … the dealerships are closed. How about Monday? You can drive my car this weekend."

Sandi squinted sideways at her husband. "Promise?"

"Promise."

Sandi smiled. "Okay. And no more beer parties, either," she said, wrinkling her nose. "It *smells* in here, like old beer. And smoke."

"Okay. Thanks," said Herb as he gave her a greasy peck on the cheek and hurried back to the garage. "Got to go."

~~~~

By dusk, the Trans/Action team had gutted and removed the Tempest's body and they were digging in, furiously examining the engine, chassis, suspension, drivetrain components and all the other stock equipment on the car now laid bare by the body's removal. Greasy and exhausted, they finally left to go home, reluctantly, at 6:30 p.m., mostly because Sandi insisted Herb join the family at the dinner table. They agreed to return early Sunday morning.

Chapter 7

AT DAWN, JEFF Young and Tom Nell stood in Adams' formerly tidy garage, each holding a cup of coffee and looking blankly at the Tempest's greasy, black engine. Hand tools were strewn across the cold, hard floor and a piece of paper bearing a handwritten "to do" list was taped to the bug-spotted windshield.

11/15/70—TO DO:
- Remove front-end sheet metal
- Remove all suspension
- Remove all interior
- Remove engine
- Remove transmission
- Remove rear axle
- Source 12 volt battery

Fifteen other tasks followed. Jeff and Tom looked at the list and then looked at each other. The men knew from experience in developing Pontiac's racing engines that converting a stock engine into a reliable racing engine was no small feat. Fortunately, they'd already made the mistakes.

"We gotta yank that thing out," said Jeff in a matter of fact way, sneering at the filthy, old, stock V-8 powerplant. The two engineers had discussed and debated their plans for the new engine daily since they signed on for this project. They had agreed on the general approach, but now the tough part had arrived: agreeing on details for the design and executing the plan.

"Yeah, we do. And when we put the new one in, Herb wants it shifted a few inches toward the rear for better overall balance of the car. He wants a 50/50 weight distribution between front and rear. First we gotta get some weight off of this baby. We really should acid dip the new engine blocks. That ought to get about 30 pounds off, which would leave us the same as the pros."

Acid dipping engine blocks was dangerous. As the name suggests, it entails slowly lowering the heavy steel engine block into a vat of acid via an overhead chain looped through a heavy-duty block and tackle. If it went as planned, the acid uniformly ate away the surface of the steel, resulting in an even reduction of weight from the engine block. The trouble was the acid; it could just as easily eat away the engineers. And the danger of a spill was frightening. But if they were to truly compete, they had to do the acid dip. The next step would be to slightly enlarge the cylinders in the engine block, a process known as "finish boring," which would increase engine power. They decided to bore them out to 4.125 inches, based on their own calculations, to accommodate bigger pistons and forged connecting rods. Connecting rods, as their name implied, connected the cylindrical piston head, which moved up and down in the cylinders, to the crankshaft, which rotated and sent power to the transmission, which in turn sent power to the wheels.

Their calculations did not end there. They also needed to ensure the proper compression ratio in the cylinders. The compression ratio is basically a measurement of the amount of increased air pressure that built up in a cylinder as the piston reached the top of its stroke, just after the carburetor sprayed a little cloud of air and gas into the cylinder. At that point the spark plug would fire, igniting this highly pressurized mix. The resulting small, controlled explosion in the cylinder forcefully rammed the piston back to the bottom of its stroke, in turn spinning the crankshaft—cranking it—to which the bottom of the piston was attached.

"We want a nice compression ratio of 11.5 to 1 or so. That's what we agreed on—right?" Nell asked, but was really stating with authority.

Young grinned. Now Nell was talking their language, the language of gearheads, the native tongue of Detroit. "Yes," said Young. But that wasn't all. The engineers knew that in order to compete, their engine's cylinders needed not only to be wider but shorter, to maximize power. They needed a short, stocky, powerful and tough engine that still met all the restrictions in the rulebook. "And de-stroke it," Young continued.

"The connecting rods got to be 7.08 inches long on center by my calculations. With a robust, forged crankshaft, that should give us the 2.84 inch stroke we talked about yesterday," said Jeff, staring at the anemic iron under the hood.

"Okay. We'll need some big main bearings too, something that can take the high rpms." The main bearings hold the crankshaft in place while still allowing it to spin, thereby delivering power to the wheels via the transmission and axle.

"Delco-Moraine makes 'em. I remember from last year," Nell said.

"Good. Order them Monday."

The two engineers spent the next few minutes discussing the details of their engine plan in the technical language that came so naturally to them. They raised their coffee cups and toasted their plan to put the muscle in the GTO's heart. Although neither admitted it openly, they couldn't really think of this car as a GTO until they were finished with the engine.

Chapter 8

WHILE NELL AND Jeff were discussing their engine plans, Adams, Harry Quackenboss, and Joe Brady stood at the rear of the Tempest gazing at the gutted Tempest body lying on the garage floor.

"No offense Herb, but the aerodynamics of this old body, well ... *stink*," said Joe.

"Then we'll make up for it in the chassis," grinned Adams, looking in the direction of the engine. "Greek? Hey Greek."

Ted Lambiris looked up from his study of the fuel pump and walked over to Adams and Joe, wiping his frozen, greasy, fingers with a shop towel.

"Greek," said Adams, "we need to get some weight off this body. Let's acid dip the front sheet metal. Maybe we can do it at the same time Nell and Jeff are dipping the blocks."

"Okay," Ted nodded. "I'll talk to 'em." He walked to the front of the Tempest, or what was left of it, as Nell and Jeff were toasting their coffee cups.

Joe turned to the chassis. "We've got to reinforce some of these weak spots here in the design," he said, pointing at various places on the chassis. "I can do that."

"Good," said Adams. "You know, we got an advantage over the pony cars with this frame. The Mustangs and Camaros have uni-body frames."

"Yeah," said Joe. "Stub frames."

"Right," agreed Adams. "But we got this open rail frame," he said pointing around the u-shaped frame with his finger. "The uni-body certainly makes manufacturing easier, but—"

"But we can stiffen this baby better," interrupted Joe. "We can patch and gusset it here," he pointed at a spot in the frame, "and here ... and here ... and here. We know exactly where, Herb, from work!"

Adams nodded, grinning at Joe.

"And we can triangulate the whole thing with a big cross in the middle," said Joe enthusiastically, envisioning the result. "Stiff as *hell* ..."

"Good," said Adams. "I'll build a roll cage with Dutch. What about the front suspension? We need some camber gain there. We got to get rid of those stock steering knuckles and use the big ones we put on the Firebird Racing machines."

"Definitely," agreed Joe, "that'll make installing the J56 Corvette brakes a lot easier, too. Put 'em on all four wheels. I'll plot revised camber curves."

Adams nodded again. "Remember—keep the receipts, we're working with a budget. We should put a better steering column on too, maybe a tilt wheel from a Firebird. Whatever it is, it better be collapsible for driver safety. Steering Gear makes them in Saginaw—not that we need a new one. I just don't want our driver impaled on the column after a sudden stop."

Joe winced at the thought. "Okay," he said. "I know a guy in Saginaw, maybe he can get us a stripped down production column."

"How about the springs?" asked Harry.

"Softer springs will get us better wheel control but more body roll. Maybe we can limit the roll by slapping a couple of monster anti-roll bars on. I mean big and stiff."

Harry nodded. "Firebird Trans Am bars, along with some better joints should do it. And those stock rubber bushings won't cut it. Maybe some more robust joints will do the trick. You know, we've got to lower the whole suspension, too, if we really want to compete, Herb. I mean we've got to really drop this baby and hug the track. We'll have to cut the springs a few inches to do that."

"Whatever it takes. For damping, I was thinking of Koni shock absorbers."

"Yes, double adjustable. They work great," agreed Harry.

Adams looked at the rear suspension. "We're lucky, you know, to have coil springs, not leafs back here." Adams rubbed his chin, thinking.

A large part of the chassis engineer's job is to design and adjust the racing suspension to keep the tires flat on the track while the suspension moves vertically and horizontally at high speed. Cambering, or tilting the front wheels inward or outward slightly, is a part of this equation and it greatly affects a Trans-Am racecar's handling. If the wheel and tire are tilted inboard at its top, a knock-kneed look, it has what engineers called "negative camber." Conversely, a wheel tilted outboard at the top, a bow-legged look, has "positive camber." Camber angle is the measure of the degrees of inward or outward tilt of the wheel and tire when looking at the front or rear of the car. Camber is important to handling, and hence the ability to push a car completely to its racing limit, because the proper amount of camber (typically negative camber) maximizes the contact between the width of the tire tread and the track. As a racecar rips around a corner, centrifugal force causes it to lean toward the outside of the turn. This makes the outside tire lean outward and gives it positive camber. Meantime, the inside tire gets negative camber. The object is to keep the outside tire as flat as possible on the track surface because it absorbs most of the cornering load. To achieve this, racecar tires are typically negatively cambered; otherwise, when the car corners, the tires lift up and lose contact with the track, which drastically reduces traction. This necessitates slower cornering, which translates into a tremendous competitive disadvantage over the course of a long, curvy, road race.

Adams wanted to achieve zero degree camber on both outside tires in the incredibly hard cornering he knew was to come. All the Trans-Am cars negatively cambered their front tires, but conventional racing wisdom limited cambering to the front end only. Why? Adams rubbed his chin again. If it works on the front, why wouldn't cambering work on the back end also? Maybe it would further reduce the G-forces as the car rocketed around the curves, too. It would certainly improve rear-end traction. That kind of handling improvement would provide the old goat with a definite competitive advantage over the pony cars on the twisting Trans-Am courses, especially on tracks without banked turns.

"Maybe we could camber the rear end, too," said Adams finally.

"What?" Joe Brady looked at his boss. "How? Bend the rear axle? Why? Who ever heard of that?" asked Joe, a note of incredulity in his voice. "Man, I *knew* you were thinking too much."

Harry silently scratched his head.

"Listen, Joe," said Adams. "If cambering on the front end helps handling—and we know it does—why wouldn't it help on the rear end also? The pony cars can't camber the rear end, even if they'd thought of it, because their leaf springs would probably get in the way. But with coil springs on the butt-end of this baby, there's nothing to get in the way of cambering the rear." Adams looked at Joe, who was also scratching his head now. "Joe, if it helps with cornering, even a little, it'll be worth it because we'll have something none of our competitors have."

Joe looked at the rear end still scratching his head. "Camber the rear end ... camber the rear end ... well, we *could* bend some axles and see what happens."

"Let's do it," said Harry. "If it fails in testing, so what?"

Adams grinned. "We'll start by cutting the axle tubes off the rear end and weld on some flanges at the correct angle to the center sections and axle housing. Then we'll bolt the flanges together to get the right camber."

"Yeah, but what *is* the correct angle? I mean, nobody's ever done this, Herb."

"Just experiment with various angles. It won't need much, I bet, one degree negative or so. You watch." Adams smiled at the concerned young engineer.

"What if we misalign it?"

"What are you worried about? Any misalignment will be taken up by the usual play between the axle and differential. Anyway, I'm the test driver, not you." Adams winked at Harry. "It'll be a quick change rear end! Okay," Adams continued, "what about the rubber? I'm thinking some big Goodyears on Minilite wheels. Nell and Jeff are going to move the engine back a few inches to improve the overall balance of the car. That backward shift should also give us enough room up front to put the big gumballs up there, same size as the rear."

Harry chuckled, shaking his head.

"Wait a minute. Why not put smaller tires up front like everybody else?" asked Joe.

"Better grip," responded Adams quickly. "With the right fat and cambered rubber up front our Tempest will stick like glue to the track, especially in the rain, I bet. No rules against it. Who cares what everybody else does, anyway?"

"But what about the fenders?" Joe pointed at the sedan's front fender. "Big rubber just won't *fit* under there."

Adams shrugged, "So we flare them." He nodded at the fender, "Yeah, just flare 'em with a blow torch and hammer. I'll do it."

Joe Brady, mouth agape, squinted at his boss for a moment, then back at the fender.

Harry rubbed his chin, thinking out loud. "The weight distribution idea is great. The high front end weight of the pony cars is a big drawback. I mean, one end of them's got to do more work than the other end, work that can't be used to transfer power to the ground."

"Precisely," said Adams with glinting eyes. "Hurts their overall traction, too."

"But big tires all around," Joe smiled, shaking his head, "and a cambered rear end—we're gonna have one funny looking old dodo bird here, boss."

"Yeah, man" replied Adams softly. "But this one will *fly*."

Chapter 9

SIX OF THE seven Trans/Action team members sat around a Pontiac
Motor Division cafeteria table eating lunch and discussing the Tempest.
"Gentlemen," said Adams, "like I said before, I have a driver in mind and I
plan to ask him to drive for us when Tom Nell and I see him in about a
month." Adams felt the anticipation among the group. All eyes were on
him. "It's Bob Tullius. He's a hell of a—"

"Tullius? You can get Bob Tullius?" blurted Joe Brady.

Adams smiled. "Well, we'll see. I think you guys know the kind of
driver he is, a real pro with an excellent record. Once I tell him about the
project, maybe he'll join us unless he's got something else going. Anyway,
he's driving at Daytona in early February. Tom Nell and I are going down
there to help Billy Joe, Pontiac's driver. Pontiac's last stand ... Pontiac's last
official stand, anyway. Unless anyone here objects, I plan to ask Tullius to
drive for us, face-to-face. It'll be tougher for him to turn me down that way,
I hope." Adams looked around the table at the nodding heads.

"Tullius ... man, if we could get him. Cool!" hooted Jeff. Brady
slapped him on the back, grinning broadly.

"Hey, it ain't done yet, boys," warned Adams. "He may actually want
to get a salary, you know."

Jeff and Joe's young faces straightened at this thought. Money problems again.

"Listen Herb, on another note," said Tom Nell earnestly, "Jeff and
I ..." he looked quickly around the table, "and the other guys here have

been working our butts off for three weeks now on the Tempest—I mean the GTO. You know—every day after work and the weekends, too. These days, a lot of the work is plain grunt work, like pulling the engine out, degreasing, and stuff. Don't get me wrong, now, I'm not afraid of grunt work."

Adams nodded, "Yeah, I know that."

"But it's the grunt work that's taking up a lot of our time. I mean a *lot*, Herb."

"So what are you saying?"

"Well, it's almost Christmas. If we're going to make Lime Rock in May, we need some help. Just a grease monkey, part-time, to do the dirty work, so we can focus more on engineering and the machining and assembly stuff."

"I agree," said Joe Brady softly. "The mundane little stuff on the chassis and suspension is eating up a lot of my time. Yours too, boss. And man, I'm exhausted. Sleep deprivation ..." Joe rubbed his bloodshot eyes.

"Yes," said Adams, "I know. I've been kicking this idea around myself. We're making good progress, but Lime Rock is right around the corner. So where can we find some good, cheap help? I mean minimum wage help. Our budget is under pressure as much as our time."

The guys looked around the table at each other. "I'll talk to Tullius about it," said Adams. "Maybe he knows somebody."

Chapter 10

THE MATTER-OF-FACT VOICE coming from the kitchen's transistor radio that October evening announced that 27-year-old rock singer Janis Joplin was dead in Hollywood of a drug overdose. In other news, a witness in the court-martial of a first lieutenant in the U.S. Army was soon expected to testify that he saw the lieutenant open fire on helpless women, children, and old men in the Vietnamese village of My Lai. Herb winced, switched it off, and sat down at the dinner table with his wife and children.

"Sandi, I have to go to Daytona in February one last time to help Pontiac's last remaining racer, Billy Joe," Herb said across the table. "I'm going with Tom Nell. It's really Pontiac business, but Bob Tullius will be driving in the 500 race so I'm going to ask him if he'll drive for us this summer."

"That's nice. Bob's very nice. Tell him I said hello."

Herb laid down his fork and looked at his wife. "I won't have to. You can say hello to him yourself. Want to go to Daytona?"

Sandi closed her eyes and thrust her fists in the air, imagining the warm, humid, sunny Florida air. "When do we leave?"

"Next week. Tom Nell's taking his wife Marilyn, too. We'll drive down together. Billy Joe reserved a block of motel rooms for his team, including us. But I should warn you now about Billy Joe. He's kind of character ..."

~~~~

"Hello Mr. Adams and Mr. Nell! Welcome to Daytona!" drawled Billy Joe loudly from across the Speedway Motel parking lot. Billy Joe had already become one of racing's most colorful characters. Well into his 50s, Billy Joe still liked fast cars and fast women, as evidenced by the fact that not only was he Pontiac's racecar driver, he was also on his second or third wife and was rumored to have a girlfriend or two. He was known as an old school driver, which mostly meant he was prone to fisticuffs after races with other drivers who happened to cut him off, bump his quarter panel, or commit untold other offenses—either real or perceived—against him on the track. Yet, being a Southern gentleman, he still referred to the two young engineers as "Mr.," never just Herb or Tom.

"How was the trip, y'all?" asked Billy Joe.

"Fine, fine," said Adams, shaking Billy Joe's enthusiastic hand. Herb introduced Sandi and Marilyn Nell.

"Pleasure to meet ya, ladies. Hey, I got a block of rooms, and two of 'em are for y'all. Check in at the office over yonder," he said, pointing to a small white cinderblock building on the corner of the parking lot.

"We'll do it," offered Sandi, looking eagerly at Marilyn Nell. Marilyn nodded quickly and the two women walked to the office.

~~~~

"Now," drawled Billy Joe. "Why don't y'all join me and my team for dinner tonight at the tavern? Catch up on old times. Enjoy some Southern hospitality after your long drive."

~~~~

Half an hour later, Sandi was settling into the motel room. Herb was in the shower when Sandi was startled by rapid, loud knocking on the motel room door. She gingerly opened it.

A 38-caliber pistol was pointed at her chest. Involuntarily, Sandi drew a sharp breath and froze.

"I'm on to you!" sneered the bleached blonde, middle-aged woman holding the shaking gun. She peered over Sandi's shoulder into the motel room. "*Where is he?*" she demanded in a husky drawl.

Sandi stood, frozen.

"I said, where is he? You cain't hide him!" said the woman, waving the gun. She was tall and tanned, with a lot of makeup around her brown, weathered, fiery eyes.

"Who? Where is who?" stammered Sandi, her heart thumping madly.

The woman sneered, "You know who I mean—Billy Joe! My *man!*"

"Billy Joe's not here. He—"

"You stay the *hell* away from my man or I swear I'll blow your head off, understand me?"

"Ma'am, I don't know what you're talking about. I—"

"*Shut up!*" she hollered. "I know you're foolin' around with him, so don't try lying about it. I saw your name on the register at the motel office. This is one of Billy Joe's rooms! I got you red-handed! I ought to blow your head off right now!" The gun began to shake violently in the woman's hand as she drew an uncertain bead on Sandi's forehead.

"No, no, don't shoot. Listen to me, please." Sandi crept backwards, her trembling palms facing the woman, her eyes riveted on the gun barrel.

"What? Listen to *what?*" The woman paused, dropping the gun's barrel slightly. "Is that the shower goin'? I'm listening to that *shower*, baby! He's in the shower! I'll blow him away too!"

"No, please, that's my husband in the shower—Herb Adams."

The woman narrowed her eyes at Sandi. "Nice try, sweetie. Now get outta the way!" She pushed her way past Sandi, walked to bathroom door and violently kicked it open. The black pistol quivered in the woman's damp, cold hand.

Sandi vainly attempted to warn her husband, shouting "*Herb!*"

It was too late. The woman yanked open the shower curtain, revealing Herb Adams, naked, white and wet with a shaking gun pointed at his head.

"*HA!* I got—" the woman stopped in mid-sentence.

"*Don't shoot!*" pleaded Sandi, quickly putting her quavering hands over her mouth.

Herb saw the woman and the gun and he yelled, almost falling in the slippery tub at this highly unexpected event. "What the *hell?*" he shouted, stunned.

The woman dropped the gun to her side, saying, "Oh … I thought you was …" the woman looked at Sandi, "I … I thought he was …"

"Who? Who'd you think I was? A runaway convict?" asked Herb, his knees together and hands over his privates.

The woman took a step back. "Billy Joe … I, I thought you was Billy, but …"

"He's *not*," said Sandi softly through deep breaths, her heart pounding. "Like I told you, he's my *husband.*"

The woman looked at Sandi, "So you ain't fooling with my man?"

"No, I'm not. We just arrived here from Detroit."

The woman raised the gun and an eyebrow simultaneously, "Detroit? Why's your name on one of Billy Joe's rooms on the motel register book then?"

Sandi struggled to control her breathing. "Because my husband is a racecar engineer for Pontiac Motor. He's here providing engineering support to Billy Joe and his team for the Daytona 500. We're part of Billy Joe's team, so he gave us one of the rooms he reserved for the team."

The woman's face fell. She lowered the trembling gun and passed it to her other hand. "Oh. I see."

The bathroom was silent but for the sound of the shower dutifully watering the naked, motionless, knock-kneed engineer.

"Well … I best be movin' along," the woman said. She turned and walked to the door saying, "Have a nice day, y'all."

~~~~

Neon light, slurred speech, cigarette smoke, and stale beer filled the air in the Daytona Tavern. Popcorn littered the floor. Three hours earlier, Billy Joe and most of his team had commandeered a large bank of tables in the small bar for a greasy dinner of burgers, fries, onion rings and cold beer. The food was now gone, but the beer kept coming, compliments of Billy

Joe, who sat across the table from Herb. Billy Joe was attempting to catch his breath, recovering from fits of laughter after hearing the story of his girlfriend and the gun.

"She was after the wrong one," said Billy Joe, winking at Herb from over his beer. "It's that 'un over there she's looking for." Billy Joe looked in the direction of the corner and nodded at a young, thin, big-haired redhead in a tight black T-shirt that read *Waylon Jennings* in white script, undulating across her large breasts. She was taking a long drag on a skinny cigarette, surrounded by beer bottles and talking to another big-haired woman at her table.

Beauty is in the eye of the beer holder, thought Adams.

"Isn't that kind of risky, Billy Joe, given your girlfriend's propensity with guns?" asked Adams.

"Yeah, but it's worth it," said Billy Joe, leering at the buxom girl. "It's perfect. I looked at every square inch of her … it's perfect."

Chapter 11

WELCOME TO THE Daytona International Speedway—Home of the Daytona 500 read the huge sign at the entrance to the parking lot. It was a warm, humid, sunny south Florida morning. The faint scent of citrus trees filled the cool air—a welcome change from Detroit's gritty snow. Adams and Tom Nell parked in the massive vacant lot and walked past the empty ticket booths to the silent grandstands.

Daytona.

Adams and Nell silently took in the view.

The huge oval track, the grandstands, the giant infield.

The turns were highly banked at about 30 degrees, Adams guessed. A freshly painted bright yellow stripe circled the inside edge of the entire asphalt track. Between the infield and the shoulder of the track was a strip of grass circling it, bright green and impeccably manicured, showing the recent tracks of large lawnmowers. Not a dandelion in sight.

The infield itself was gigantic, with a good-sized pond near one end. Around the entire outside edge stood a short, white retaining wall marked by occasional smudges of various colors, reminders of the speeding violence that lived here. A high chain link fence and evenly spaced light poles rose from the short wall. Behind the wall were the grandstands. This was NASCAR racing.

Along with Trans-Am and the open-wheeled USAC cars, NASCAR was big time racing. Big crowds. High speeds. *Maybe one day*, thought

Adams. The roar of an engine from the nearby pit road broke the silence and Adams' daydreaming.

"I'm goin' over to help out the guys on the Pontiac," said Tom Nell, pointing to a stock car in a garage surrounded by a group of men in parkas peering into its open hood. Nell, in a white T-shirt, hustled off in the direction of the Pontiac.

Adams nodded, looked down pit road in the other direction and saw an athletically built man climb out a car's window. He was 50 yards away, but Adams recognized him as the man he had come to see—not for Pontiac, but for Trans/Action. The driver was about six feet tall, maybe a little less, with a confident, relaxed air about him. Adams waved his arm in the air, walking down the grandstands toward the driver, attempting to attract his attention. The driver didn't see him; he was looking at the car with his hands on his hips, still wearing his helmet. The driver removed his helmet, revealing short, sandy-blonde hair. Yes, that was him, definitely. Adams whistled loudly, still walking toward the pit. The driver turned around and looked. "Hello, Bob!" yelled Adams, waving.

Bob squinted. "Herb?"

"Yeah. Surprised?"

"Herb Adams! Hello buddy! What in hell you doin' here?" exclaimed Bob Tullius, grinning widely, walking toward his old friend on the other side of the chain link fence separating the grandstand from pit road.

"Oh, just came to see an old friend. Supporting Billy Joe, too," said Adams.

"That's unfortunate. Hey, come on, come over here through the door." Bob opened a door in the fence and the two men eagerly shook hands. "You come to see me win the 500 in a few days? You know old Billy Joe can't beat me—not on the racetrack, anyway."

"Ah … well, sure Bob. Just between us, I'm sure you'll win. Always do, don't ya?"

Bob slapped Adams on the shoulder, winking, "You bet! I'll get you a pit pass, so you can see me wallop 'em up close! Got a real good car this year. Running good. Good crew, too. So how've you been? How're Sandi and the kids?"

"Fine thanks, everyone's fine. How about you?"

"Great. Man, I love Daytona. The crowds, the TV, the competition—takes a lot out of ya, but it's just a great race."

"Yeah, sure is. You're a real pro now, racing with the big boys full-time. I'm real happy for you, man. I know how long you've wanted this."

"Yep—I'm very fortunate to do something I love full-time. Dream come true. Beats the hell out of selling cameras. Hey, we're finished for the day here. Car's in good shape for qualifying. Let's go to dinner, what do you say? I can't drink much though—got the race ..."

"Yeah, yeah, I know. I'll keep an eye on you."

Adams squinted into the garage toward the Pontiac stock car, looking for Nell. Next to the Pontiac, a small group of men in winter parkas were standing near a little fire burning in a steel drum, rubbing their hands together and occasionally warming their palms over the drum's heat. Another man in a white T-shirt and jeans was leaning into the Pontiac's engine compartment, his arms working furiously at some belt, bolt, or screw. Adams grinned. Tom Nell at work again.

~~~~

Herb and Bob sat in a booth in the greasy spoon and ordered their burgers. Adams took a sip of beer. "Listen, Bob," said Adams sullenly, "Pontiac pulled the plug on racing last year."

"So I hear. Too bad. I mean, I know they had a bad year with the driver's death. Guess I can't blame them. I hear the Firebird racing team is disbanded," said Bob softly.

"Yes. I can't blame 'em either." Herb looked into his beer. "Listen Bob, my guys at Pontiac Special Projects and I provided engineering support to the Firebird racing team for the last two Trans-Am seasons. We developed a lot of stuff for them, including some engines that put out 460 horses. They didn't get a chance to really prove themselves, though. We had a great suspension, too. Anyway, my guys took the end of Pontiac-sponsored racing pretty hard. Me too. So I got an idea."

Tullius smiled. "Knowing you, I got a pretty good guess."

Adams nodded at his friend. "Yes. We're doing it ourselves."

Bob leaned back in the booth with a slight frown. "What's the car?"

"My '64 Tempest ... I mean *GTO*. We're hopping it up good, Bob. We've got a great team."

A smile eased over Bob's face. "And you want someone to drive it?"

"Well ... yes. It will be very competitive with these pony cars, Bob. I mean the car's got an open rail frame—not uni-body, so we can stiffen it up better with gussets. And we know exactly where to do it because we're the factory guys. We're gonna triangulate the whole thing with a big cross through the middle ..."

Bob scratched his head, staring out the window though narrowed eyes. The smile faded.

"I'll build the roll cage myself," continued Herb. "We're slapping some big steering knuckles in the front suspension for camber. And four, big J56 Corvette brakes, Bob. We'll plot new camber curves. Installing a new steering column from a Firebird—collapsible. Putting big sway bars in it, too. Koni shocks ..."

Bob took a deep breath and exhaled slowly, shaking his head. "I don't know, man. What about the engine?"

Herb continued the pitch. "The engine's gonna be a 303 short deck, just like last year. Ram Air IV heads, four barrel carb with a high performance intake ... lots of horses, man. You get me?"

Bob pursed his lips, faintly nodding. "I see ... how about the transmission?"

"Muncie M22 rock crusher with a Hurst short-throw stick."

"What about a decent seat?" asked Bob.

"I'll fabricate the seat myself—plenty of support for you." Herb studied the driver's face. "We know how to do it, man ..."

"You don't have to tell me that," interrupted Bob. "If Herb Adams and his Pontiac guys are behind it, I know what kind of ride it's gonna be." Bob looked out the window again, a thoughtful expression in his eyes as he weighed the unasked question. "That old tub's gonna move, despite the aerodynamics."

"Yes. It'll move, all right. So what do you say? We can't afford to pay you a salary, just a share of the purse. The first race is at Lime Rock in May."

"You got sponsors? Unless you're surprisingly well-financed, Herb, you're not even going to be able to afford to get to the races." Bob leaned back and crossed his arms, still appearing uncertain.

"That might be a problem. We are burning through the bread kinda quick. But we're buying as much used componentry as possible—good stuff. And thanks to the work with the Firebird racing team for the past couple years, we've got all the contacts necessary to get the best components."

Bob looked out the window again, frowning. "You need sponsors. Maybe I could lean on some … Lime Rock will be on TV …"

"So you'll do it?" asked Adams, a hint of eagerness in his voice.

The driver turned his attention from the window with a smile. "You bet, man. You bet. For you."

Chapter 12

IF TULLIUS, A pro, was going to drive, Adams knew he had to make him comfortable in the car. He had to deliver on his commitment to make Tullius the right seat. He examined the frame, thinking. Seating is very underrated in racing. The wrong seat, whether poorly fitted, loose, poorly positioned, or myriad other reasons, could lose the race by causing the driver to tire prematurely, thereby leading to a loss of driver concentration. Some say a well-fitting seat is worth half a second per lap. Since Adams was an occasional driver himself at Waterford near Detroit, he knew from personal experience the value of a good seat. A bad seat adversely affected the driver physically and, eventually, mentally. The mind could only absorb what the ass could endure.

The seat was also a source of the car's feedback to the driver. Good seats transmitted the vibrations and G-forces drivers needed to interpret the cars' reactions to the drivers' actions. The seat provided "feel." This feel influenced the control, sensitivity, and power the driver exerted over the steering wheel, the pedals, and stick shift. Ergonomic efficiency in the cockpit translated to faster lap times, and it started with a good seat.

Adams' goal here was to get Tullius' body *in* the seat, not just on it. He had to give him the maximum lateral support possible without interfering with Bob's ability to move his arms around. Tullius would need to get his right hand quickly from the wheel to the stick and back with minimum effort, and he had to do it blind, absent the luxury of actually looking at the stick. He also had to smoothly crank the wheel 180 degrees with no interference and with minimal movement of his hands from their positions on the wheel. Adams' seat would put Bob low and nearly upright. Bob needed the ability to ram the pedals all the way to the floor without fully extending his legs. The seat also needed to provide sufficient support to stop him from sliding forward or even "submarining" completely under the dash during hard braking.

Okay, he had the plan. Now for the execution. Adams deliberately donned a welding mask, lifted the welding torch and lit it.

~~~~

A few hours later Adams picked up the ringing phone in his living room.

"What if I can get us a sponsor? Maybe a few?" said Bob Tullius' voice on the other end of the phone.

"Sponsors? For us?" asked Adams incredulously.

"Hell, yeah."

"Great!"

"Just one hitch. One of the sponsors has a kid. And he wants the kid to help out on the team, kinda."

Adams eyes narrowed. "Help out?"

"Just grunt work, you know. The kid needs some work experience. Needs to learn about deadlines and hard work. He's a local kid. Detroit area. Not far from you."

Adams paused. "... I see ... a kid. How old?"

"Eighteen or so. Just have him help out a little. Like I said, grunt work."

"Well, we are looking for some help with grunt work. My guys asked for help."

"Perfect. I'll tell the sponsor it's a deal." Tullius hung up.

~~~~

A day later, Adams walked into his cold garage followed by an 18-year-old, tall, athletic-looking boy with light brown hair, big green eyes and chiseled features. Even under the loose T-shirt sporting a Corvette Stingray logo, the kid's well-developed upper body was apparent. But most importantly, Adams noticed something else, something less obvious: The kid had black grease under his fingernails. "Okay kid, here it is ..."

The kid looked around at the gutted chassis and car body lying next to it. A man was leaning into the empty engine compartment, fiddling with something. The chassis had no engine and was up on blocks. The vehicle had been disemboweled; it barely resembled a car chassis at all. No seats, no dashboard, no steering column, and no axle; it also looked as if extra supports had been welded on the frame in weird places. And the body was a wreck, with spots of exposed sheet metal, rust, and Bondo dotting the dirty gray paint. It was an older body style, too, a regular sedan of some kind— not the red or yellow Firebird he'd expected.

Taped to the windshield at a cockeyed angle was a smudged piece of paper with a handwritten list of some kind, and sporting the day's date: December 15, 1970. A dirty chrome *Pontiac Le Mans* badge was stuck on the rear. Not even a GTO. How could this hunk of junk ever win *anything*? There was no *way* this thing could compete in Trans-Am even if these guys could put it back together by May. The disappointment and enormity of the hopeless job was all over the kid's face.

A small, tinny, transistor radio knocked out a rock tune from the corner. At least they listened to good music, even if they weren't going to pay him. The garage was well-lit and relatively clean, too. They also appeared to have an extensive assortment of tools and machinery.

"Welcome to Trans/Action," said Adams, patting the kit on the back.

The kid smiled weakly, still staring at the spectacle before him. "Uh ... thanks."

"Let me introduce you to Ted Lambiris. Greek—hey, Greek."

The man lifted his head out of the engine compartment. "Yeah?"

"Ted, let me introduce our new assistant, Jim. The Greek is our fuel systems, dash gauge and body man."

"Pleased to meet you sir," said the kid, offering his hand.

"Likewise," responded the Greek, grabbing the teenager's hand and giving it a cold, greasy shake. "We need the help. Listen, Herb, I got some ideas on the fuel system. I found a used 22-gallon Firestone safety cell bladder that would fit in here real good. And I talked to a guy about how to … how to … well …"

"What?" asked Adams.

"Well, sort of tweak it a little."

"Tweak it?"

"Yeah. Ya know, to squeeze a little extra gas in it."

"Don't exceed the dimensional limits set by Trans-Am."

"I won't. Anyway, I figure a couple of Holley centrifugal fuel pumps, about 110 gallons an hour or so, should do it. I also found a joint that sells surplus aircraft supplies. It's brand new stuff. They got braided fuel lines and fittings. And they're cheap."

"Good, buy 'em. Don't forget to keep the receipts, I'm watching the budget. Give 'em to me—I'm keeping them in a folder."

"Okay. One more thing. The filler neck on the gas tank. I should configure it so it can be switched 180 degrees. That way we can fuel this baby from either side, depending on the layout of the pits at the various racetracks."

"Do it. We need every advantage we can get against the pros, especially in the pits."

Adams glanced at the new helper and saw the unmistakable look of despair on the young man's face. "I know it doesn't look like much now, but we've got a plan. Believe it or not, Jimbo, we'll make this car real competitive. You'll be proud to say you helped."

Jim raised his eyebrows and tilted his head slightly, examining his greasy right hand. "Uh … okay, Mr. Adams."

"Remember, amateurs built the Ark—professionals built the Titanic."

The kid managed a thin smile.

"Really, kid, you watch," Adams smiled confidently. "You watch. You'll see."

~~~~

Two weeks later, the kid stood in the garage watching his breath in the cold, oily garage air, waiting for an assignment, reading Mr. Adams' long list taped to the windshield. *Man ...* they had a lot to do. From the corner workbench, the tinny transistor radio played a rock tune.

"Gimme an adjustable end wrench, kid," said the voice from under the chassis.

Jim picked up a wrench from the toolbox and handed it to the out-stretched arm. "Here you go, Mr. Nell."

Tom Nell took the wrench under the car, grunted a few times and said, "There. That oughta do it." He slid out on his back from under the front end of the Tempest. "Let's fire it up, Jeffie."

"You're going to start the engine?" asked Jim, surprised.

"You think we're just going to stand here admiring it?" retorted Jeff Young, settling into the Tempest's narrow, newly constructed racing seat. "Jim, go find Herb for this."

Jim shrugged, lumbered inside the house and soon re-emerged with Adams, who was chewing cereal.

"We're gonna turn it over, Herb," said Nell.

"Okay. Let me open the garage door." Adams opened the door and nodded at Young, peering over his shoulder from behind the wheel.

Jim was not prepared for the sound. He'd never heard anything like it—not from a car, anyway. The 303 V-8 sounded more like a jet at very close range. "*Jeez!*" hollered Jim, but he was not heard over the roar of the Tempest's new, unmuffled, enormously potent powerplant. Nell squinted over Young's shoulder at a dashboard control.

The entire car shook violently. Jeff peeked around the right side of the racing seat at Jim. The teenager, wide-eyed with hands over his ears, was saying something again. It looked something like, "*Oh my God ...*" Jeff slowly pressed down on the accelerator, grinning through the car's increasing shudder and thunder. Jim stepped back against the garage wall, still mouthing something at the engine and grimacing, hands pressed tight over his ears.

Jeff felt a finger tap on his left shoulder. He looked around at Adams, who was making a cutting motion across his throat. Jeff switched off the ignition. The garage fell silent.

"Oil pressure looks good," said Nell finally.

"Yeah," responded Jeff. "*Now* it's a GTO!"

Nell cracked a smile in silent agreement.

"Congratulations, gentlemen," said Adams, beaming.

"Kind of noisy, huh Jim?" asked Nell, looking at the young helper stilled pinned against the wall with hands on ears.

"What?" hollered Jim, easing his hands to his sides.

"Noisy," repeated Nell, chuckling.

"Oh … yeah," said Jim, slowly approaching the engine under the open hood, awestruck. "*Man!* Wow! Didn't expect that! *Wow!*"

"You were hoping for something a little quieter?" asked Nell.

"Maybe we could get a muffler to protect your sensitive young ears," offered Jeff.

"All right," said Adams, "take it easy on the kid, now."

"Unbelievable," muttered Jim, oblivious to the teasing and continuing his utter admiration of the engine. "How much horsepower?"

"Not enough, probably," said Adams. "It'll need some tweaking, right boys?"

"Yeah," said Nell. "Probably only 440 or so horses right now. With the right touches, we'll get it higher."

"Higher than *440*? Man … maybe you guys—" Jim stopped himself.

"Maybe us guys what?" asked Jeff, exiting the car.

Jim looked at the floor and put his hands in his pockets. His cheeks flushed.

"Maybe we guys really *do* know what we're doing?" Jeff winked at Nell.

"Uh … well, I …" stammered Jim. The garage fell silent again.

"Can you blame the kid?" asked Adams. "He didn't know anything about this project before he walked in this garage two weeks ago, and then all he saw was a gutted chassis and an old sedan body lying next to it. That scene wouldn't inspire racing confidence in anyone. Anyway, he's a believer now, right kid?"

"Absolutely!" blurted Jim.

Chapter 13

JOE BRADY DROVE straight to Adams' house after work and parked his car in the frigid January twilight. Holding a few thin, gray sticks, he crunched across the snow, entered the garage through the side door, and saw Dutch Scheppleman alone with the GTO, staring at it with his hands on his hips. The butt of an unfiltered cigarette was clenched between his teeth, emitting a wisp of smoke.

"Hey Dutch!" said Joe Brady. "Look—I bought these welding sticks. A welding engineer at work told me about 'em. See, they turn colors when you burn 'em and indicate if you're welding at the proper temperature. This one turns orange at 2,000 degrees ... I *think*. This one turns green at 1,800 ... or something ..." Joe scratched his head, fumbling with the sticks.

The veteran machinist's eyes narrowed at the sticks, then Joe. Dutch slowly lowered the cigarette from his yellowed teeth.

"No, really, Dutch. He says they work great. I mean, he's an engineer and—"

"So *what?*" interrupted Dutch. "Some book-smart Poindexter with a pocket protector and slide rule hangin' on his belt? He don't know shit about the real world." Dutch looked at the ceiling, closed his eyes and slowly shook his head. "*Engineers,*" he muttered.

"Well, I ..." stammered Joe.

Dutch scratched his head. "No offense, kid, but some of you school-taught gearheads spent too much time in the classroom." A small grin crept across Dutch's weathered face. He looked at the young engineer, "Ya know, *I'm* gonna enroll in college."

"Really?" asked Joe.

"Oh yeah."

"But, how come? I mean ..."

Dutch's face straightened as he leaned close to the young engineer. "To find out how they suck all the common sense outta ya." Dutch slapped Joe's back hard and let out a thick, rasping, laugh.

Joe smiled thinly, gazing at the welding sticks in his hand.

"Come here, kid, I'll show ya how to weld. Here, put this on yer brainy head." He tossed Joe a welding mask and took one last draw from the cigarette before flicking it to the ground and perfunctorily grinding it out under a greasy, steel-toed shop boot. Dutch donned his own scratched welding mask, lit the welding torch, and began carefully welding a bracket to the GTO's frame.

Joe watched carefully. In a few minutes the machinist was finished. The result was two uniform, elegant, rippled weld beads at the seams between the bracket and frame.

Dutch shut down the torch, flipped up his welding mask, and squinted at Joe through an acrid blue haze. "See kid ... weldin' ain't science—it's *art.*"

Chapter 14

HERB ADAMS SCANNED the morning newspaper on his desk. Gas prices in the U.S. were predicted to rise after OPEC's early-February threat to set oil prices without consulting buyers. Bad news for the V8 pony cars, thought Adams as the ringing phone interrupted his thought. He picked up the receiver on his desk, saying "Special Projects—Adams speaking."

"Special driver—Tullius speaking."

"Hi Bob," said Herb through a chuckle. "Caught me by surprise here at work. How are ya? Congratulations on Daytona."

"Thanks. We had a good run there. Hey, how's your car?"

"Coming along pretty good. Making good progress. Engine's ready and installed—turned it over last week and it sounded real good. We're working on a second engine now. Suspension is almost done, body and fuel system coming along. The body's back on. We'll take it for a first test drive this weekend, weather permitting. Just around the block."

Bob laughed, "Oh, the neighbors will love that. Anyway, it's March now, so we only got two months left. You on schedule?"

"Yes, we'll make it. The time commitment is taking its toll on the guys, but they knew what they were getting into. We haven't had a weekend off all year. We're busting our butts after hours, too. They've got a lot of energy, especially Nell. Man, that guy's a maniac. Anyway, this car will go."

"Good. I'll take care of it on the track."

"To *hell* with that, we want ya to win!"

Bob laughed, "Of course, of course I will! Hey, Herb I got some good news here. I've been calling around to some more of my sponsors. I got some more for us."

"More sponsors? You got more sponsors for us? Who?"

Tullius rattled off the names of four well-known companies: an oil company, a tire company, a car wax outfit and a Swiss watch maker. And none of them asked for their kids to join the team.

"Free tires?"

"Yeah. Oil, too. Maybe even a watch or two, but I'm not sure all the wax in the world will help the body, even if we do get it free."

Adams chuckled again. "Outstanding! How'd you swing that?"

"Just my contacts. I'll get the tires delivered ASAP."

"Great. Hey, what's that watch company?"

"It's Swiss. They make chronograph watches. Expensive."

"Oh, yeah," Adams said unconvincingly.

"They'll pay us two or three hundred—I forgot which—each race. Same deal with the oil company. It ain't much, but—"

"So, they're going to pay us ... I like it. No money excuses for us now."

"Good," said Bob, "they'll take care of paying for spare parts, entry fees and towing, too. It's not much, but ... anyway, glad to help."

"You know, Bob, we really only hoped that you'd drive for us. These sponsorships are icing on the cake. Appreciate it. Really."

"No sweat. Just make that machine hum and we'll call it even. And make sure you paint it—ya know, make it look nice."

"Yeah, paint. It's a deal."

~~~~

"We got to paint it ..." said Adams, staring at the dull aqua-marine car with its to-do list taped to the windshield. "We been focused on all the engineering, and rightly so because that's what will win the race. But we've got to get it *looking* good, too. For Bob." He glanced around the cold garage at his crew. Grinning, Adams turned and lifted a can of paint from the corner of the garage. A light yellow-green color was splashed on the can's side and lid. "I got this chartreuse paint here …" He peered at the astonished faces in the garage.

Someone laughed.

"Char-what?" asked Dutch, squinting at the can.

"Chartreuse!" said Adams enthusiastically, holding up the can for the group. "See?"

A loud snort emanated from the corner.

"Herb, you're kiddin', right?" said a voice.

"Hey," Adams said, looking at the label, "it's good stuff!" He looked around the room quickly, grinning. "It's high quality paint and it'll be … different."

Silence. They collectively studied the seven-year-old car body. "Don't ya think we're gonna be different enough already?" asked someone.

Adams dropped the can, mildly dejected. "Well, what color do you want to paint her? Gray or something?"

Shoulders shrugged and someone said, "Well, it's cheap." Heads nodded, looking at each other in the dim garage. Adams immediately regretted the suggestion.

~~~~

Monday evening, the day after Easter, Adams looked at the dull gray GTO in his garage. "All right, time for a test drive around the block," Adams said, rubbing his exhausted eyes. He tore the latest to-do list from the windshield. "Tom, follow me in the Suburban so I can see where I'm going. And remember, I've got no lights, so don't rear-end me. It's dark out there."

"Okay," said Goad, quickly turning and trotting out the side door toward the Suburban parked in the driveway.

Nell opened the garage door and the team was greeted by a blast of biting cold, dry air. Adams, sitting at the controls of the GTO, turned the key. As the engine roared to life among the happy, tired faces of Tom Nell and Jeff Young, Adams realized that Sandi's face might not be so happy now, after hearing the unmuffled roar of 450 horsepower emanating from her garage at 1:15 a.m. He hadn't realized it was so late, but too late now,

thought a guilty Adams as he slowly backed the rumbling, shaking GTO
out of the garage. He looked around at the neighbors' houses in the dark,
still April night. They wouldn't be too happy either.

So what. This test drive had to get done to stay on schedule. With its
huge, new Goodyear slicks on each wheel, the big gray sedan now took on
the appearance of a steamroller. It rolled slowly backward down the driveway, hunched closely to the ground, quivering with raw power, snarling and
puffing blue-gray smoke from its gaping twin tailpipes.

Adams backed into the neighborhood street. He slipped the Hurst
stick into first gear, eased off the clutch, and the dark GTO growled down
the street, past Sandi's "new" 1961 Bonneville parked at the curb, and dis-
appeared quickly into the cool night, followed by its calming stable-mate,
the Chevy Suburban.

A window in the house across the street opened.

"Engine sounds better than ever," said Nell to Jeff as they stood together at the end of the driveway, his breath visible in the frigid air. "Hope
the oil pressure stays up."

"Yeah, it—"

"*HEY!* What's all the racket?" shouted a voice from the open window
across the street.

"Let's get outta here!" whispered Jeff loudly, turning to run.

Nell, laughing to himself, ran after Jeff, to the sanctuary of the garage.
The window across the street slammed shut.

"Hey, what are we," said a breathless Nell, "men or wimps?"

"Yeah, but that's not *my* neighbor!" replied Jeff, huffing. "I mean, let
Herb deal with him."

While the two chuckling men caught their breath, the distant rumbling
of the Tempest soon returned as the racecar crept up the dark street toward
the garage. A dog barked incessantly in the distance, from the same direction as the reverberating GTO. Then a sharp whimper and the barking abruptly stopped.

The rumbling of the GTO grew closer. "It *is* kinda loud. Especially for
one-thirty in the morning," said Nell, trying unsuccessfully to suppress his
laughter.

"Naw," said Jeff. "Just neighbors with no sense of humor."

Nell, punch-drunk with fatigue as they all were, began to laugh hysterically. "Killjoys!" he managed to blurt between fits of laughter.

The GTO slowly thundered up the driveway and into the garage. Adams switched off the ignition. Goad pulled up behind him in the driveway, got out, and immediately looked at the front bumper of the Suburban. Then he squinted down the darkened street from where they'd just driven, looking for something.

Adams cut the engine. "What's so funny?" Adams asked the hysterical Nell and Jeff as he exited the GTO.

"HEY! I'm tryin' to get some sleep here!" hollered the voice from across the street. Adams turned in that direction. "Shut that thing up!" the voice yelled.

Adams now spied his neighbor leaning out the second story window in the dark. He turned back to Nell and Jeff, who were laughing hysterically, but quietly, and pointing at the neighbor. "All right, shut up you guys. Keep it down," Adams turned in the neighbor's direction. "I'll handle this." Adams began walking down the driveway toward the neighbor.

"Uh ... Herb?" said Goad.

"Not now, Tom, I got a problem here," snapped Adams.

"But Herb, I think you should know something," insisted Goad, still looking down the dark street.

Adams stopped in the driveway, turning to Goad and giving him a hard stare, "Listen, Tom, I'll be right back. Can't you see we got a *problem* here?"

Goad shrugged his shoulders and looked at the front bumper of the Suburban again.

"Who are you?" asked the neighbor in the window to the shadow below.

"It's me, Frank. It's Herb."

"Oh ... Herb. Was that you makin' that noise?"

"Yeah—sorry Frank. It's for a race, we just lost track of time."

"I'm calling the cops!"

"No, Frank—wait—I shut it off already," said Adams urgently.

"Shut what off?"

"The car."

"That ain't no car. It was a tank or somethin'."

"No Frank, it's not a tank," Adams said. "It's a race car. We're making a race car and I just took it out for a little test—"

"Well, test the thing someplace else or I'm callin' the cops!" The window slammed shut. A light in the second story of the house next door suddenly switched on. Adams walked back across the street.

"Oh, you handled that real good, boss!" said Nell, doubled over in sleep-deprived giddiness.

"Real funny. You don't have to live across the street from him," said Adams, managing a smile. "Anyway, let's get some sleep, we're all exhausted. We got a bump steer problem. Got some suspension work to do tomorrow, gentlemen."

"Uh, Herb, I think we got another problem," said Tom Goad awkwardly.

"What now?" asked Adams, rubbing his bloodshot eyes, patience running thin.

Nell and Jeff stopped laughing.

"You know that dog that was chasing you down there?" Goad pointed down the street.

Adams nodded, "He ran right out in front of me back there, barking like hell, just like he does every day on my way home from work. I barely dodged him, dumb dog. Hardly saw him with no lights." Adams shook his head, rubbing his fatigued eyes again, "What about him?"

Goad winced, "well, I think I ... uh ..."

"What? Spit it out, Tom."

Nell and Young had stopped laughing.

"Well ... okay ... I ran over the damn dog!" Goad blurted. A brief moment of silence passed as the men took in the news. "When you dodged the dog Herb, it ran behind the Tempest, right in front of me. I didn't mean to ... Hell, the last thing I expected was a damn dog at two in the morning jumping out right in front of me as I'm trying to give you some light ..."

Adams' jaw dropped. "You killed the dog? Are you *sure*?"

"Oh, I'm sure. I mean, first I hear the barking, then you swerve and I see the dog real close to my bumper, then 'BANG!' I hear the whack, then I feel the bumps. Then, no more barks ..."

Nell and Jeff howled in laughter. "Dog murderer!" shouted Jeff, pointing at Goad.

"Shut up, Jeff." Adams scratched his head and managed a brief chuckle. "Shit. Better the Suburban than the GTO. We can't afford any dents on the fancy bumper of our racing machine."

The four men laughed uncontrollably together. "Listen," said Adams, catching his breath, "we'd better get the dog. If we don't pick it up, the neighbors will know we squashed it, and they'll tell the owner. Then I'll have even more neighbor problems."

"I'm not picking up any dead, smashed dog!" said Nell indignantly. "I'm an engineer, not a … a … pet mortician."

"Me either. And the sight of blood makes me barf … guts too, even dog guts," agreed Jeff. He looked at Goad, "I say he who squished it, scrapes it."

"Yeah," said Nell enthusiastically. He turned around, lifted a shovel hanging neatly from the garage wall, and handed it to Goad, saying. "Good luck, Buddy!"

~~~~

Adams and Goad found the dog, about half a block from the garage. It was an unpleasant sight for the two exhausted engineers. "You know, maybe if we just left it here, some other cars would run it over a few times and it would be unrecognizable—I mean a real road Frisbee," whispered Goad.

"No way," said Herb flatly, "not enough traffic around here." They pushed the dead dog into a large garbage bag.

"Well, what now? I mean, what do we do with it, Herb?" asked Goad sincerely.

"I'll think of somethin'."

Chapter 15

THE NEXT MORNING, Adams and Joe Brady, holding a cup of Diet Coke and a mug of coffee respectively, stood in the garage watching Ted Lambiris hold a smallish, square decal against the door of the Le Mans. The decal was white with the number 49 printed in black. The Greek was eyeing it, tilting his head from side to side. The chrome *Pontiac Le Mans* emblem had been pried off and the original rear license plate had been removed. In its place, a metal plate in the form of a license plate was affixed. It read, **"Trans-Am GTO"** in large, block letters.

"Engine is okay, but we got a bump steer problem," said Adams as he stuck the latest to-do list to the windshield, yawning. "Noticed it last night on the test drive. Every time I hit a little bump in the road, the car changed direction by itself." He looked at Harry and a yawning Joe Brady. "Not good, gentlemen. The new knuckles that give us the inclination on the front tires are a lot taller than the stock ones. They're causing at least some of this problem."

Joe popped open the hood and peered inside with Harry. "The relative lack of directional stability of the big tires up front isn't helping either, I bet," said Harry somberly.

"Well, let's fix it. The way I figure it, we should tweak the steering linkage, steering arm, and intermediate rods," said Adams.

Joe furrowed his brow, "And flip the knuckles." Seeing the confused look on Adams' face, Joe continued, "I mean reverse the steering knuckles so the linkage is ahead of the wheel centerline. You know—GM is doing that now on their production vehicles." Joe took a big slurp of steaming coffee. It was much better than the vending machine stuff at the office.

Adams grinned, nodding at the young engineer. "Yes, of course. Let's do it. Good, simple solution. But we'd better hurry, only four weeks to Lime Rock."

"Far out. I'll get on it now."

"And let's keep lightening up this baby; the entire car's still too heavy. I want to test drive her at MIS next weekend. I talked to the general manager of MIS. It's all arranged."

Joe looked at his boss, eyebrows raised, "MIS?"

"Yeah. You know—Michigan International Speedway."

Joe paused, dropping his eyes to the car. "Yeah ... Yeah ... *MIS*," he said through a grin and another yawn.

~~~~

"Hey Herb," said Ted, still holding the decal against the GTO's door, "whaddaya think?"

"Looks good," smiled Adams. "Stick it on."

Adams spied a clean, new sponsor's decal resting on the floor, ready for peeling and sticking to the car and he thought of Tullius and the work he'd done—on his own—to get these sponsors. Adams was grateful to Tullius. The sponsors had replenished Trans/Action's kitty and eliminated the need for other expenditures, like tires and oil. "How 'bout the other decals?" asked Adams.

"Over there—in the other boxes," said Ted, motioning with his head to the other corner of the garage.

Adams carried his Diet Coke over to the corner. Each of the many boxes contained two identical shining stickers. Adams picked up one, the stylized logo of a car wax company. "How 'bout we put these just behind the front wheel well, on the fender?"

"Yeah, okay," Ted replied absently, focusing carefully on peeling the backing off the number 49 sticker.

Adams reached down into another box and picked up a second sticker sporting the unmistakable logo of a well-known tire and rubber company. "Let's put these on the rear fenders, behind the wheels on each side."

"Fine," said Ted distractedly, gently and fastidiously smoothing out the number 49 on the door. Adams picked out two more stickers. Squinting at the GTO, his head cocked slightly, Adams held the stickers in front of him, each proudly bearing the name of an oil company, in large capital letters, in a circle partially framed by a checkered flag.

"These go in front of the rear wheel well," said Adams. Another sticker was in the shape of a pentagon. "Greek, put the Swiss watch sticker on the front part of the front fender, as far forward as it'll go. It'll fit nice there. One on each side."

"Okay. How 'bout this smaller number 49 on the hood, about like this?" Ted laid the sticker on an angle on the driver's side of the hood.

"Fine. Stick it."

"Nell and Young did such a great job on the engine, I thought we'd brag about it a little by sticking a couple of decals reading *'Pontiac 303'* along each side of the hood here." The Greek pointed along the uneven edge of the hood.

"Yeah, good idea."

The car was taking shape, beginning to look like a race car. Granted, thought Adams, it wouldn't win any design contests, but with all the decals covering the dull gray paint, it would be a little less out of place among all the new pony cars. Not that looks mattered. Engineering was what mattered, and this car had it. Plenty of it.

~~~~

The instant young Jim heard the GTO's new racing engine turn over, he abandoned any plans of quitting the Trans/Action team. In fact, he was now so sure of the car's future success that he'd told all his friends. Now he hoped they'd let him stay on for the racing season, even though the grunt work was almost finished. To hell with tuition money. Jim opened the side door of the garage, took one look at the GTO and immediately lost his train of thought. *"Far out!"* he said.

Ted Lambiris, smoothing the bubbles out of a sponsor's sticker, looked up quickly and smiled at the teenager.

"Oh yeah, this is cool! Number 49!" said Jim. He quickly scanned the sponsor's stickers. "Outta sight!"

Ted went back to his smoothing job, grinning. "These decals won't make us any faster, ya know, kid."

"Yeah, but they *look* good." Jim continued to stare at the new graphics on the Tempest.

"Glad you approve of the decals, Jimbo, but the reason we're sticking these on ain't for looks. We have to—sponsors want the adverting exposure in exchange for the money they gave us."

"Advertising exposure? So there's going to be a lot of people at these races."

"Yep. TV coverage, too."

Jim nodded, still grinning at the Tempest's new look. He examined the watchmaker's sticker. "Wow, TV. Hey, since we got free tires and oil, can we get free watches, too?"

"'Fraid not, sport. Sponsors only give us what we really need—money. Maybe I better leave my old Timex at home come race time, though, just in case." Ted held up his wrist and winked at Jim.

Adams entered the garage from the house. "What do you think, James?" he asked.

"Outta sight," said Ted smiling. "He says its outta sight, man."

Jim looked at Adams, nodding enthusiastically and oblivious to the sarcasm. "Yeah. Far out, Mr. Adams!"

"Listen Jim, Joe and I need your help on some more front end work," said Adams, nursing a recently skinned knuckle. "Got to correct a bump steer problem."

"Yes sir. I'm ready. Uh … Mr. Adams? I was wondering about something," said Jim, picking nervously at a Band-Aid on the back of his calloused tender hand. "I know that just about all the work you hired me for is finished now and I … well, sir, I was wondering if I could stay on as part of the team during the racing season."

Ted stopped smoothing the sticker and looked at Jim. Ted and Adams glanced at each other.

"Jim," said Adams, "I appreciate your interest, but we just can't afford to pay you, so—"

"You wouldn't have to. I'd be a volunteer, just like you guys."

Ted and Adams looked at each other again, smiling this time. "You'd do that for us?" asked Ted.

"You bet. Man, this machine is so far out it's gonna tear up Lime Rock and every other track! I mean, I've heard you guys talking and seen you work over the past few months. And the sound of that engine ..." Jim looked respectfully into the GTO's open engine compartment. "Jeez," he muttered, shaking his head.

"Appreciate your confidence in us, Jim," responded Adams. "We'd be happy for you to join us as a volunteer."

Jim shot his fist into the air, "*Far out!*"

Chapter 16

THE MICHIGAN INTERNATIONAL Speedway, or "MIS" as it is more commonly known, is a two hour shot west out of Detroit on Interstate 94 in an area of southern Michigan's rolling countryside known as the Irish Hills. MIS is a big, banked, D-shaped oval that in 1971 could also be laid out in road track, which coursed over part of the main straight, through the infield, across the back straight, out into the country and back again.

In the early spring of 1971, Adams and the Trans/Action crew eased the GTO off Tom Goad's groaning trailer and onto MIS's pit road, surrounded by empty grandstands. Adams squeezed an old helmet onto his head, eased himself into the old gray car and twisted the key. It rumbled to life. He winked nervously at the staring crew, eased the Hurst shifter into first gear and rolled onto the vacant track. He swallowed hard and reminded himself that this was no longer Sandi's car; it had a full racing suspension, and according to Tom and Jeff, an engine with 460 horsepower and a red line at 8,000 RPM.

Adams had a competition driver's license, but he'd never driven anything like this. His mouth dried and his heart pounded as he watched his right hand throw the Hurst into second. He stood on the gas and was mashed into the seat. He felt his cheeks being involuntarily pushed back toward his ears. "*Christ,*" he muttered.

Adams fought to contain his emotion as he shifted into third and squeezed the gas. The old car hurtled toward 60 mph and Adams drew a deep breath. On the back straight, he jammed the stick into fourth, stood on the throttle, and was again pinned to the seat. The machine rocketed past 110 mph carrying its wide-eyed driver. "Yeeee *haaa!*" hollered Adams from under the helmet. Adams now genuinely believed the GTO might actually have a winning chance in the Trans-Am events.

~~~~

A few weeks later, Adams and Ted Lambiris drove the Suburban towing the GTO on the open flatbed trailer for twelve hours when they passed a sign on the right that read: "Lime Rock—Drive Slow." The Greek smirked from behind the wheel, "I thought the point was to drive fast here," he said to Adams, pointing at the sign.

"That's for other guys," said Adams from the passenger seat as they pulled into the motel parking lot. Although Lambiris, Adams, and the other Trans/Action team members didn't know it, some of their competitors were already at the track. Two of the professional teams had each been at Lime Rock for almost week, each with two racecars and a mule car, driving the track every day, getting a feel for it, and adjusting their cars, strategies, tactics accordingly. The drivers rounded the first turn 100 times, until they knew every square inch. Then they moved onto the next turn for another 100. By race day, their drivers knew this year's Lime Rock track like their own backyards. And their well-funded, sparkling, factory-sponsored racing machines were tuned to perfection.

~~~~

Next morning, Adams and his team gulped down their motel restaurant breakfast at six a.m., walked out into the cold, wet morning and drove to the track in the misty rain. The GTO was filthy from yesterday's long drive on an open trailer and the frigid light rain was not enough to clean it up, so on the way to the track, the Trans/Action team stopped at the nearby Housatonic River and quickly rinsed their grimy race car.

Adams turned a corner in the Suburban and squinted at a sign reading, "Welcome to Lime Rock Park. Road Racing Capital of the East."

~~~~

Lime Rock was built in 1957 on 325 rolling acres in the foothills of the verdant Berkshire Mountains in Lakeville Connecticut. It is a beautiful track
with an almost stadium-like feel, the result of its setting in a small, natural
valley—a big outdoor theater. Adams and the crew made their way to Lime
Rock's paddock road and unloaded the GTO at their assigned spot: the end
of the road. Adams read a large banner hanging on the low retaining wall
displaying the name and familiar logo of a national TV broadcasting company in big block letters. His stomach flipped. This sort of nervousness had
never hit him at a race before. It was different when you were here as the
owner—the creator—of the car, not just an advisor. And this was not just
qualifying day. It was press day, too.

Adams donned a windbreaker, pulling the hood over his head in an effort to shield himself from the cold rain. He was as nervous and excited as
he'd been in a long time. All their work over the last five months was now
coming to fruition. Jim held the racing program in his hand, studying the
cover. "*Schaffer Trans-Am Lime Rock Park*" it read above a photograph of the
number 6 Javelin followed by the number 6 Mustang. Beneath the photo it
read, "May 6, 1971." Jim briefly flipped through the program before tossing
it aside, picking up a shop rag, and wiping the remaining damp dirt from the
GTO.

"Hey guys," said Adams sternly to his huddled crew in pit road.
"Tullius is gonna talk like a driver, not an engineer. He's not gonna roll into
pit road and say shit like 'well the left front camber is off by 1.7 percent, the
oil pressure is 33 percent low on right turns and the tires require less tow-
in.' He's gonna say something like, 'I'm loose and the pressure's low.' That's
it. That's all we're going to get, because he's not like us. He's no engineer.
He's a driver. And he's busy as hell trying to navigate the track, beat the
other guys at high speed and win. For us."

Adams glanced at the raised eyebrows and creased brows studying
him. "So here's how you decipher driver-speak. It's very simple. The first
thing he mentions is the first priority we have to work on and fix fast in the
pit. The second thing he mentions is our second priority." Adams glanced
around at blank faces. "I know it sounds dumb, but in the heat of the race,

when Tullius is in the pit, we're gonna ask him how the car's handling, see? And he's gonna blurt out some crazy shit—two or three problems he's having with the car—after he chokes down a huge gulp of water. It's our job to immediately recognize and prioritize this feedback and act on it. Fast. We gotta be practical. We gotta listen to him hard. So we act first on the first item he mentions. We don't engage in some kind of esoteric discussion about it or ask him if he's really sure. We do it—immediately. Real quick. Then, if we have time, we fix the second thing he mentions. Fast. No time for any conversations or clarifications. It's your job to figure out what the hell he's talking about and fix it—now. Got it?"

The crew nodded their heads in unison.

"You Herb Adams?" a voice asked from behind Adams.

"Yeah—that's me," said Adams, turning around.

"I'm from SCCA." He introduced himself and another guy. "We'd just like to do a technical inspection. Take a look at your vehicle to make sure it meets specs."

Adams briefly and stiffly shook their hands, smiling weakly. Each of the men was holding a clipboard.

"Tech inspection … yeah … go ahead," said Adams. The pit crew slowly dispersed, eyeing the inspectors warily.

"Would you pop the hood, please?"

"Of course." Adams and Jim each released a hood pin and jointly pulled up the hood. The SCCA men peered in at the engine.

"It's a 303. The carburetor's regulated. It's all in spec," said Adams helpfully.

The men continued to study the engine, frowning.

"I called SCCA and Trans-Am a few months ago and told them we'd be here and described the car …" offered Adams.

"Yeah, I know. That was me you talked to," said one of them flatly. "Pop the trunk." Adams nodded at Jim, who quickly walked to the back of the GTO and opened the trunk. The men quickly looked in the trunk. One of the men crouched down on one knee, looking under the chassis, still frowning.

Adams began to feel uneasy. These guys weren't going to disqualify them for some technicality, were they? After all the work? Adams struggled to contain his emotions as the two men continued to pore over the GTO. Now they were inside, looking at seemingly everything in the cockpit.

From a distance, the Greek watched the technical inspection, fidgeting. When one of the inspectors pulled a measuring tape from his pocket, extended the metal tape from the roll and leaned in toward the fuel cell, the Greek held his breath.

"It's a GTO. It's homologated," offered Adams.

"We're aware of that," one of them said, staring without expression at the dash gauges. He looked at Adams, "It's just that some of the, uh ... independent teams' cars don't quite make tech. We don't want to see anyone ... well ... *injured.*" He exited the GTO. The other inspector rolled up his measuring tape.

The Greek exhaled slowly.

"Turn it over," said one of the inspectors bluntly.

Adams looked at him, puzzled.

"The engine ... start it."

"Oh! Oh yeah," sputtered Adams as he hurriedly entered the car and twisted the key. The car growled to life. The inspector raised his eyebrows and walked slowly to the rear of the car, examining the exhaust. He bent down and sniffed the smoke briefly.

"What's he doing?" whispered Jim to Adams.

"Checking for nitro," responded Adams quietly. "In the fuel. Any fool can smell it—even him."

"Okay," coughed the inspector from around the rear bumper. "Cut the engine."

Adams complied, turning the key. The car immediately fell silent.

The inspector dropped to one knee, leaning his nose close to the driver's side tailpipe. He took a deep whiff and cocked his head for a moment before standing up. He waved over the other inspector with a finger and together they walked a few feet away, whispering.

Adams exited the car and strained to listen in, but another car further up pit row started its engine and ruined any hope he had of hearing anything the two men were discussing. Those guys got *ice* in their veins, thought Adams.

Joe Brady, rubbing his sleep-deprived eyes, and Tom Nell approached.

"Just one thing," said one of the inspectors returning, pointing at the large, chrome, exhaust pipes protruding slightly from under the bumper. "You piped the exhaust out the rear, not the sides."

"Yeah?" said Nell defensively. "So what?"

"Well, you might … well, uh … overheat the cars behind you."

"*Overheat?* With *exhaust?*" blurted Joe incredulously.

"Well, you generate a lot of heat out of there …"

"Listen," said Adams calmly. "We moved the pipes from the sides to the rear because the car shook like hell with 'em on the side. The move to the rear cut the vibration—a lot. Safety issue. That's not gonna cause any burning—overheating—of the guys behind us. I mean, we're not runnin' a rocket engine or anything. It's just a little 303 short deck."

Looking at the pipes, the official scratched his head, motioned with his finger for the other official to join him and turned his back on the quizzical, slightly hostile, stares from Adams, Brady, Lambiris, and Nell. The officials resumed their whispering while slowly walking away a short distance and stopping.

Joe turned to Adams and whispered urgently, "What the hell is this? They looking for a way to DQ us?"

"They'd better get more creative than that to disqualify us," said Nell through gritted teeth, squinting at the huddled officials.

"Not cool," muttered Jim. *The man is trying to keep us down.*

Bob Tullius approached the huddled race officials. Smiling, Tullius shook the officials' hands and spoke to them for a few moments.

"I think our position has just been successfully advocated for us, gentlemen," said Adams as he watched the two officials turn and walk back toward them. Tullius winked at Adams from behind the officials.

"Okay," said an official, handing Adams a small piece of pink paper, "you're good."

"Thanks," said a smiling Adams, visibly relieved. He admired the paper before looking up. "Hey, why the cops?" Adams motioned in the direction of two state troopers standing nearby.

"Oh. The State of Connecticut says pit road is a public highway. That's the law, I guess. So the troopers patrol it."

Adams flashed a puzzled look.

"Just don't go running across pit road during the race, they'll nail ya."

Adams glanced at the troopers and shrugged.

"You know, this vehicle is different than most independents we see," said the official, looking at the GTO with his hands on his hips. "It may not look like much, but I suspect you really got something here."

"Hope so," responded Adams, pleased at the compliment, albeit backhanded.

"Yeah," agreed the other official, "looks like you've done your home-work. Well, maybe we'll find out tomorrow for sure. Good luck." The two men walked down pit row, past three men standing next to a heavily de-caled, shining pony car. The three men with the pony car were looking at the GTO, but not looking. One of the men, the oldest, was clearly a driver, wearing a driver's two piece racing suit bedecked with sponsors' patches. Adams recognized him. He was one of the best drivers on the circuit. Their eyes met briefly, the men exchanged nods, and Adams turned to work on the car.

~~~~

"What a *joke!* Look at that thing," snorted one of the three young men qui-etly as he polished the glinting pony car.

"You don't know who that is?" asked the pony car driver, giving the young man a sharp stare.

"Another amateur, by the looks of his old wreck." He cupped his wet hands around his mouth and exhaled slowly in an effort to warm his frozen fingers.

"That's Herb Adams. He ain't no amateur."

The young man gave the driver a startled look. "You know him?"

"I know him. He and his team of nerds at Pontiac Engineering were the brains behind Firebird Racing the last few years. Those geeks next to him are from Pontiac Engineering, I do believe. They know what they're doing, gentlemen."

"In that old tub? Come on, man!" whispered the other man loudly, still looking askance at the GTO.

"I'm tellin' you, don't judge that car by its body. I suspect there's some muscle under there. Racing suspension, engine, drivetrain, too. They passed tech inspection."

The two men looked at their driver skeptically. "Firebird racing fell flat last year. Even pulled out this year. We'll smoke 'em," said one of the young men, pointing his thumb in Adams' direction, "and all the other so-called independents, too."

"We'll beat the other independents. But don't be so sure about that one," warned the pony car driver. "Hey—look at this." The pony car driver nodded in the direction of the old gray sedan. He was looking directly at a driver walking toward the GTO and Adams. The GTO driver shook Adams' hand and began examining the car. "Know who that is, boys?" asked the pony car driver.

"Tullius? They got *Bob Tullius* to drive that thing?"

"That's Tullius all right. And he won't drive just anything."

The two young men, with a new hint of reverence in their demeanor, watched Tullius enter the old gray car.

"Listen to this," said the pony car driver, squinting hard.

Tullius turned the ignition and the GTO roared to life, billowing a din of humid exhaust toward the three men.

"I think we may have an unanticipated problem here, boys," coughed the pony car driver above the GTO's raucous 460 horses.

Chapter 17

AT 41 YEARS old, Bob Tullius knew how to drive. And he knew how to race. He knew the Trans-Am tracks also, all of them. They were road-like courses scattered all over the country and Canada with a seemingly infinite variety of turns, hills, straightaways, surfaces, and difficult braking conditions. For the Trans-Am series, these tracks attracted some of the best drivers in the world. On the straights, the Trans-Am racecars ripped along at well over 150 miles an hour. Horsepower was important on the Trans-Am circuit. But the hills and sharp turns, in both directions, significantly increased the challenge of Trans-Am racing. This was very different than simply standing on it and turning left like they did in stock cars on the steeply banked, high-speed ovals.

This was road racing.

For this reason, the handling of a Trans-Am vehicle was very important. The snake-like chicanes, or successive turns, were sometimes within a few feet of each other. Some were called switchbacks because of the way they cut back and forth so rapidly and sharply—sometimes at 180-degree angles to each other—demanding premium driver skill and chassis engineering. And Trans-Am racing was punishing on the brakes. It was common for a driver to rapidly squeeze the brake pedal nearly to the floor, slowing the car very quickly to 20 miles an hour from a screaming straightaway run in order to negotiate some of these hairpins.

As he walked toward the GTO—the old goat—and Herb Adams standing next to it, Tullius had no concerns about this car's engineering.

Adams was one of the best racing chassis engineers Tullius had ever met. That's why Tullius had agreed to drive for him. "Everything okay?" asked Tullius.

"Yeah, yeah. Fine. Thanks for your help with the officials. Whatever you told them worked. We passed the tech." The men shook hands.

"No sweat," said Tullius, examining the car. "I knew we'd pass."

Adams' stomach flipped at the sight of Tullius looking at the GTO. What if Tullius thought this was a practical joke? A brief wave of insecurity washed over Adams.

Tullius put his hands on his hips. "So here she is, eh?"

Adams shrugged. "She's a 50-50 car, like I told Nell."

"A *what?*"

"A 50-50 car. She looks good at 50 feet away going 50 miles an hour."

Tullius threw Adams a half grin before returning to his study of the vehicle. "What's with the big slicks in front?"

"Makes it stickier."

"Kind of unorthodox, but ..." Tullius examined the front. "Hood's kinda cock-eyed."

"We were more concerned with the guts than fit and finish. The hood'll hold on."

Tullius paused, rubbing his chin. "Okay, let's see what she's made of."

Adams quietly drew a sigh of relief. "It's got no power brakes or steering. 303 short deck under the hood. Now, be sure to keep it at or below 5,000 rpms this time around ..."

Tullius, only half listening to Adams, was aware that three men standing next to a gleaming pony car in the next pit were watching them, unsuccessfully attempting to be inconspicuous. One was his long-time rival behind the wheel and a very formidable competitor. Tullius hated to admit it, even to himself, but the pony car driver was good—maybe better than good.

Tullius eased into his car through the driver's side window, settling into the seat. Felt good. The steel, spartan interior of the car was a medium blue. He approvingly examined the brushed aluminum dashboard sporting a checkerboard pattern. On the dashboard's far left was a large, unmarked red plastic light protruding slightly from the dash.

"What's this?" asked Tullius.

"Oil pressure warning light," responded Adams. "When the pressure drops below 20 psi, it'll light up. Nell's idea."

Tullius grunted softly, continuing his study of the dash. Five round, black gauges with white needles were set into the checkerboard dash. The first gauge on the left was the oil pressure. Next, directly over the steering column, was a larger gauge—the tachometer. Next to it on the right was the oil temperature, followed successively by the water temperature and fuel pressure gauges. To the right of the column, below the last three gauges, were five toggle switches, each labeled with a little blue plastic strip, with white embossed letters: starter, ignition, fuel pumps, wipers, and master. The car lacked a speedometer. No matter. It wasn't the clock Tullius would race—it was the other cars.

"See, to start it, you—" Adams began.

Tullius depressed the clutch, quickly flipped some toggle switches, and turned the key. The sound of 460 horses from a single 303 short deck filled the damp, cold early morning air at Lime Rock.

"*Like that?*" shouted Tullius through a broad grin. He goosed the throttle.

Adams mouthed something as Tullius looked in the mirror and the gray machine rumbled to life. The pony car driver and company were getting a face full of GTO exhaust. "Take that, hotshot," Tullius muttered to himself as he glanced in the rear view mirror, still grinning. This thing sounded good, anyway. He put on his helmet, gave Adams the thumbs up, and slowly pulled the car out of the end of pit road and onto the track.

Another little blue embossed label, just above the steering column, caught Tullius' eye: *When in doubt read instructions.*

~~~~

Tullius didn't know the car, but he knew Lime Rock very well from personal experience. A narrow, undulating short course of just over a mile and a half, and fast—a real horsepower course. Lime Rock was raced clockwise and laid out basically in the shape of a pentagon, except for the big hook-shaped leg that ran out the lower left of the course. Instead of a nice, sensibly angled leg connecting the bottom of the pentagon to the upper left part, this big, long hook stuck out. It was as if the track designer's hand—or bulldozer—became apathetic on the 2,800 foot long main straightaway at the bottom of the course and simply kept on going, until realizing he overshot the point where he should have turned right and up. So the track had to double back to reach the lower left part of the pentagon. To achieve this, the designer created a sharp right 180 degree turn known as the "Big Bend" at the end of this longest straightaway, which connected to a short straightaway before bending back left again to connect to the lower left side of the pentagon. This series of turns made for a fairly difficult right, left, right combination—a chicane. Tullius caressed the growling, gray GTO around the unbanked Big Bend. All the turns at Lime Rock were unbanked, placing a premium on the suspension.

After Big Bend, the track quickly bent back to the left, joining what remained of the lower left part of the pentagon. This area was known as the Esses, which led into the upper left part of the pentagon: No Name Straight. The car handled well mid-way through the snaking turns of the chicane. Tullius coasted through the Esses, fluidly shifted the Hurst stick into third gear, squeezed the accelerator down smoothly and quickly at the start of No Name Straight and immediately felt his body jamming back into the seat. This acceleration was surprising.

Tullius laughed out loud under his helmet.

Halfway along the straightaway, and in a seemingly single motion, he quickly let up on the gas, tapped the clutch, finessed the stick back into fourth gear and squeezed down the pedal again. Tullius was a master at smooth shifting, despite his bad left knee, the result of a football injury years earlier. More than a decade of competitive driving experience taught Bob Tullius that gentle, smooth operation of the controls—the wheel, accelerator, brakes, and stick—made for balanced, faster racing. The guys who kicked at the pedals, rammed the stick around, and spun the wheel wildly were rewarded with sliding, jerking, unsettled cars that lost traction, durability, and—most importantly—*time*. If they actually finished the race before destroying the brakes, engine or chassis, these drivers were absolutely exhausted. And they wondered why they didn't win. After all, they'd *worked* the hardest. Those guys confused effort with results. They confused wild emotion and brute force with *feel.* As a result, when they weren't flailing around in the cockpits, shoving their cars beyond their limits, they often were running their cars at well below their limits because they were out of balance, skidding, sliding, losing speed and occasionally spinning out.

As Tullius briskly squeezed the gas pedal, the GTO's muscular powerplant again responded immediately, screaming toward the slightly uphill curve at the top of the pentagon known as Climbing Turn. In a rapid, fluid, series of movements, Tullius braked and downshifted.

Downshifting in racing is not intended to slow the car. Brakes do that, and brakes don't wear out the engine either. Rather, Tullius downshifted in his approach to corners to get into the right gear, at the right RPMs, so as to maximize acceleration when he exited the corner. Downshifting was really about anticipation. But in racing, downshifting was complicated by the fact that while downshifting, the driver must also brake, and it must all be done smoothly, gently, without nose-diving the front end. If the driver just shifts into a lower gear and pops the clutch while standing on the brake, the car will surely nose-dive and maybe even lock up the rear driving wheels as a result of the braking effect caused by the engine's compression. Hence, good drivers increase the engine revolutions slightly, or "blip" during the downshift to match the engine RPMs with the rear wheels' RPMs, all the while braking. Unfortunately, blipping requires the simultaneous manipulation of three pedals with only two feet. Since even the best drivers are not three-legged, the driver must operate two pedals, the brake and accelerator, with one foot. He must brake hard and smoothly while blipping the throttle just enough after squeezing the clutch and shifting the stick.

To perform all this, drivers use a technique called "heel and toe" downshifting; they swivel or pivot the right foot onto the gas while braking as hard and as smoothly as possible. The ball of the driver's right foot is placed on the brake pedal and begins to push down while the right outside portion of the same foot rests on the accelerator. The left foot then depresses the clutch, and the stick is fluidly moved into the lower gear (all while the ball of the right foot is continuing to brake). The right foot then rolls quickly over on the gas and pushes or "blips" it to increase engine RPMs. The left foot rapidly, but smoothly, lets out the clutch and the gears mesh at the same revolutions while the right foot continues to brake. If the blip is too weak, the rear driving wheels lock up when the clutch is re-engaged. If the blip is too strong, the car will accelerate at a time when the driver is attempting to slow it with the brakes. Proper heel and toe down-shifting requires practice, athletic ability, sensitive hearing, and *feel*.

The GTO blipped easily with Tullius at the controls. It held the track and, despite very big g-forces in the turns, even at relatively high speed. This was good. Tullius gassed it again in the middle of Climbing Turn and roared into the Back Straight. Quickly and fluidly snapping the Hurst shifter into fourth gear with a practiced hand, he gassed it and was again pushed back into the seat, estimating his speed at 125. This was *very* good. Approaching the next curve, West Bend, Tullius braked hard and heel-toe downshifted again. The GTO responded smoothly, rounding the curve effortlessly. He stood on the gas again briefly, eased off, rapidly squeezed the clutch, and finessed the stick quickly back into fourth. The GTO thundered toward the final turn, a gradual wide right bend called Driving Turn. Tullius eased off the gas, leaving the car in fourth gear—75 miles an hour, he guessed, coasting around the turn. This was definitely a *very* good suspension. The g-forces were at their maximum rounding the all bends. Halfway through the curve, he gently, swiftly, mashed the gas pedal to the floor, preparing to enter the longest straightaway on the track, the Main Straight. Now it was time to test the engine. "Let's *go,* baby," muttered Tullius from beneath his helmet, gripping the wheel tighter, his hands at nine and three o'clock. The GTO blasted out of Driving Turn, accelerating fast into the Main Straight. Tullius felt his heart quicken as his body was once again pressed back into the seat. In an instant he was halfway down the Main Straight, still accelerating. The tachometer read 4,800 rpm and was rising fast. He roared past pit row at 121 miles an hour before braking hard again for Big Bend.

"Hot *damn*, baby!" shouted Tullius.

Chapter 18

"JEEZ," SAID THE young man standing to the pony car driver's right, gawking as the old gray GTO roared past them on its first test lap around Lime Rock.

"Told ya," muttered the pony car driver. "Time that thing on the next lap. Let's see what these gearheads did to the old goat."

The driver's initial surprise upon first seeing Herb Adams and Tullius with the GTO had now turned to genuine, albeit mild, concern. He estimated its speed on the main straightway at 130, and this was just warm-up. He wouldn't have believed an old tub could move that fast, even with Herb Adams and his engineers behind it. It just didn't *look* fast. But looks don't get you anywhere in racing, he reminded himself. It's the suspension and the drivetrain. This so-called amateur car clearly had plenty of both, unlike the other amateur jalopies he'd raced against in the past. The old gray sedan took the turns surprisingly fast. These guys had a driver, too, a very, very, good one.

"All right, let's go, boys. Back to work. We're next on the track."

The two men continued to gape at the GTO tearing around Lime Rock on its second leg. "HEY!" shouted the pony car driver.

"Sorry ..." they said together, turning their attention to him.

"One minute you're laughing at that old goat and the next you're pissin' your pants over it. Listen, no amateurs are going to beat us, *got it?*" The two heads nodded. "We're an experienced, professional team with factory support. No amateurs have *ever* beaten us and they won't here, either. We got a huge car company backing us and we're not gonna let 'em down."

"Yes, sir," they quietly agreed in submissive unison.

"Now, a few warm-up laps to get any bugs out, then we qualify for tomorrow. Let's fire it up," the pony car driver barked as he climbed into his car.

The two men knew there were no bugs in the pony, but they weren't about to argue. They'd been at Lime Rock for exactly a week now, personally getting every bug, real and imagined, out of the mule car and the racecars, too. And their driver knew the track like the back of his hand. He should; he'd driven it close to 150 laps over the last week.

The GTO, still roaring around the track, passed the three men. One of them clicked a stopwatch at the gray, growling blur.

~~~~

Tullius pulled into the pit after four very rapid trips around Lime Rock. Seven men greeted him as he exited the GTO. A Connecticut State Trooper watched them from a distance.

"How's the oil pressure?" asked Tom Nell urgently.

Tullius was astonished at the car's performance. "Oil pressure? Dunno. I was focused on driving—no little red light."

"Well, what do you think?" asked Adams, surrounded by the pit crew.

Tullius pulled off his helmet and grinned at the eager faces. "I think we can compete with this old baby. I mean *really* compete. But maybe you could straighten out the hood and adjust the clutch. Got a bad knee, from football."

The Trans/Action team quietly congratulated themselves with back slaps and handshakes.

~~~~

During the next few hours, the crew adjusted the clutch linkage, reducing both the height and travel of the clutch pedal. After they had adjusted the clutch to Tullius' liking, he entered car 49 again for a few more practice laps.

"Okay," said Adams to his driver, "take it up to 8,000 rpm now. I mean *redline* it."

"Here we go," said a grinning Tullius as the GTO's engine thundered awake. As the big gray GTO rolled onto the dry track, a few dozen spectators sat in the stands under the gray Saturday sky. One of the many big name professional drivers was widely expected to take the pole position in the qualifying race to follow and few in the stands paid any attention to old car number 49. But the car's crew watched closely. The nervous faces of Trans/Action stared as their car entered Big Bend and smoothly negotiated the Esses, cutting the corners, into No Name Straight. Tullius' acceleration and downshifting was drowned out by the pony cars roaring around it. The GTO vaulted up Climbing Turn on the far side of the track and roared down into the Back Straight, hugged the inside of West Bend and accelerated into Driving Turn. The Trans/Action team watched as Tullius screamed past them in a blur, accelerating on the Main Straight. Tullius hit 141 miles an hour before braking hard at Big Bend.

Ted Lambiris clicked his stopwatch as the gray blur whizzed past. He glanced at the lap time on the stopwatch and performed a quick calculation in his head just for kicks: 90.5 miles an hour average speed for that lap. Four more laps at this rate and they'd qualify for sure. Tullius again smoothly rounded Big Bend and the Esses, but as he hit the gas into No Name Straight, a loud noise came from the engine compartment and the car lost power. Tullius' heart sank. He'd heard this sound before. It could mean only one thing: a blown engine. He eased off the gas and nursed the GTO back to the pit. Seven furrowed brows greeted him.

"Blown engine," Tullius said, exiting the car.

A collective murmur of sharp curses emanated from the team.

"Pop the hood," said Tom Nell, doubtfully.

"Yeah, let's see," agreed Jeff Young.

Nell and Young opened the hood and squinted into the engine compartment, with Adams looking over their shoulders. Everything but the fan belt, which had fallen off, looked okay. The fan belt alone wouldn't have caused this problem. Maybe there was some serious internal damage. But how? This thing was engineered right, built right, too. If there was internal damage, it would be unlikely the engine could be repaired in time for tomorrow's race, let alone qualify for it today. They had one spare engine, but it would take all night to pull this one and replace it. They had to find and fix it, whatever the problem; and they had to do it fast. Tom Nell quickly checked the compression on each cylinder, rotating them all twice, or so he thought. All but one of them seemed fine. The bad cylinder appeared to have a compression problem, said Nell. Nell, Young and Adams discussed the matter briefly, decided to load the GTO back onto the trailer, and find a garage where they could further diagnose and repair it fast. With any luck, they would still have time left to qualify today.

The GTO was quickly loaded onto the creaky trailer and hauled to the nearest Pontiac-GMC-Chevrolet-Buick-Cadillac car dealer, who, after hearing their story, allowed the Trans/Action Team to use one of the two dirt floor repair bays in the tiny dealership. The car was hastily unloaded from the trailer onto the dirt and Nell and Young immediately dug into the engine, removing it from the car and dropping the oil pan, frantically searching for the source of the compression trouble. An hour passed without success. The engine was further disassembled. Another hour passed, still nothing to indicate the source of the compression problem. After another hour, the engine had been completely disassembled. Nell and Young were perplexed. During the next few hours, they re-assembled the engine. Finally, Nell checked the compression again on each cylinder, and this time they all checked out fine. Nell scratched his head, staring blankly at the underside of the hood, when he noticed an unusual black streak on it. He picked up a shop light, shining it at the streak. It looked like rubber, made by a belt. After a brief puzzlement, it dawned on Nell. In his haste to find the trouble, he hadn't rotated one of the cylinders two full turns. The result was a misdiagnosed problem. This engine had no compression problem, it was just the damned *fan belt!* The black streak on the underside of the hood was made by the fan belt as it flew off the engine. Nell cursed repeatedly as they hurriedly reinstalled the engine and new fan belt. Adams turned the ignition. The GTO roared to life, with no sign of compression trouble.

"Well I'll be a … I'm sorry guys … I …" muttered Nell sheepishly, wiping his filthy hands and muscular forearms with a shop towel.

Adams looked at his watch: 4:55 p.m. The last qualifying laps at Lime Rock were over. It would be a long drive home. Hell of a way to spend a vacation day, he thought. Adams walked over to Nell, who was staring at the greasy floor, shaking his head. Adams silently patted Nell on the back.

"Hey," said Jeff Young softly to his engine partner, "let's get back to the track, buddy."

~~~~

The men thanked the dealer's owner, loaded the GTO back on the groaning trailer, and climbed into the Suburban with Jeff Young at the wheel. They snaked their way through the gas station parking lot, choked with parked cars awaiting repair. A Volkswagen Bug was parked at a corner. As Young rounded the corner, a loud screeching sound came from the trailer. He immediately stopped and looked in the rearview mirror and saw that the trailer was scraping a parked Volkswagen Bug. The three men jumped out of the Suburban and looked at the damage. The trailer was fine, but the bug's quarter panel was deeply scratched from the trailer.

"Don't worry about it," said the dealer. "It needed some body work anyway."

The men apologized profusely and jumped back into the Suburban. Jeff Young backed the trailer away from the Bug and negotiated his way around it. The Suburban pulled up to the street, waiting for traffic to clear; as Young made a right turn out of the lot onto the street, another scraping noise emanated from the trailer. A Camaro. Young winced at the rearview mirror, drew up his shoulders around his neck, and drove on.

~~~~

Tullius knew that his biggest competitor had just qualified at an average speed of 92.72 mph, despite previously blowing two transmissions, both of which were rapidly replaced by the professional pit crew. That crew set the standard for pit stops; they were incredibly fast. Their driver's speed around the track was rumored in pit road to be a new course record. And there were more challenges, like the aggressive driver in his Mustang. Tullius couldn't let them bother him.

"Hey buddy!" yelled Tullius, walking toward the race promoter.

The promoter of this year's Lime Rock Trans-Am race was watching the last qualifying car of the day pull into pit row. He looked in Tullius' direction. "Bob! Bob Tullius! How are you, buddy?"

"Not so good after this afternoon."

"Yeah. Bad luck."

They exchanged the usual pleasantries and brief small talk, and then Tullius got to the point with his old friend. "Hey, I have a favor to ask of you."

"Shoot."

"That old GTO is very competitive. I had it up to 140 on the Main Straight today. It's got a great suspension, too. Average speed of 90.5 mph on one lap. I mean, it handles as good or better than any pony car I ever drove. 450 horses. Consistently, too."

"Don't look like much," said the promoter, chuckling.

"Don't let that fool you. I'm telling you, that machine goes like a striped-assed ape. The guys behind it are Herb Adams and his engineers from Pontiac. They're factory guys, except for one thing: they got no factory backing. No factory money. They gave technical support to Firebird racing the last few years. Those guys know what they're doing."

"I saw the old goat go today," said the promoter, nodding.

"Well, I thought we blew an engine. We didn't—just a belt problem. My guys fixed it, but during the fix we missed qualifying. So how about letting us give it another go? Another shot at qualifying."

The promoter looked at the ground and shook his head. "Can't do it. SCCA and Trans-Am would both go nuts. Open Pandora's Box. We make an exception for you guys, and then everybody wants an exception for every little thing."

"But these guys drove all the way from Detroit. I mean, it's no big deal to me 'cause I'm just doing this for kicks, but these guys put a lot of blood, sweat, and tears into this machine."

"I can't bend the rules for you, buddy." The promoter looked at the infield, thinking. "But there is another way. There's this thing called the 'promoter's option.' As the track promoter, I got the option of adding a few cars—any cars—to the field in the last positions."

"No need to qualify?"

"Nope."

"Well, all right then buddy! Thanks!"

"Wait a minute. You gotta start dead last, understand? And you got 30-some new pony cars ahead of you on this tight track, in an old tub without no factory support." The promoter looked up at the threatening evening sky, "And maybe in the rain."

"Yeah, yeah, no sweat. Just give us a chance."

"Okay, okay," grinned the promoter. "Number 49 will be the promoter's option tomorrow. Just don't embarrass me, Bob."

"Embarrass? Hell, we're gonna *win*."

Chapter 19

RACE DAY GREETED the Trans/Action team and the other 30 cars with pouring, cold rain, typical for a New England May. The announcer sat in the relative shelter of the press booth, perched above the grandstands, halfway down the Main Straight. The veteran sports announcer wore a blue blazer with a patch on the left breast sporting the circular sports TV broadcasting logo of his employer. Wearing a headset, holding a corded microphone, and smiling into a television camera, he said in a smooth, practiced tone, "Thank you and welcome again, ladies and gentlemen. Today, we're in Connecticut at the beautiful Lime Rock Park Raceway for the opening race of the 1971 Trans-Am racing season—the Schaeffer Beer Trans-Am. Twenty thousand spectators and all the top teams and their drivers are on hand, including Ford, Chevrolet, and American Motors—and if the past is any guide, this race promises to be a highly competitive and exciting affair. On the pole for today's 200-mile race in the over two liter class is the all-American red, white and blue Sunoco/AMC Javelin. The driver set a course record of 92.72 miles an hour during one lap at yesterday's qualifying rounds. He'll have his hands full, however, with last year's Trans-Am series drivers' champion and winner here and his orange Mustang, starting second today."

The announcer continued describing the well-known drivers in the second and third rows of the starting grid. "So the orange Mustang will share the front row with the patriotic Javelin for today's exciting race. Detroit's pony cars—Mustangs, Camaros, Firebirds and Javelins—have dominated the Trans-Am series since its beginning in 1966 and there is no reason to doubt that they won't dominate today at Lime Rock, despite the threatening skies. So stay tuned for 131 laps of exciting Trans-Am racing action after these important messages."

~~~~

During his first practice lap Saturday morning, Tullius quickly noticed the inside of the GTO's windshield begin to fog up in the rain-drenched air. He vainly wiped the windshield with his hand before realizing the hopelessness of the effort and pulled slowly into pit road, squinting through the windshield.

"What's the matter?" asked Adams.

"Fog." Tullius pointed at the windshield. "Can't see ..."

Adams ducked his head into the cockpit, quickly spying the windshield. "Oh ..." He ducked back out, looking to his left, then right. This was not the time to tell Tullius that they'd removed the car's heater and defroster in an effort to save weight. "Dutch! Hey Dutch!" called Adams.

The mechanic peered through the misting rain, "Yeah?"

"Come here ..." Adams shouted, motioning Dutch to approach the car.

Dutch took a long draw on his cigarette as he walked to Adams at the driver's side of the car. "What ya need?" he asked.

"A de-fogger. And quick."

Dutch glanced at the inside of the windshield. Tullius wiped it with the side of his hand, leaving a narrow, damp streak on the glass.

Dutch tossed his cigarette to the ground, rubbed his chin and said, "Yeah. Okay ... be right back." The machinist walked deliberately to the team's Styrofoam cooler and opened it. Fishing around inside, he removed two cans of beer, pulled the ring tab on one, and began guzzling the can's contents without pause.

"*Hey!*" said Tullius to Adams. "I need a de-fogger and he's gettin' *drunk* ..."

Adams put his finger to his lips, "Wait a minute ..."

Dutch carefully set the empty can on his tool chest and belched loudly. He wiped his mouth with the back of his hand, popped open the other can, and with a practiced motion, began rapidly gulping it down as the other members of the Trans/Action team looked on with a mix of amusement, awe, and concern.

Dutch belched again. He set down the second empty can and methodically removed a pair of tinsnips, a riveter, and a roll of duct tape from his tool chest. He picked up the first can and began carefully cutting it in half lengthwise with the tinsnips, then he did the same with the other can. He then carefully cut out the bottoms and tops of each section. After placing the tinsnips back in the tool chest, he picked up the riveter and pop riveted the four halved cans together lengthwise. Grabbing the roll of duct tape, the machinist walked to the car with the cans. Silently, Dutch bent the cans, forming a U-shaped scoop, and duct taped the cans over the rivets. He heavily taped one end of the scoop to the upper left corner of the interior windshield and the doorframe. The other end of the scoop jutted from the car into the exterior air, facing forward. Dutch stepped back, admiring his handiwork. As the car sped along, air would be forced into the scoop from the exterior, rammed around the bend formed by the inside of the beer cans, and forced across the interior of the windshield, effectively keeping it fog-free.

Dutch belched loudly. "There. De-fogger. Union made, too. And it'll even provide Tullius with that nice used car smell." Reaching for a cigarette in his shirt pocket, the machinist glanced at Adams, "Ya know, boss, I'm feelin' pretty *good* …"

~~~~

Undeterred by the rain and 45-degree temperatures, the few hundred Lime Rock fans who paid two dollars to enter the pre-race pits ogled the decal-laden 1971 Mustangs, Camaros and Javelins. This was professional racing and the real fans wanted to get as close as possible to the racecars and drivers they read about in the car magazines and saw on television. Some were awestruck by these seemingly superhuman men and their incredible, glossy machines. The fans studied every inch of the cars and stared at the valiant drivers, whispering, pointing and talking excitedly to each other. They strained over each other to hear their heroes and see the bright new professional racing machines gleaming in the rain. A few brave souls even asked for autographs from the drivers.

At the far end of the paddock, behind a barricade of motor oil company signs, sat a wet, old, gray sedan sporting a smallish number 49 sticker on its doors and a few oddly placed sponsors' decals. About half a dozen ordinary-looking men, in ordinary raincoats and windbreakers, some of whom appeared fidgety, surrounded it. One of them was very young, a teenager. They nodded from under their little black umbrellas, smiling, at the fans walking by. Wearing his racing garb, Bob Tullius stood under an umbrella talking to a lone reporter who was casually jotting notes on a damp pad of paper. All the other racing journalists who weren't crowding around the drivers at the front of the starting grid—and the drivers themselves—had sought the shelter and comfort of a scotch distiller's tent on the infield. The tent was very well equipped to meet the needs of the ironically sodden, yet thirsty writers.

Thank God for distilled spirit race sponsors.

"It really handles well," Tullius told the journalist through the frigid rain. "And it should be good on short tracks like this one. On the longer courses, we'll be giving something away with the aerodynamics, however." While Tullius continued to talk up the GTO to the solitary writer, most fans simply ignored the relatively motley looking Trans/Action Team and their old gray GTO—or at least tried to ignore them. Other fans greeted them with stone faces, occasional sniggers, and more than a few outright laughs. Before long, Herb Adams felt a vague empathy for sideshow circus freaks and zoo animals.

Chapter 20

AFTER THE PITS were closed to spectators and press, Bob Tullius confidently donned his helmet, fastened his seat belt, and looked through the rain-streaked windshield at the rear ends of 30 professional racecars. The rain continued, and now the wind began to blow. The damp 45-degree air felt sub-zero now. He had driven the GTO a total of eight laps around Lime Rock, and in the first five he'd really just felt out the car and got it warmed up for the hard stuff—and that was just yesterday. But even before the seat was warm, he was sure he could get this baby down to a 1:03 lap. If the fan belt hadn't fallen off yesterday in qualifying, he knew the car would have made a one-minute flat lap here. That would have given him third place on the grid, directly behind the pole sitter. Tullius trusted himself, the Trans/Action Team, the GTO, and the four big gumballs in this rain. Some of the best automotive racing engineers he'd ever met created this machine. And even better, what was there to lose? He had no pressure to win because nobody expected this seven-year-old, last place tub to compete. They didn't understand. This car's a jackrabbit wearing a turtle shell.

~~~~

The Greek, disguised in a hooded windbreaker, approached Adams next to the car. He lifted the bottom of his windbreaker, revealing a glass Coke bottle jammed into his right front pants pocket. Only the bottle's top protruded from the pocket.

"Hey," said the Greek, "watch this ..." Ted cast quick, furtive glances up and down the pit and casually removed the gas cap from the GTO. He grabbed the top of the Coke bottle with his right hand, pulled it out slightly of his pocket and leaned into the car, tipping the contents of the Coke bottle into the tank.

"*HEY!* What in hell ..." shouted Adams, wide-eyed.

The Greek quickly put a finger to his lips, "*Shhhh* ..."

A look of puzzlement passed across Adams' face. He squinted at the liquid pouring from the pocketed Coke bottle. It wasn't the color of Coke. The Greek chuckled quietly and looked quickly over his shoulder, still pouring.

Then the realization hit Adams. The crazy Greek was topping up the tank with extra gas. This was potentially illegal, since each car was only allotted a 22-gallon tank. Adams looked up and down the pit quickly. No race officials in sight. A Connecticut State Trooper ambled away from them; he couldn't care less. The other teams were focused on their own cars. They were probably cheating, too. And the Greek *did* look like he was just leaning on the car. Sort of.

The Greek furtively squeezed the empty Coke bottle back into his pocket and screwed the gas cap back on the car. He winked again at Adams, grinned broadly, and walked away, whistling softly. Adams blinked rapidly at the gas cap, mouth agape and heart pounding.

~~~~

"Okay, now listen," Adams said to Tullius as the driver settled in behind the wheel. "One hundred thirty-one laps total. We got two planned pit stops for gas—every 44 laps or so. So look for our pit board—we'll tell you when to pit. Okay?"

Tullius wiped the inside of the windshield with a rag. "Yeah ..." The cars ahead of Tullius roared to life and began easing onto the wet, cold track. Tullius flipped the ignition. He heard and felt the rumble and shake of the GTO's engine as he slowly saluted Adams, eased the shaking machine into first gear, lumbered out of pit road through a huge cloud of damp, blue-gray exhaust and onto the slick track. Tullius' throat tightened with excitement.

As the field of racers made their way around the track in the first warm-up circuit, the rain fell harder until Tullius could actually hear it pounding the roof, hood and trunk—even above the roar of the GTO's engine and the quick beating of the windshield wipers. The rain fell so hard it rebounded from the track, spattering back up and creating a thick mist just over the track. The cars made one circuit around the track, remaining in order, waiting for the green flag at the starting line.

They made a second lap, still cruising in order. The rain continued.

As the Javelin and the orange Mustang on the front row approached the starting line, the starter, a smallish man hunched over in a vain effort to avoid the downpour, quickly left the shelter of a small shed at the edge of the track and furiously waved the green flag. The race was on.

The two cars in front of the pack gunned their engines and roared toward the Big Bend at the end of the Main Straight. The starter, after waving the wet, heavy, green flag for what seemed like an eternity to him, stopped his frantic waving and ducked back into shelter to avoid a further soaking as the pack roared past. As he cruised passed the starting line seconds later, Tullius squinted through the watery windshield and the rapid beating of the wipers for some sign of the starter with his green flag. He saw nothing like a green flag. Tullius kept cruising around the track, still at the rear of the pack, making a full circuit. Approaching the starting line, again he squinted for the green flag and once again, nothing. Unusual, he thought. How many times are we going to tiptoe around here, waiting for the green flag? *"Let's go!"* Tullius said out loud.

As he worked his way methodically through the Esses, Tullius saw it—action on No Name Straight. The cars in front of him had not only broken their starting formation, they were passing each other! *"Son of a bitch!"* hollered Tullius, realizing the race was on and immediately mashing the accelerator to the floor. Tullius looked quickly to his right and saw the pole sitter in front, rounding Driving Turn and gassing it into the Main Straight. The Javelin had a three-quarter-lap lead on him *already*, and Tullius had just started racing. Tullius cursed loudly again. But then, as he downshifted and rounded Climbing Hill, Tullius saw the orange Mustang facing the wrong way in the muddy infield. It looked like the number two car in the starting grid. Even Tullius' quick glance told him that something was seriously wrong with the Mustang's front end. The number two guy was out on the first lap of the race, but the GTO showed no sign of fishtailing or traction loss of any other kind. Tullius gently snapped the stick into fourth gear and took a deep breath to calm his anger at the bumbling starter. A bad start, but one serious competitor had spun out already while the GTO was sticking like glue to the track. Tullius passed a car on the Back Straight and another on the Main Straight.

He was no longer in last place. This would be okay, he reassured himself. This would be okay.

On the fourth lap, the GTO was greeted by more disconcerting news—another Mustang was in the ditch. This one, previously running with the front of the pack, was stuck in the mud at the front of the Esses and looked to be another car piloted by a well-known driver. Tullius drove on, carefully but quickly and smoothly, through the downpour. He passed eight more cars in rapid succession during the next few laps. The GTO was handling very well. Maybe he could push it a little …

By the tenth lap, Tullius and the GTO had passed 18 cars. He was in tenth place and the car felt better and better. He was passing everywhere on the track—curves and straightaways, inside and outside. Tullius now felt justified in his self-confidence and his confidence in this car. He rounded the West Bend, glanced into the rearview mirror, and saw something unexpected. The red, white and blue Javelin being driven by Mark Donahue was nearing the end of the Main Straight and had closed on the GTO. A yellow Javelin was right behind the red white and blue Javelin. Unless Tullius got on it *right* now, the pole sitter was going to lap him. With renewed determination, Tullius smoothly stuck the Hurst shifter into fourth gear and rapidly squeezed the accelerator to the floor. The GTO, as usual, immediately roared its approval and rocketed out of the bend into No Name Straight and then into Driving Turn. Tullius eased off the gas, rounded the turn and again smoothly put the gas pedal to the floor. As the GTO screamed past pit row on the Main Straight at 143 miles an hour, it left a plume of heavy, blinding mist in its wake.

"You ain't lappin' me, pole boy," said Tullius out loud.

As he entered the Esses, Tullius did a double take at someone on the infield dragging what looked like a kid's red wagon with a car jack in it toward the Mustang stuck in the mud off the track near the Esses. He was going to try to jack his car out of that mud?

On lap 21, Tullius noticed a Javelin stuck in the mud at the end of the Main Straight. Moments later, Tullius saw a driver with a jack under his orange Mustang, working hard, by himself, to get unstuck. The light, relatively unbalanced pony cars with their skinny front wheels were clearly having difficulty on the drenched Lime Rock track.

~~~~

In the press booth, the announcer spoke in a polished tone into the television microphone. "So after lap 21, it's the red, white and blue Javelin, followed closely by another Javelin—the yellow one. Stay tuned, ladies and gentlemen, for more racing action from Lime Rock, after these messages." He removed his headset, picked up the lap charts and began studying them. Was this going to be another relatively boring Trans-Am race with a predictable winner? That wouldn't be good for ratings. Within moments, his experienced eye recognized from the charts that car number 49, which had started in last place, had moved rapidly through the pack.

Who was this? Bob Tullius the chart said.

The announcer wasn't aware that Tullius was even driving today. He looked up from the charts and onto the track, searching for car 49. As the pony cars streaked by, he noticed what looked like an old, gray, clearly amateur entry near the front of the pack. It looked like a GTO. An *old* GTO with long flanks and square edges. It sported a small number 49 sticker on the door. The announcer looked back at the chart. Car 49 was a 1964 GTO, the chart said. *1964?*

He looked at the chart again, blinking, to verify the year, and then glanced back at the track. Now that he'd seen the old GTO, he wondered what had taken him so long to notice—it was such a sharp contrast to all the new pony cars. But *man*, it moved. To come from 31st to near the front in only 20-some laps, was remarkable for any car. Yet, this thing was seven years old. He glanced back at the charts. The oldest professional pony car was listed as a 1970 model and a couple other amateur teams were racing 1967 model pony cars. As the pack streamed past him on Main Straight, the TV announcer heard cheering from the stands. He looked at the soaking wet fans through the blowing rain and noticed they were much more animated than they'd been earlier in this race. They were cheering as if this was nearly the last lap. Some were standing in the nearly horizontal rain, waving their arms in the air as the pack roared by. They didn't seem to be focused on the leader; it was a car behind the two leading Javelins they seemed to be cheering for. The GTO?

A finger tapped him on the shoulder. "Ten seconds," said the cameraman. The announcer quickly donned his headset, spun around to the camera, and heard the producer in his ear, "... and 5, 4, 3, 2, 1 ..." The producer silently pointed his finger at the announcer.

"Welcome back, ladies and gentlemen, to Lime Rock Park Speedway for the Schaefer Beer 200—the opening race of the 1971 Trans-Am series," he said in his smooth, trademarked baritone. "At the end of lap 26, it's still the pole sitter in the lead followed closely by another AMC Javelin. But the real story here seems to be another car—car number 49, a *1964* Pontiac GTO, the old goat, yes, you heard it right, 1964, driven by the talented Bob Tullius. Despite the fact that he's competing against brand new Mustangs, Camaros, and Javelins, Mr. Tullius, in his old goat, has managed his way from last place to fourth place in just 26 laps. The GTO, Pontiac's only entry in this race, has passed nearly everyone on the track and has passed them nearly everywhere on the track. While a half-dozen new pony cars have spun out in these wet conditions and found themselves stuck in the mud, the vintage car number 49, with Tullius at the controls, has snaked its way through the remaining competitors into the top four in only the first quarter of this wet race. Clearly, anyone here at Lime Rock who judged this vintage GTO by its dated cover made a big mistake."

~~~~

At the end of lap 37, the GTO, charging hard, had moved into third place. The yellow Javelin was still second behind the pole sitter, but Tullius was now looking at both of them through his windshield, not his rear view mirror. And he was closing the gap on the yellow. Tullius had put the screwed-up start out of his mind. He was third with 90-some laps to go. This was very satisfying.

~~~~

At the next commercial break, the TV announcer studied the grandstand's reaction as the leaders ripped past them in the rain. They still weren't focused on the Javelins. They were soaking wet and definitely cheering for the GTO. Some of them were wildly cheering—on their feet and waving fists in the wet air as the old gray GTO streaked through the plume of spray left by the two leaders in front of it.

This was remarkable. The announcer grinned and slowly shook his head in amazement. He had been following and covering racing for decades, but he'd rarely seen anything like this show of populist support for an underdog.

~~~~

At lap 43, Adams held up the pit board at the edge of pit road. It read GAS in large, white letters. Tullius screamed past without hesitation in an envelope of spray. At lap 44, Adams held the board higher. Tullius drove on. "He can't see me," Adams said to the Greek. "Too much damn spray."

The Greek glanced at his fuel chart, "He's gonna be on fumes soon. I mean even *with* the extra Coke."

"I gotta get closer." Adams quickly looked up and down pit road. "Closer to the track so Bob can see the board." A Connecticut State Trooper stood nearby, shoulders hunched and arms crossed in the cold rain. "I'm going across pit road to the track." Adams whispered loudly to the Greek.

"What about the *cops?*"

"Screw the cops. We need gas, man."

"But, what if they … I mean, we ain't got the *bread* to post your bail."

"Here he comes!" shouted Adams from under his hooded blue wind-breaker as car 49 emerged rapidly out of the mist and approached the straight outside of pit road. Adams ran across pit road to the edge of the track and thrust the pit board high in the air as Tullius roared past.

Tullius saw the board and understood the instruction to pit.

Adams, soaking from spray, trotted back across pit road in full view of the trooper, who dropped his hunched shoulders, uncrossed his arms and stiffened his stance as he squinted at Adams.

"Tullius saw it," announced Adams to the Greek.

"Yeah. So did the cop."

On the following lap, car 49 pitted and Tom Nell, physically the strongest member of the team, rapidly hoisted the big gas can and rammed its spout into the fuel filler neck of the car's tank. Adams, holding the pit board in his left hand, held a steady open right palm at Tullius as Nell gurgled the gas into the thirsty car. A photographer snapped a shot of the scene from behind the car.

Nell finished re-fueling and pulled the can from the car, backpedaling fast. Adams furiously waved the driver to go, stepping back quickly. The car peeled out of pit road in a swirling, moist cloud.

Adams cast a furtive glance at the cop, whose shoulders were hunched up again, and his arms were crossed as he stared sullenly out at the sodden track.

"No jail for you this time, boss," said the Greek through a wet grin. "And remember—things go better with Coke ..."

~~~~

On lap 64, the seemingly inevitable happened; Peter Revson in his yellow Javelin pitted and Tullius moved into second place. The TV announcer had a story and he was excited. "Ladies and gentlemen, we have a remarkable story in the making here at Lime Rock. It's lap 64 and the seven-year-old gray GTO, with absolutely no factory support and only a few sponsors, has incredibly woven its way through the rain-soaked field from *dead last* into *second place* behind the pole sitter! Each time the two leaders accelerate past the grandstands, the soaking wet crowd leaps to its feet to cheer on the old, amateur underdog GTO. The yellow Javelin, formerly in second, just entered the pit, which allowed Bob Tullius in the GTO to streak into second place. Despite the continuing rain, this grandstand crowd here at Lime Rock remains at near capacity and roared its approval upon witnessing the GTO just move into second. An otherwise potentially ordinary race—made even more mundane and difficult to watch by the incessant rain—has become a truly exciting battle: a battle of David and Goliath. I must say, ladies and gentlemen, that in all my years of covering automobile racing I have rarely seen anything like this."

~~~~

The yellow Javelin, supported by its professional pit crew, was quickly out of the pit and back on the track. On lap 67, Tullius was forced to pit for gas again and yellow regained second place. The grandstands quieted. The Trans/Action team, manning the pits, did their best to fuel their car and get it back on the track fast, but it took almost twice the time for the Trans/Action engineers to do the job yellow's pros had taken three laps earlier.

Nineteen laps later, the TV audience heard unmistakable excitement in the announcer's voice. "The old GTO, continually pressuring Peter Revson's yellow Javelin since yielding back second place, is now very close to the Javelin as they absolutely *roar* down the wet main straightaway, nearly neck-and-neck in a fight for second place with 45 laps to go! The drenched crowd is on its feet again, cheering madly for their underdog hero, the seven-year-old gray GTO driven by Bob Tullius. And now they enter the Big Bend at the end of the Main Straight ... it seems—yes the GTO has pulled along on the outside of the Javelin ... now Tullius is *passing* on the *outside* of the turn! Incredible! Tullius is extending his lead on the yellow car through the curving Esses. The GTO, now in second place, is pulling away from the Javelin, heading into No Name Straight and seemingly closing on the leader! I can't *believe* what I'm seeing!"

From the pit, the soaking wet Trans/Am team cheered their car wildly, but they were drowned out by the deafening roar of the crowd. Fifteen laps later, in the relentless rain, Tullius quickly looked in his rear view mirror as he rounded Driver's Bend and gunned it for the Main Straight. The yellow Javelin was falling further behind. Tullius glanced again at the rearview mirror; yellow looked as if he were coasting now and heading for the pits off the Main Straight. Yellow coasted into the pit and stopped. The ignition system on the yellow Javelin, soaked by 100 laps of rain and mist, was shot. Despite his crew's best efforts, the Javelin refused to re-start.

After 101 laps, and with 30 more to go, Lime Rock was now littered with motionless racecars, stuck, broken, or both, immobilized just off the track and in pit road. As he chased the leader around the Big Bend and into the Esses, Tullius saw another Javelin mired in the deep shoulder mud of the escape road at the end of the Main Straight. Just off the Esses, a driver was still at it, prying his Mustang out of the muck. A quick glance told Tullius that the orange driver now had a big stick of some kind, like a fence post, that he was using to lever the Ford out of the gumbo. It looked as if he nearly had the car out. Regardless of this race's outcome, that guy clearly deserved the perseverance award for this effort. A Mustang, its front-end busted from the spinout on the first lap, was off the track just ahead. Another Mustang was at a dead stop with its front wheels askew, facing the wrong way on the infield next to the track.

Tullius appreciated the GTO's handling more than ever.

~~~~

The announcer, struggling uncharacteristically to retain his journalistic objectivity in the face of this developing underdog story, leaned into the TV microphone. "It's lap 124—only seven more laps to go—and Bob Tullius in his vintage GTO, who failed to qualify for this race and started *last* in this field of 31 cars, continues to close on the man who started *first* and has held first nearly ever since. A Mustang follows the GTO in a very distant third with the rest of this rain-soaked pack not far behind him. The 20,000 fans that turned out to see this race in the rain are—remarkably—still in their seats cheering wildly for the old gray goat. Ladies and gentlemen, it's been a long, long time since I have had the privilege of seeing such an exciting race. As I said earlier, this is a classic battle between David and Goliath: the amateur-built, low-budget, seven-year-old GTO against the new, well-funded, professional Javelin. Regardless of which of these great drivers and cars you're rooting for, this Lime Rock race has turned out to be a real beauty. But wait—the GTO is slowing—it's entering the pits with what appears to be smoke or steam from under the hood. This is an unscheduled stop for the classic Pontiac, which may cost Tullius any chance at winning the race. As you can see on your screen, the GTO pit crew has popped the hood and appears to be pouring water into the radiator. Now they've slammed the hood back down, secured the pins, and Tullius is off again!"

Tullius had begun feeling the car's horsepower loss a lap earlier. The engine's lightning quick responsiveness and thundering power had vanished. The smoke from under the hood confirmed the bad feeling: the engine was leaking power somehow. He was losing ground quickly now. The leader was pulling ahead. Tullius had no choice—He had to make an emergency pit stop. He cursed and he pulled into the pits. As he slid to a long stop on the wet asphalt, Tullius pointed at the hood, screaming at the Trans/Action guys manning the pit from under his helmet, *"Power loss— power loss!"* As soon as Tullius popped the hood, Tom Nell and Jeff Young dove into the smoldering engine compartment. One of them jerked his head back out, grabbed a bucket of water, and began pouring it in the radiator.

A voice shouted from the grandstands, *"Only four laps to go Bob!"*

Nell and Young slammed the hood back down, fumbled the hood pins back into place, and in a single motion, jumped off to either side of the car, waving Tullius on frantically. Tullius smoothly mashed the accelerator to the floor. Instead of the neck-snapping jolt and squealing rubber he'd expected, it sluggishly rolled out of the pit and back onto the track.

No amount of water in the world could fix a blown head gasket.

The Trans/Action crew, soaked to the bone after three hours in the 45-degree dripping air, shuddered and sneezed in the cold, raw elements. The downpour continued. The crowd hushed.

Lime Rock had ended too soon for the old goat.

~~~~

Half an hour later, after the race finally ended and the pole sitter was declared the winner, an American Motors public relations representative strolled down pit road under an umbrella, accepting congratulations on behalf of the winning team. He didn't appear particularly happy, certainly not for a PR guy whose team had just won the opening race in the Trans-Am season. After a *Motor Trend Magazine* reporter congratulated him, the PR man's response explained his demeanor. "Yeah we won, but I'm glad Tullius dropped out." The PR man managed a slight smile. "After all, how would it look to say in a release, 'An American Motors Javelin won the Trans-Am opener at Lime Rock, Connecticut? Second place went to a '64 Pontiac Tempest.'?"

Chapter 21

ON THE MORNING of Monday, May 10, 1971, Herb Adams sat at his Pontiac desk rubbing his tired eyes, drinking Diet Coke and trying to forget the weekend. The words of the track official echoed through his mind: "Gee, if you'd only been able to complete one more lap and had at least been *rolling* when the checkered flag waved, your GTO would have finished seventh and would have driven away with $1,400." Instead, the team earned a measly $150 for being 19th and was classified "DNF"—did not finish. Adams winced. All that work for $150. He drew a deep, steady sigh, staring into the warm, weak java. Still, not bad considering they started dead last.

Clearly, engineering know-how alone wasn't enough in racing. He'd have to bone up on the rules. No matter, Adams told himself. The second race of the Trans-Am circuit—Bryar, New Hampshire—was scheduled at the end of the month. The GTO had proven itself at Lime Rock and after a simple head gasket replacement, it would be ready to compete at Bryar. Hell, at least they wouldn't start last. Adams rubbed his chin. The crowd at Lime Rock had liked number 49 after seeing it run. The press still didn't care much, but so what? And who needs press anyway?

The phone on Adams' desk rang. "Special Projects, Adams," he said flatly into the phone.

A voice on the other end said he was a reporter for a big-name car enthusiast magazine. Adams sat up in his chair. "What can I do for you?"

"Well, sir, I was wondering if you had a few minutes to talk about your car's performance at Lime Rock last Saturday."

"Uh, sure," Adams absently pushed the Diet Coke aside.

"Good! Your old car ran quite a race in that rain. I was there, very impressive. The program says it's a 1964 GTO. Is that correct?"

"Well, yeah. Ya know, the GTO was built on the Tempest/Le Mans chassis. The Tempest was the basic model, the Le Mans was the luxury version of the same thing, and the GTO was the performance version. Truth be known, it's really a Le Mans."

"A 1964 Le Mans?"

"Yeah, 1964. It was my wife's."

The caller paused. "I see. And how many miles did it have before you modified it for SCCA racing?"

"About 80,000."

"*80,000 miles?*" the journalist asked in an incredulous voice.

"Yes sir, 80,000."

The journalist continued, "And as I recall, and if my information is correct here, your car didn't qualify, so it started last in the field of 31 cars."

"Yes. I'm not sure, 31 or 32. We were last, though, I'm sure of that. We had a little trouble with a belt on qualifying day. Fortunately, Bob Tullius knew the race promoter, who agreed to let us in as his entry—the promoter's entry."

"So, Mr. Tullius took this 80,000 mile, seven-year-old, former grocery shopper—with no factory support—from dead last to second with four laps to go in the driving Lime Rock rain against a bunch of brand new, factory-supported pony cars?"

"Uh … well … it was more than just a grocery shopper."

The reporter laughed on the other end of the line. "Yeah, but you're racing against brand new Mustangs, Camaros, and Javelins!"

"Hey, I don't think making a race car out of '64 Tempest is any funnier than making one out of a Javelin."

The reporter laughed again. The men talked a little longer and the reporter thanked Adams for his time.

"Wait—you gonna run an article about the GTO in the magazine?" asked Adams.

"I'm sure going to try, Mr. Adams."

Adams resisted the temptation to ask the reason. "Okay, well, thanks and good luck." The men hung up. Adams scratched his head. *That magazine didn't give us a second look before the race. The GTO didn't even finish, yet now the big magazine was calling him about it. Maybe press attention would be helpful after all.*

No more than 20 minutes later, the phone rang again. This time, it was another auto enthusiast magazine. The "eastern editor" introduced himself over the phone and said he wanted a phone interview with Herb Adams, the man behind what the reporter called the "real star" of Saturday's Lime Rock race. Before the day was over, three other journalists had spoken to Adams on the phone.

~~~~

The following day, Adams found a copy of a car racing magazine on his desk. He opened it to a dog-eared page. There was a picture of Bob Tullius under the headline, "Tullius, in a vintage GTO, outran all but one." Adams' eyes widened. The first three paragraphs described the winner's victory at Lime Rock two days earlier. But paragraph four made Adam's heart skip.

> *The highlight of the day, however, was Bob Tullius, the Falls Church veteran. Tullius, who could not qualify for the race on Friday because of engine trouble, started in last place in the 32-car grid with his strange looking 1964 Pontiac. Tullius steadily splashed through the pack and by the halfway point, had secured third place, behind only Donahue and Revson. With 30 laps to go, he moved into second when Revson retired due to ignition trouble in his Javelin. Tullius looked like a sure bet for second when he entered the pits with steam from under the hood. Despite his amateur team's best efforts, he was done for the day with an overheated engine.*
>
> *The Pontiac's performance, the best ever for an independent entry, established it as a serious contender for the balance of the 1971 Trans-Am racing season.*

Adams looked out his office window as the words rung in his head, "the *best ever* for an independent entry."

Later in the week, more press accounts rolled in. One headline shouted, "Tullius Stars ... in Show." Another read, *"The Gray Ghost Rides Again."*

The Gray Ghost? The article described the gray GTO as a "ghost from the past," which came to haunt the new pony cars at Lime Rock with its surprising speed and handling. Adams grinned. The press had laid a moniker on the GTO. *The Gray Ghost.*

More press reports poured in later:

> *... the real highlight of the race was the performance of the '64 Pontiac Tempest handled by Bob Tullius. Bob reports that the car belonged to his crew chief, Herb Adams' wife, and had 80,000 miles on it before it was decided to turn it into a racer. We hear that there are some GM engineers involved in the preparation of the machine and it runs like a factory car, better than any Firebird we've ever seen.*
>
> *Bob Tullius stole the show by running second for much of the race in this 1964 Pontiac Tempest until mechanical ills sidelined him.*

Another magazine's headline on Lime Rock read, "When the rains came, so did the Tempest. It took ... untold dollars to win the Lime Rock Trans-Am, but in the end all they really beat was a 1964 Pontiac." Adams grinned with quiet delight.

Beneath a picture of the GTO, yet another magazine wrote, "The 'old goat.' A 1964 Pontiac GTO entered by Herb Adams and driven by Bob Tullius. Pretty surprising car! The team is anxious to try it out in the dry."

Another journalist wrote:

> *The Salvable spectators—those who could be saved from their numb, waterlogged state—were becoming aware of the real race ... The Tempest, with its long tail and flat flanks, was unstoppable, passing on the inside, the outside, all the while closing the gap on Revson's second place Javelin. It was only a matter of time until that distance was cut to zero—the Tempest out-deeped the Javelin into the hook and drove away. What none of the spectators*

realized during all of this was that the Tempest is actually Herb Adams'
wife's car—which explains everything. Adams is a Pontiac engineer, rare in
his ability to produce simple solutions to complex problems with his own two
hands.

It seemed apparent that the Gray Ghost's sponsors were going to get
their money's worth. Maybe they already had.

~~~~

A week later, the Adams' doorbell rang. Sandi opened the door and saw the
neighbor from across the street standing at the door holding an armful of
magazines. His eyes were wide and eyebrows high. "Sandi! Look! Herb's in
here! This one, too!"

"Yes, we know. We saw. Won't you come in?"

The neighbor quickly stepped across the threshold. "Oh my *God!*
Herb's famous! My neighbor's *famous!* And I'm in his house!" His eyes
darted about the walls, floor, and ceiling.

"Well, I don't know about that ... I mean he just ..."

"Is he here? I gotta talk to my buddy!"

Sandi squinted at him, "Sure, I'll get him. Have a seat." Sandi motioned to a chair in the living room.

A minute later Herb appeared, wiping his dirty hands with a shop
towel. "Hi—"

The neighbor jumped to his feet, the magazines raised high in his
hand, "Hey buddy! You're famous! Look!" He eagerly held up the magazines. "You're in here! I knew you could do it, Herb!"

"Well ... uh ... thanks ..."

"Man, you really tore 'em up at Lime Rock! And with Sandi's old car!
The Gray Ghost! Unbelievable, buddy! I was with you all the way!"

"Well, thanks. Uh ... no offense, but as I recall, you threatened to call
the cops on us for making all that noise in the middle of the night."

"Me? Oh hell, Herb, I was only *kidding.* I wasn't *really* going to call the
cops or anything. I mean, I didn't know what you were doing."

"Building a tank, as I remember."

"Oh yeah—well, that was then, Herb. Now you're famous! Right alongside these famous racers! I can't *believe* it." He looked at the magazines in admiration, shaking his head. "I really knew you could do it. Hey, would you sign these magazines? For the kids, I mean. I got a pen right here."

My first autograph, thought Adams, and for the guy who threatened to call the cops on him at two in morning a few months ago. "Sure. Billy and Suzie, right?" asked Adams.

"Uh … yeah, but just sign your name, that'll be fine."

Adams signed his name on the covers of the magazines.

"Great! Great! Thanks buddy. Anything I can do to help with the car, just let me know! Hey, how about you and Sandi join us for dinner some night? See ya." He scampered out the front door and jogged across the street, clutching his paper treasures.

"What was *that* all about?" asked Sandi from the kitchen.

"The price of fame," responded Herb dryly.

Chapter 22

TWO WEEKS AFTER Lime Rock, amid the Gray Ghost's continuing press attention, the Trans/Action team gathered at Waterford Hills Race Track on a Saturday morning in mid-May to test and break-in a backup engine on the Gray Ghost. They also planned to test some recent chassis adjustments.

The Waterford Hills Race Track in Clarkston, Michigan was a road track, similar to a Trans-Am track. It was also close to home for Trans/Action. Standing in Waterford's pit row next to the GTO, the Trans/Action team members discussed the continuing press attention and congratulated themselves. But Herb Adams was concerned.

"Listen boys," Adams said with a frown. "All this press attention is nice, but have you considered the practical result? At Lime Rock, no one knew who the hell we were—they thought we were just another bunch of shade-tree hacks. Well, they found out different." The guys grinned and nodded their approval.

"Yeah!" said someone, "We got the *Gray Ghost!*"

Adams shrugged. "I'm not so sure, gentlemen. Now that the competition knows us, maybe Tullius won't be able to sneak through the field so easy. This press attention will motivate them to gun for us. Jealousy. See, the Javelin *won* the damn race, but *we* got all the press attention. Nobody in the press even mentioned the other hotshots. They finished behind the red white and blue Javelin and *way* ahead of us, and the press ignored 'em. You think they like that? How about their sponsors? After all the dough they spent on their cars? I don't think they dig that. I'm guessing they'll be *real* unhappy with us at Bryar. They're going to want to beat us, boys, and beat us bad. Put us amateurs in our place. They're gonna want to prove we were a just a fluke."

Adams glanced around at the sober faces. "So we've got to prepare for it by getting the GTO in tip-top condition for Bryar," he continued. "We gotta lighten it up more—a lot more—and get this new engine broken in. We've now gotta do everything else we can to make the car as competitive as possible. If we sit back on the laurels of our newfound fame, we'll get our teeth kicked in at Bryar, and the whole world will see it on TV. And we don't want that. We come to *win*. Everybody got it?"

The somber team expressed their understanding in muffled tones.

"All right. Let's get this baby—the *Ghost*—on the track." Adams climbed in the Gray Ghost and started the engine. The new powerplant rumbled to life. After a few circuits, Tom Nell and Jeff Young made some minor adjustments. Joe Brady, camera in hand, took photographs of the Ghost rounding a 180-degree turn. He and Adams would study the photos later to judge the wheel camber relative to the roll of the car. They suspected the negative camber on the rear wheels was working, but wanted to ensure a zero degree angle of the outside tires during some hard cornering.

After a few more rounds, Nell and Young pronounced the Ghost's new backup engine ready for racing and the team began to pack up for home. "Hey, Herb ..." said the earnest voice of Tom Nell from behind Adams.

"Yeah?"

Nell wiped his hands with a greasy shop towel. "Listen ..." he looked at his shoes, wiping his hands faster. "Bryar is on Memorial Day weekend and ... well ... I got a wife and four kids ..."

Adams placed his hand on the engine man's shoulder, smiling. "And headquarters won't let you get out of town."

Nell nodded sheepishly.

"You can't blame her," said Adams. "I mean, all the time you been spending after work and on weekends at the dyno with the back-up engine lately, it's a wonder she hasn't left you, man. I'm hearing the other guys are having some trouble at home too, and it's because of that." Adams nodded at the Ghost, which was being loaded onto the trailer by the team. He took a deep breath and exhaled slowly. "Taking up a lot of time. Personal time. Family time. That car is a jealous mistress, and our lousy DNF last week didn't help. Maybe we should have just bit the bullet and bought one of last year's Trans-Am cars; that would have been a lot easier. Way less work and time."

Nell shook his head. "No, no, no ... I mean where would we have gotten the bread to buy a car like that? Anyway, working on this old goat—and with you guys—it's great." Nell rubbed his shoulder and continued, "We got to know each other a lot better. And talk about team building. Marilyn has been supportive of me but—"

"Yeah," said Adams, examining a scab on his knuckle. "You're not alone. The other guys' wives are the same, and the girlfriends of the single guys are pissed, too. Heck, sometimes I think Sandi has just written me off. It's like we're living separate lives or something. She hasn't said anything, but I can tell. I can see in it in the other wives, too. Same thing. They understand the racing and the desire and the challenge, but they're wondering if all the effort is worth it, if all the sacrifices we're *all* making will be worth it. And I see where they're coming from, the wives and girlfriends. Kids, too. When was the last time any of us so-called dads went to a little league game? I mean, once you get past a certain invisible point, you start to wonder 'what the hell am I doing?'" Adams pulled hard on a tuft of his own hair.

"Hey, don't talk like that, man," said Nell, looking around nervously. "Listen man, I may not be so good at expressing my feelings—that's what Marilyn says anyway—but I gotta tell you now something you already know; we're competing against the big boys. We may never have this chance again. And if we do it half-assed, we shouldn't even bother. So we go as hard as we can or not at all. Nothing in-between. Just like engineering, man: no gray. It's go or no-go. It's simple. Pure. That's why it's beautiful."

Adams looked up from his shoes and into his friend's eyes. "Ah, Tom Nell; philosopher-engineer."

Nell smiled. "I prefer 'engineer-philosopher.'"

"And now that you've philosophized about the importance of all-or-nothing," grinned Adams.

Nell raised his palms in defeat and chuckled. "I know, I know … after all that, I still need to split for a while."

"I dig, man," said Adams sincerely. "Stay home. Spend some time with Marilyn and the kids. Take it *easy* for a change. We'll be okay at Bryar." Adams squinted at his sullen, guilt-ridden teammate. "Listen," said Adams slowly. "I know from personal experience that it's a lot easier to get grease off your hands than a wife's wrath off your heart."

Chapter 23

THE BRYAR MOTORSPORT Park was situated in Loudon, New Hampshire, a long way from Detroit. After a two-day drive towing the old GTO, Adams and Goad arrived at the Loudon motel well after dusk on Friday of the Memorial Day weekend. Early next morning, Adams and Goad choked down their motel breakfast and hurried off to the track on Route 106 North in Loudon. It was qualifying day. And press day.

Their reception at Bryar was markedly different than at Lime Rock three weeks earlier. As the Suburban, towing the Gray Ghost, rolled to a stop in pit road half a dozen people instantly gathered around. Adams was immediately greeted by a beaming reporter who quickly blurted an intro-duction and the name of a car racing publication Adams didn't recognize. The reporter asked question after question about the car and the team and before long, another writer, then another, and yet another, joined him. A number of other people who didn't appear to be reporters were ogling the Gray Ghost chained to the trailer. Adams did his best to answer the rapid-fire questions from the press. Within five minutes, a dozen reporters were crowded around Adams, whose back was against the Suburban. The writers were now shouting questions, competing with each other for Adams' atten-tion. Adams spied his bleary-eyed teammates who had just arrived from their 16-hour ride from Pontiac. Tom Nell was conspicuous by his absence.

Adams raised his hands and shouted above the reporters, *"Hey! Hey! Hey!"* The crowd quieted. Adams continued, "Listen, gentlemen. I appreci-ate your interest, but we have to get the car off the trailer and ensure it's ready for qualifying right now. We gotta have a tech inspection by the race officials, too. So please give us half an hour or so. The guys and I will be happy to answer your questions then."

"What about Bob Tullius?" asked an inquisitive voice from the small crowd.

"Bob should be here in about 30 minutes. He'll talk to you, too, if you'd like." The reporters looked at each other, nodding and whispering. They began to slowly disperse. One took a photograph of the Gray Ghost on its trailer, then he took a quick shot of Adams before walking slowly away. "Thanks for your cooperation," said Adams.

Ted Lambiris elbowed Adams. "Christ, you'd think we were rock stars or somethin'," he whispered. "Crazy. Three weeks ago they didn't say boo to us. Some even laughed. Now look at 'em!" The Greek shook his head in disbelief, watching the reporters reluctantly scatter.

"Guess we make good copy," smiled Adams.

"Yeah. Look at this," said the Greek, handing Adams a thin newspaper. "They like us, all right."

Adams took the paper. "LIME ROCK ... Javelin Laps Entire Lime Rock Field."

The Greek snorted. "Look inside ... *inside* ..."

Adams shrugged as he opened the paper. The name of the article's author appeared, in small print, between the headline and the article. "Hey, I talked to that guy on the phone after Lime Rock," muttered Adams.

"*Read it, man!*" said the Greek, hopping up and down slightly.

Adams re-focused on the paper, "Yeah, yeah, cool it, man." Adams glanced over the words describing the winner's triumph and the top five finishers. *"But the real star of the race, as far as the rain-soaked crowd was concerned, was Bob Tullius."* Adams shot a quick smile at the Greek.

"Read on, man!" shouted the hopping Greek.

"He was running second in a 1964—that's right, 1964—Pontiac Tempest until about 10 minutes before the race ended. He retired in (continued on page 22)." Adams fumbled the paper quickly to page 22. *"... a cloud of steam, a blown head gasket suspected as the reason for the overheating engine."* On the opposite page appeared a black and white photo of car 49 followed by the winning Javelin. Adams

grinned as he flipped to page 24 and chuckled at the headline, *"Tullius Stars in Donahue Show."*

~~~~

Half an hour later the Gray Ghost was parked on the pit road tarmac and the press—and some members of the other pit crews—had returned in force. Adams and Tullius were attracting the most attention. Tullius whispered in Adams' ear, "Our sponsors are eating this up, man. Been talking to 'em. They know they're getting their money's worth and then some already! It's not just a car anymore—it's the Gray Ghost."

Adams looked up pit row at all the multi-colored, shiny new pony cars, sporting the large decals of their corporate sponsors. Some of their crews, with arms crossed, were looking at the crowd around the Ghost. Only a few journalists were with the pony cars. "Yeah, but the competition can't be too happy about this," said Adams quietly.

"To hell with them. Not my fault if I got a better car."

"No, Bob. I mean all the press attention we're suddenly getting."

"So what? We're a great new story, they're the same old boring story. That's not our fault either. We can't control the press. And don't worry about the race. If any of them rich boys in their fancy little ponies try to take it out on me and the old goat—I mean the *Ghost*—on the track, I'll handle 'em." Tullius winked and grinned broadly at his friend. "Now let's talk up the GTO some more for our important sponsors." Tullius, exuding confidence, turned to the reporters and smiled. A camera flashed and Tullius raised his palms into the air. "Who wants an interview?" he shouted.

~~~~

Dutch stood next to Adams and squinted at the track in the crisp, mid-morning, New Hampshire sun. Joe Brady had said Bryar was a tight, small track, another road course—a twisting layout with mostly unbanked turns, a long straight, and three other near straights. It measured exactly 1.6 miles, and its shape defied easy description, with seemingly random curves connecting the four north and south straightaways. The layout was akin to the outline of a pulled tooth—a molar—with two legs at the bottom and a concave crown at the top.

"Hey, what kind of spring load you got?"

Dutch turned and saw a guy dressed in a fancy pit crew uniform from a competitor's pit crew looking at Adams.

"Oh … well, our metallurgist did some computer analysis on that," responded Adams.

"Computer?"

"Yeah, our metallurgist. *Confidential.*"

"Oh—well, we all know you got support from the factory," the man winked.

"Oh, no," Adams shrugged, "we got no help from them."

"Anyway, how 'bout your rear stab bar?"

"Big Firebird. Very robust."

"What kind of shocks ya got?" asked the man, leaning over to catch a glimpse of the Ghost's undercarriage.

"Konis …"

The man scratched his head. "Okay, thanks." He took a long look at the Ghost before turning and strolling away.

"How 'bout that, man?" whispered Adams. "The pro is askin' *us* about what makes the Ghost go!"

Dutch cocked his eyebrow at Adams and whispered, "But I just cut the spring and bolted it back on, no computer analysis. You poindexters only got slide rules, and I sure as hell didn't even use them on the springs. And who's the metallurgist? Some Pontiac salaried guy?"

Adams grinned and put his hand around the fabricator's shoulder. "Don't worry about it, man. That's what ya call 'pre-race psychology.'"

~~~~

The Greek handed Adams an orange booklet. "Here," said the Greek. "Race program."

Adams glanced at the cover. *Bryar 200 TRANS-AM. Sedan Championship Races.* A photo of the patriotic number 6 Javelin appeared in the center. *Bryar Motorsport Park. Loudon, New Hampshire. May 31, 1971. Price $1.00.*

Adams flipped open the program, glancing at a Corvette advertisement on the inside cover before briefly studying the race schedule on the opposite page. He flipped the pages, stopping at a photograph of the Javelin driver next to an article about him. He flipped another few pages, stopping at the driver biographies. Tullius wasn't mentioned.

Adams turned the page. Another Javelin driver photo, followed by a team owner photo, followed by a two-page color photo of the team owner hawking auto parts. Adams flipped through the rest of the program, pausing at a full color ad of an orange Javelin on the back cover. *"American Motors … specially prepared and modified the new Javelin-AMX, so you don't have to. If you had to compete with GM, Ford and Chrysler, what would you do? American Motors."*

Adams snorted and began looking for a trash can. He saw a man standing near the Ghost. Even from a distance, Adams knew the face immediately: It was the red white and blue Javelin driver, Mark Donahue. He was talking to his friend Tullius as they stood next to the Ghost. The driver pointed at the Ghost's big front tires. Adams, walking toward the Ghost, overheard the driver tell Tullius the big tires up front won't work. Tullius grinned and shouted something unintelligible at the driver, who responded with an uproarious laugh. A photographer snapped a photo. The driver approached the Ghost, gave it the once over and placed his left hand above the passenger side window, leaning on the car while smiling at his buddy Tullius.

The camera shutter snapped again.

Adams curled up the program and stuffed it in his back pocket. Donahue's not so bad.

~~~~

At eleven o'clock, Adams dispersed the inquisitive members of the press again so the Ghost could qualify. Tullius donned his helmet, climbed in, flipped the toggles and started the engine. A camera flashed as the Gray Ghost growled awake and spewed a blue plume from its trembling, oversized tailpipes. Tullius gunned the engine for the press and grinned at them. Some writers winced and recoiled from the thunderous blast.

More photographs.

Tullius felt a tap on his left shoulder. It was Adams.

"Listen, hotshot," Adams hollered over the din. "We lightened her up a little since Lime Rock. Otherwise, she's the same."

"Best news I heard all day, gearhead," shouted Tullius, smiling. "But can't you straighten out that crooked hood?" He gave Adams the thumbs up, eased the Ghost into first gear, and rolled it toward the track as the press corps watched in silent admiration.

Tullius slowly accelerated onto the main straight and shifted into second. The track was dry and warm under the late May New Hampshire sun. He rounded the first curve and headed into the first 180-degree bend to the right. With its four big slicks and well-tuned suspension, the Ghost stuck to the track just like at Lime Rock. Tullius carefully negotiated the remaining turns at the north end of the track—the molar's crown—and gently snapped the stick into third as he tapped the clutch and smoothly mashed the pedal to the floor at the beginning of the back straight. The Gray Ghost responded instantly, pinning Tullius into its narrow seat as it rocketed toward 80 miles an hour. In a split second, Tullius let up on the gas, hit the clutch, fluidly moved the shifter into fourth and smoothly bore down on the accelerator again.

The Ghost ripped past the 100 mile an hour mark in an instant. In another moment, the gray behemoth hit 126 miles an hour, then 138, before Tullius braked hard for the U-turn to the right at the southeast corner of the track. The Ghost rumbled around most of the bend in second gear before Tullius caressed the stick into third and gently stood on the pedal again. The Ghost screamed out of the curve and up the short straight. Tullius downshifted into the hairpin to the left and roared back down the next straight until he came to the last bend, this one at the southwest corner of the track. The main straight was next. The Ghost's chassis was as good as ever, tires, too. Now it was the engine's turn.

"Let's go, baby," said Tullius to his ride. The Ghost came blasting out of the last bend on to the main straight in third gear, accelerating fast. Tullius quickly, smoothly slid the Hurst stick into fourth, slammed the gas to the floor and held on; 146 miles an hour and the Ghost was only halfway up the straight, blaring past pit row.

Two dozen heads near the Trans/Action team in pit row, all belonging to journalists, swiveled quickly from left to right as they watched the Gray Ghost whistle past them on the main straight.

Tullius jumped off the gas, downshifted, and braked smooth and hard again for the first bend. "Oh yes … oh yes," he said, patting the steering wheel. After the next few circuits, the green flag waved as the Ghost tore across the starting line.

Tullius was qualifying. Now he drove very aggressively, pushing the Ghost to its limit by alternately and repeatedly caressing the brake pedal, rapidly easing the Hurst forward and back smoothly, and blipping the clutch and accelerator.

Bryar, with its plentiful U-turns, was a demanding course. The old Gray Ghost responded beautifully. By the end of qualifying day at Bryar, the Ghost, at an average speed of 112 mph, had earned a respectable tenth place on the starting grid of 33 cars for the next day's race.

Chapter 24

MAY 31, 1971 greeted the Bryar Motorsport Park with sunshine. Since the Trans/Action team knew their car could run in the wet, their spirits were not particularly lifted by the blue New Hampshire sky; the Gray Ghost was simply untested on an arid track. Their nerves were exacerbated by the continuing press attention after Lime Rock and yesterday during qualifying. No longer were they anonymous amateurs; now they were minor celebrities, at least in the small world of Trans-Am racing, and this added pressure. Every action they took on the car, from merely popping the hood to wiping a mirror, seemed to be newsworthy. Yesterday they'd reveled in it. Today— race day—it became distracting and slightly unnerving. And the spectacle of failure was frequently on their minds, but seldom on their tongues.

Joe Brady, taking a break from rubbing his tired eyes, looked up and down pit road at the competition. One guy in the next pit appeared to be brushing touch-up paint on a sparkling Javelin. Another guy further up the pit was holding something heavy behind the open trunk of a Mustang. The man was bent over slightly, struggling to hold the weight. In full view of a race official, the man clumsily placed the load on the ground and looked around briefly. Then, one by one, he put the heavy pieces in the trunk.

Bricks? What the hell? These cars had specific weight restrictions and this guy was clearly cheating. And the race official was winking at it! This had to be stopped.

Furious, Joe turned, looking for Adams. Instead, he saw the Greek. Something in the Greek's expression appeared to be different, and it momentarily distracted Joe from the cheating Mustang. Joe watched the Greek walk up to car 49 with a bulge in his right front pocket. Only the top of a Coke bottle was visible from the Greek's pocket. Joe froze, and all thoughts of reporting the cheating pony car vanished. Lambiris unscrewed the gas cap, casually looked up and down pit row, and leaned awkwardly into the car, fumbling slightly with his pocket. The Greek winked at Joe and put a finger to his own smiling lips. The Greek furtively inspected his pocket jammed hard against the car, before darting his eyes up and whistling softly. After a few moments of fumbling, Lambiris casually pushed away from the car, screwed the gas cap back on and strolled away with an innocent, empty Coke bottle in his pocket.

Joe looked sheepishly back at the Mustang.

~~~~

Moments later, Bob Tullius, confident as ever, took a deep breath and climbed into the Ghost. "Here we go boys!" said Tullius as he turned the ignition, flipped toggles and pushed buttons. The Ghost shook to life and rumbled onto the track, joining the gleaming new pony cars before 18,000 spectators.

"Welcome, ladies and gentlemen, to Bryar Motorsport Park and the 1971 Trans-Am race," bellowed the loudspeaker. The announcer introduced the pole sitter in his Mustang and the remaining competitors in the starting grid. The crowd applauded politely after each driver was announced. But when he announced the tenth starter, "Car number 49, a 1964 Pontiac GTO driven by Bob Tullius," the crowd erupted, cheering wildly, before the announcer was finished. The announcer paused, waiting for the cheering to subside, but the roaring continued. Some in the crowd were even standing. A homemade sign, made out of a dingy bed sheet, hung on the chain link fence behind the grandstands. It read, *Go Ghost! # 49.*

The Trans/Action guys, now the Gray Ghost's pit crew, beamed at the cheering spectators. The Greek waved back at the crowd, both hands extended in the air. Tullius, surrounded by the din of racecars slowly rumbling around the track and concentrating on the coming race, was oblivious to the raucous greeting. Finally, the cheering quieted enough for the announcer to continue. Ten minutes later, the green flag waved as 33 racecars flashed across the starting line. The 1971 Bryar Trans-Am was on.

At the race's start, Tullius immediately gunned the Ghost. He quickly maneuvered past a Javelin into ninth place, and by the end of the fifth lap number 49 was running eighth, just behind a Mustang.

At lap 35, the front running car, the red, white and blue number 6 Javelin, retired with carburetor trouble. The favorite was out of the race. A big, growling Mustang took the lead and the Gray Ghost moved into seventh, drawing a bead on the front-running Ford.

At lap 50, trouble reappeared for Tullius and the Ghost. As Tullius rounded the hairpin in second gear, he attempted to shift into third but was met with resistance and the harsh grinding of unmeshed gears. Tullius glanced in the rearview mirror at a Javelin closing on him. He pressed the clutch and attempted to ease the stick into third. More grating. He tried again, jostling the shifter. The stick bucked violently, refusing any effort to engage third gear.

This was a major transmission problem. The Ghost's third gear was shot. Tullius cursed loudly. He wasn't going to quit now, not at the halfway point. Not ever.

Tullius had been coasting now for a few seconds—far too long—and was rapidly losing speed while attempting to find third gear. He took another glance in the mirror and cursed again, this time at the closing Javelin. He rammed the stick back into second. It meshed immediately and Tullius slapped the gas to the floor and held it there until the tachometer was nearly redlined. As he prepared to shift from second gear directly into fourth, Tullius knew he must avoid under-rotating the engine to avoid serious damage to the motor. The only way to do this was to rev it high, but not too high, in second gear before shifting directly into fourth. He was halfway down the straight with the Ghost's engine screaming near the redline when he shifted fluidly from second to fourth gear. Tullius smoothly mashed the gas pedal to the floor and the Ghost instantly complied, roaring toward the next curve. No signs of shuddering or the low engine groaning indicative of under-rotation.

The Javelin began to shrink in the Ghost's rear view mirror.

Tullius took a deep breath and slowly exhaled. He had avoided over-rotating the engine in second and under-rotating it in fourth. Now he, and the remaining gears in the transmission, had to do it repeatedly for another 55 laps while continuing to close in on the leader.

By lap 75, a number of other pony cars had been permanently parked in the pits for various mechanical, electrical and other myriad problems. But the handicapped Gray Ghost rumbled on.

Even without the benefit of third gear, Tullius had managed the Ghost into fifth place and he was closing on the shiny new Camaro in front of him. By this point, racing in the absence of third gear was becoming second nature. Tullius no longer had to think about revving the engine high in second gear, lifting the stick up from second and immediately meshing it back down into fourth. His body simply did it while his mind concentrated on the race. And the Ghost complied.

Adams called Goad to his side, "Bob's going quicker now than he went in qualifying isn't he?"

Goad fumbled through the clipboard. "Uh … let's see …"

Adams nodded his head, watching the Ghost rip past pit road.

"Yeah," Goad said, "much faster." He looked up at the gray blur, "*Man!*"

Despite Tullius' pressure, the Chevy, with the benefit of a third gear and a dry track, was able to stay just ahead of the Ghost for 25 laps. At lap 109, Tullius had enough of the cat and mouse. As the Ghost entered the Main Straight on the Camaro's bumper, Tullius steered to the outside, fluidly threw the stick from second to fourth and smoothly bore down on the gas. But the sleek Camaro also accelerated, and midway up the straight, the two machines were even.

The grandstand spectators were on their feet, roaring their approval for the Gray Ghost as it whipped past them, neck and neck with the young Camaro. The Ghost began to pull ahead when Tullius, on the outside, was forced to jam the brake pedal nearly to the floor in order to negotiate the first turn. The Camaro also braked hard, but with the benefit of the inside position was able to take the inside of the curve and maintain fourth place. The Ghost stayed on the Camaro's bumper, like a lion chasing its prey, during the last lap.

As the two cars entered the last turn, Tullius deliberately took the outside in an attempt to get around the Camaro. He had no time now; the checkered flag was close, only one more turn and half a straight. The Ghost's wide slicks squealed in protest as Tullius accelerated around the last turn, right on the edge. The g-forces pushed him hard into the left side of the seat, virtually into the door. The hot slicks on the left side were taking a terrible beating, nearly tearing off the wheel rim as the big Ghost tracked fast and hard to the right. Tullius strained, leaning hard away from the centrifugal force mashing his body into the left side of the seat while simultaneously fighting to avoid a collision with the eager Camaro.

The gamble was paying off.

The squealing Ghost was nearly alongside the Camaro halfway through the curve. Burning, smoking rubber spewed from the big, scorching gumballs as Tullius continued to press his lumbering machine hard around the last bend, pushing his car to the very limit of its cornering ability. The big sizzling tires continued their howling, squealing protest as the two cars barreled out of the last turn and onto the straight in a dead heat, the smoking Ghost on the outside, still in second gear, with its searing engine screaming at the redline.

The grandstand crowd, still on their feet, had just witnessed the first three cars finish but were focused on this race—the real race: The Gray Ghost's pursuit of fourth place against a tenacious young Chevy unwilling to yield.

The Camaro shifted from third to fourth and began its hot, powerful sprint to the finish line. In a fluid instant, Tullius smoothly hooked the Hurst from second to fourth one last time and put his right foot on the floor. The Ghost and Camaro accelerated alarmingly toward the wildly waving checkered flag only seconds away. Tullius grimaced and squeezed the wheel, willing his car to go.

The crowd roared.

The screaming Ghost closed the gap.

As the checkered flag madly waved over the roaring racecars, Tullius finished half a car length ahead of the Camaro. To the delight of the crowd, the Gray Ghost had taken fourth place at Bryar.

Chapter 25

IT WAS NOT until the first cool-down lap immediately after the race that Bob Tullius realized the roaring grandstand crowd was cheering for him. The people leapt to their feet, yelling and waving wildly as the old GTO rolled past them. Grinning, Tullius thrust his left hand out the Ghost's window and waved at the grandstands as he slowly rumbled past them. Their emotion was unmistakably directed at the Ghost. They remained on their feet, cheering wildly for Tullius and the old gray GTO. The winner, in his Mustang, received a more polite, restrained ovation as he drove past the grandstand holding the checkered flag out the window.

A few minutes later Tullius coasted into the pit and parked the Ghost. The acrid smell of burnt rubber emanated from the old gray sedan as the Trans/Action pit crew accosted their driver, slapping his back and yelling congratulations.

Tullius pulled off his helmet. "How'd you like that finish? Not bad for having only three gears ..." he shouted to Adams.

"What? Only three gears?" asked Adams, suddenly serious.

"Yeah—lost third gear about halfway through after the last pit stop. Had to shift from second straight to fourth. But the old goat came through," said Tullius as he shot an admiring glance at the car.

"What do you mean you 'lost' third gear?" asked Adams.

Three members of the press were trotting along pit row toward them. Tullius grinned at them.

"Hey Bob …" said Adams, demanding his driver's attention before the press arrived and monopolized him. "What are you talking about?"

"Like I said, man. Third gear, just lost it, couldn't get the damn stick into third gear. Man, it ground and bucked like all hell. Almost got passed tryin' to jam it in, so I said to hell with it—I'm just shiftin' from second right into fourth. So I did, no problem. I was a little worried at first about revving it too high in second and rotating it too low in fourth." Tullius quickly nodded at the track. "Probably some transmission teeth out there somewhere."

Jeff Young approached them and asked, "How was the oil pressure?"

Tullius squinted at Young. "Listen Jeff, I was focused on the race, not the damn—"

"Excuse me, Mr. Tullius?" interrupted a winded, urgent voice from behind him.

Tullius turned to look at the reporter. "Yeah—want an interview?" A camera clicked at the smiling, triumphant Tullius.

Adams left his driver to the reporters and laughed out loud. Tullius and the old car managed fourth place without a third gear. Unbelievable. What if he'd had a third gear for the entire race? He looked at the grandstands. They would have rioted if Tullius had won.

Ford Motor, thanks to their winning driver and his Mustang, had earned nine points toward the manufacturer's championship for finishing first. Even though another Mustang finished second, pursuant to the scoring rules prohibiting multiple point awards to the same manufacturer in a single race that Ford was not awarded any more points. Rather, AMC earned four points for taking third, Pontiac was awarded three points for fourth, and the eager Camaro earned two points for Chevy.

Adams' mind quickly turned to the Ghost. Hopefully there was no engine damage from over-rotation or under-rotation. He studied the car. They must quickly repair the transmission and replace the burned, stinking, halfbald tires. The next race was only six days away at the Mid-Ohio Track.

~~~~

The drive home to Detroit seemed much shorter than the way out to Bryar for the happy Trans/Action team. They'd proven that car number 49's performance at Lime Rock was no fluke and the press and fans alike had taken notice. This car could run in the wet and the dry. The team was also $2,200 richer for their effort at Bryar and they'd earned three points for Pontiac in the season's standings. Not that the Pontiac Division cared much.

The following week in Adams' garage, Tom Nell and Jeff Young, after listening to the engine with a screwdriver pressed to their respective ears, pronounced the engine to be fine. No damage resulted from the extra strain, if any, placed on it as the result of third gear failing. Tullius had babied the engine well. The engineers appreciated this, because none of them wanted to exert the time and money required to rebuild an engine after hours and in less than a week, unless it was absolutely necessary, particularly since the transmission required a re-build.

The team's confidence in its driver was also cause for happiness. If Tullius could bring the Ghost home in fourth place without the benefit of third gear, and without burning up the engine, the Trans/Action guys figured he and number 49 could do just about anything. Now the engineers' job was to ensure no further mechanical failures would handicap their car and driver in future races. They resolved to go over the Ghost with a fine-toothed comb in preparation for Mid-Ohio. After all, as Adams reminded them, the other guys would be improving their cars too as the season wore on.

~~~~

The following week was busy for Trans/Action. The workdays at Pontiac dragged on interminably for the team, but their time in the evenings at Adams' garage flew by. Adams' ever present to-do list taped to the Ghost's windshield grew shorter every night. And the grass in the yard grew longer.

By Monday night, they had replaced the tires. By Tuesday, the transmission had been removed and was nearly rebuilt. On Wednesday, the transmission re-build was finished and it was reinstalled. Thursday was spent reviewing each other's work, testing the transmission, and waxing and polishing the body. Nell and Young announced that the back-up engine was as good as ever.

Friday, the Ghost was ready to race again.

Chapter 26

THE FOUR-HOUR DRIVE to Mid-Ohio Sports Car Course was
a breeze for the Trans/Action team relative to the two-day treks to Lime
Rock, Connecticut and Loudon, New Hampshire. This race also promised
to be more fun than the first two because many of the team's friends and
Pontiac co-workers planned on driving down from Detroit to watch the
race. The team left Detroit for Mid-Ohio after work on Friday and rolled
into a Mansfield, Ohio motel, between Lima to the east and Canton to the
west.

The next morning the team engaged in their now-familiar ritual: wolf-
ing down their motel breakfast at six a.m. and hurrying off to the track. It
was Saturday, June 5, 1971—qualifying day at Mid-Ohio and, of course,
press day.

~~~~

Mid-Ohio is set in the verdant rolling hills of America's heartland. It was
built in 1962 by a group of Mansfield Ohio businessmen who were looking
for a place to race on the weekends. In 1967, the first Trans-Am race was
held at Mid-Ohio and a Mustang won it. Nine years and 30 races after it
opened, Mid-Ohio was the site of the third Trans-Am race of the 1971
season.

As the team unloaded the recently waxed and polished Ghost from its
trailer, Adams overheard his driver speaking to the press. Bob Tullius was

good at it. "We wanted to race, but didn't want that initial investment. These guys wanted a top racing car and they put the work into it, about $20,000 worth. It's a youthful crew and they have done a job well done on this car. A lot of work made this a top car," said Tullius confidently to the scribbling reporter.

Before long, a throng of reporters gathered around the Ghost and its crew in pit road. As various members of Trans/Action spoke to reporters, the mottled gray sky began to spit rain. After the reporters left Herb Adams momentarily, young Jim approached him.

"Good thing it's raining—the Ghost does good in the rain, right?" he asked Adams.

Adams looked up, considering the cloud cover. "Well, yeah, but we want a lot of rain or no rain at all." The young assistant furrowed his brow and cocked his head quizzically at Adams. "See, the Ghost runs real well in the rain—we know that from Lime Rock," Adams explained. "But we also know it can run in the dry, like last week at Bryar. Trouble is, we run different sets of tires according to the weather conditions. When the weather changes in the middle of a race, we have to change our tires in the pit ..."

Jim looked up pit road. "Yeah, but so do they," he said pointing at the bright new pony cars parked further up the row. "Anyway, we got rain tires and dry tires—"

"Yes, but they have professional pit crews and equipment, and we don't."

"But we were pretty quick in the pits at the first two races," protested Jim.

"We didn't have to change any tires though, did we? Just a quick gas-up and off she went." Adams looked at Trans/Action's lone jack and hand wrench next to the trailer and continued, "Changing tires fast is much more difficult."

Jim's expression changed to understanding, then slowly to concern. "So tomorrow, if it rains and then stops or vice versa, we'll have to change tires. But if it rains all day or it's dry all day, we won't," said Jim.

"Precisely," said Adams flatly.

Jim looked down pit road again. The teams with the factory backing were unloading their equipment from trailers—loads of it. He wiped a small spit of rain from his forehead, looked warily at the dappled gray, damp sky and swallowed hard.

~~~~

After Adams shooed off the press, Bob Tullius squinted out at the Mid-Ohio track over the three-foot high pit wall. He knew Mid-Ohio very well, just like the other Trans-Am tracks. This one, like the others, was a road course with unbanked turns, straightaways, and curves galore: 15, to be exact. The track was only nine years old and in good shape. It was 2.4 miles around, run clockwise, 40 feet wide, and followed the undulating contour of the green countryside. Pit road and the start/finish line were on a straightaway running in an east-west direction. Driving out of the pit to the west, the cars drove a short distance until reaching a left 90-degree turn that took them southward down a long straight toward what was known as Keyhole Chicane, a right-left-right combination. Then the track immediately bent back to the right into a 180-degree turn to the north. This was the Keyhole. At the end of the Keyhole, the track headed directly north into the longest straightaway at Mid-Ohio. Halfway up the straight, it bent slightly to the right, past the grandstands. A lot of action took place here in typical races and the fans knew it. The grandstands also provided some shade.

At the end of this straight were a series of chicanes known as the Esses, which headed northeast. This area was another favorite of experienced fans because it spilled off the fastest curve of the track and much of the passing took place here. After five snaking turns through the Esses, the track straightened briefly at its northernmost portion and headed directly east. It then took a 90-degree turn south before bending slightly to the right, then back to the left before entering the 180-degree right turn known as the Carousel. The Carousel emptied onto the last straight with the start/finish line, adjacent to pit row on the left and the timer's stand on the right.

Tullius slowly traced the course with his eyes, visualizing the shifting, braking and accelerating that was to come. Adams looked at his watch: 8:03 a.m. Practice for the Trans-Am cars was from 8:00 to 9:05. "Bob ... hey, Bob. Bob?"

Tullius broke his focus on the track and turned to the voice behind him, "Wha'?" he said foggily.

"You okay?" asked Adams.

"Yeah, yeah. Just concentrating on the track."

"Well, it's time to drive now, not think. It's our turn to practice."

Tullius beamed at his friend. "Good—I'm better at drivin' anyway." Tullius donned his helmet and climbed into the Ghost's familiar cockpit.

"Now listen," said Adams to his driver. "We didn't make any changes since last week—just fixed the transmission and slapped some new tires on. No time for anything else, and no need. You got third gear back. You got the rain tires on now."

"That's nice. But I see you still haven't straightened out the hood." Tullius flashed his teeth and started the engine. The Ghost awoke, growling and shaking with power. His throat customarily tightened with excitement as he gave Adams the thumbs up and engaged first gear.

Car 49 rumbled down pit row, through the misting rain, and onto the slick track. A few laps later, back in the pit, Tullius pronounced the Ghost ready to go—no changes needed. He looked at Tom Nell, "Oil pressure too." The Ghost was ready for qualifying today and the 75-lap race tomorrow—all 180 miles.

~~~~

At 12:15 p.m., the Trans-Am cars were summoned for qualifying. Tullius took the big gray sedan around the circuit deliberately, warming up amid the crowding pony cars. At the end of the carousel he gunned it, shifted quickly and smoothly into third gear with no problem, roared past the furiously waving green flag, and the qualifying race began.

The Ghost rounded the big bend to the left and rocketed down the straight in fourth gear to Keyhole Chicane. Tullius downshifted into third, quickly negotiated the chicane and ripped around the Keyhole. The Ghost stuck to the wet track, just like at Lime Rock. He gently pressed the familiar Hurst shifter into fourth and smoothly bore down on the gas. The Ghost pressed Tullius back in the seat as its engine screamed up the back straight.

The car hit 142 miles an hour before Tullius eased off and rounded the slight right bend to the next straight.

The Ghost sounded good. It *felt* good. Tullius downshifted into third again, almost a luxury after last weekend, and snaked through the Esses, cutting the apexes closely and leaving a plume of fine spray behind him. He accelerated along the short straight at the top of the track, followed it south around the bend, lightly threw the stick into fourth and squeezed the pedal to the floor. The Ghost thundered down the straight and hugged the corner into the Carousel. Tullius downshifted, rounded the Carousel hard on the inside, and gently mashed the pedal again. He quickly finessed the stick into fourth as he roared past pit row and the start/finish line.

Tom Goad clicked a stopwatch at the passing gray blur. He performed a quick calculation in his head: 83.15 miles an hour average speed for the first go-round. That would likely get them into the top ten on the starting grid.

After four more laps, Tullius pulled into the pit with one of the best qualifying runs of the field. At four-thirty p.m. the starting grid for Mid-Ohio was announced and Goad's prediction proved accurate; the Ghost would start seventh. Its best starting position yet.

Chapter 27

RACE DAY GREETED 25,000 fans at the Mid-Ohio Sports Car Course with light rain falling from a low, dark sky. Deep puddles had formed on the track from the nearly constant rainfall throughout the night.

The motel's TV told Adams that the forecast called for gradual clearing. The rain was expected to stop in mid-afternoon, just before or during the race. If the forecast was accurate, the Ghost would need its tires changed during the race. Adams grimaced at the thought.

What the hell do they know? Adams glared at the little black and white TV. They can't forecast anything.

~~~~

At 3:19 p.m., 33 Trans-Am racecars drove the parade lap in formation around the damp Mid-Ohio track, waiting for the start. A light rain fell. A soggy, homemade sign hung on the grandstand fence reading, "*Go Gray Ghost!*" After the loudspeaker's introduction of each car—punctuated by the crowd's huge ovation for car 49—the starter grasped the green flag.

The field was led by the pole sitter in his mustard yellow Mustang. Next to him was the red white and blue Javelin. Behind them, in third and fourth places respectively, were a Mustang and a Javelin. The Ghost, shod in rain tires, took seventh position surrounded by pony cars: Mustangs in front and alongside, Camaros behind. Tullius was on the outside in the fourth row.

The light rain became heavier. Then, a downpour. The track puddles deepened.

Tullius felt good. Very confident. If the rain persisted, the Ghost would surely beat them all, except, perhaps those two in the front. He'd learned that the Ghost's 142 mile an hour straightaway sprint yesterday was within three miles an hour of the Mustang in the front row, which was the fastest car on the track during qualifying. This could prove to be a three car race.

As the field approached the starting line, the green flag waved furiously. The collective roar of 33 racing engines erupted in the moist air over the verdant, wet country landscape. The 1971 Mid-Ohio Trans-Am was on.

The cars immediately broke formation and roared toward the first turn. With the advantage of starting on the left, Tullius cut the apex of the left turn in heavy traffic, eased the stick into fourth, squeezed the gas pedal down and easily retained seventh place as the pack streaked down the straight toward Keyhole Chicane. Tullius squinted past the windshield wipers, downshifted, and braked to avoid bumping the Mustang in front of him as he rounded the Keyhole. Had it not been for the Mustang, the Ghost could have taken this semi-circle turn much faster. No matter—the pack would soon spread out and allow the Ghost to move at its own, more rapid pace around the wet bends. For now, Tullius had to be content with simply avoiding a collision.

The downpour slowed to a steady rain.

Tullius shifted back into fourth and smoothly stood on the gas, racing up the back straight through the spray left by the six cars in front of it. Through the Esses, the Ghost passed a Mustang and began closing on another. This was typical of the Ghost and its driver—passing pony cars in wet curves.

The Ghost was now in sixth place.

As the pack rounded the Carousel and tore toward the end of the first lap, Tullius began closing in on the Mustang in front of him. He recognized it—the pole sitter. Dropped to fifth after only one lap? Clearly, something was wrong with the 'Stang. The Ghost ripped past him at the first bend.

After the second lap, the Ghost was running fifth.

After the fourth circuit, Tullius had the Ghost in fourth place and was closing on another Mustang, which was also having handling problems on the wet track. The soaked crowd cheered wildly each time the Ghost whistled past.

By the seventh lap, the rain had let up completely and the Ghost had passed the Mustang to move into third place. Another Mustang was now directly ahead in second place. Tullius and the old gray beast began closing in on it.

The sun broke through the thinning cloud cover for a moment.

Minutes later the Ghost took the inside of a turn with a Camaro on the outside. A photographer snapped a photo of the scene. A short distance behind them a Javelin was on the inside and a Mustang was on the outside. Suddenly, the Mustang lost control on the wet track, sliding counterclockwise in front of the Camaro. As the Mustang's right wheels slid off the track into the mud, it stopped spinning and began tracking backwards along the edge of the track, facing a fast approaching Javelin. The Javelin driver smoothly but quickly braked and maneuvered to the right, narrowly averting a head-on collision with the yellow Mustang. The Mustang driver quickly spun around and rejoined the race.

~~~~

During the next fifteen laps, the water on the track dissipated so quickly that some cars began pitting to change to dry weather tires. As the warming track dried, the water on it rose in wisps of steam, quickly scattered by passing racecars. On lap 27, as the Ghost screamed past pit row in third place, Tullius glanced at a chalkboard held by one of the pit crew. In big, white, handwritten letters, it read *"TIRES."* Adams wanted the Ghost to pit and change tires on the next circuit.

Tullius cursed. Pitting would guarantee the loss of third place, maybe worse, but that would only be temporary. With dry rubber, he could soon catch up. Hell, the Ghost tore up the dry Bryar track last week. Okay, he'd pit.

At lap 28, Tullius rapidly guided the Ghost into the pit and quickly screeched to a stop. Tom Goad clicked his stopwatch. The amateur pit crew immediately swung into action, with two guys thrusting their lone floor jack under the right front end and furiously working to remove the tire with the hand wrench. Another two guys were working on a second tire with a cross-handed T-wrench. Tom Nell was already pouring gas into the tank, his lean, muscular arms flexing as they held up the heavy fuel tank, chugging gas into the parched Ghost. Adams handed Tullius a cup of water, which the driver downed in a single gulp.

"How's it running?" asked Adams.

"Good. Real good. Kickin' ass as a matter of fact," said the driver wiping his mouth. Nell finished filling the tank and rapidly set the fuel container aside.

"Third gear okay?"

"Yeah—fine."

Tom Nell's concerned face, next to the empty gas can, appeared at the window. "What's the—"

"I don't know how the damn oil pressure is, Tom," interrupted Tullius. "I'm tryin' to drive here."

Nell cocked an eyebrow and glanced at the oil pressure gauge on the dashboard.

The hand wrench was still working on the right front tire. Tullius sat up, straining over the cockeyed hood to see the activity surrounding the tire change. It had been nearly a minute since he stopped. "What's the problem down there?" asked Tullius, motioning to the right front tire.

"Nothing. They'll get it done," answered Adams.

"Hope it's before the race is over."

The jack let the car down with a thud and the team quickly moved to the left front, repeating the process. Adams looked briefly out at the pony cars whizzing past on the straightaway. "They'll get it done," he repeated.

A Boss 302 Mustang from the pit in front of Trans/Action pulled off the track, streaked past the Ghost in pit row and screeched to a stop in its pit directly in front of the Ghost. Its crew began swarming all over the car as Tullius looked on. Two crewmembers attacked each tire simultaneously, each with a jack and impact wrench. Another crewmember was refueling it, and yet another was wiping down the windshield.

"Go Ghost!" yelled a distant voice from the crowd.

As the Trans/Action crew began working on the Ghost's next tire, Tullius looked at his watch. He'd been standing still for two and a half minutes—an *eternity* in racing.

The Mustang in front of him was nearly finished. Tullius bit his lip, squinted, and shifted in the seat, his face revealing his frustration.

The Mustang's crew dropped their car to the tarmac and the car roared away to rejoin the race, leaving the Trans/Action crew in a blue-gray cloud of exhaust and burnt rubber. Tullius looked at his watch again. The 'Stang spent forty seconds for that pit stop. The Ghost had been sitting there for three minutes. This was agony.

A member of the Mustang's pit crew smirked at Tullius sitting in the Ghost. Tullius flashed him the finger.

Tullius took a deep breath, slowly exhaled and began whispering to himself under the helmet. *We'll come back—still plenty of time left in the race. Forty-seven more laps left. Yeah, plenty of time.* Tullius squeezed the steering wheel hard, looked at the pony cars streaming past on the straightaway and gritted his teeth in anger.

At last, the Ghost's fourth tire, the right rear, was replaced and the crew jerked the jack from under the car. The Ghost's right rear corner began falling to the tarmac as Tom Nell pointed his right hand down pit road toward the track and furiously wind-milled his left arm in the direction of the track like a madman. Tullius popped the clutch, stood on the pedal and the big, suspended, right rear tire began spinning in the air for a split second. The spinning new slick hit the tarmac with an ear-piercing squeal as the crew hurriedly backpedaled away from their impatient car. The Ghost fishtailed away in a pungent cloud of blue-white smoke.

Tom Goad clicked the stopwatch. Three minutes, fifty-three seconds.

~~~~

The instant he reentered the track, Tullius felt better. Taking out his frustration and anger on the car, Tullius jammed the stick into second and hit the gas, accelerating fast down the reminder of the straightaway. Seconds later, he rounded the first bend and roared down the next straight toward

Keyhole Chicane, concentrating and pushing the Ghost hard. The agoniz-
ing pit stop was, for now, forgotten.

The sky was clearing. The Gray Ghost was back in the race.

By this time, the Ghost had been lapped so many times Tullius had no
idea of his position in the race. No matter, just *drive*, and the rest will take
care of itself. Drive *fast*.

The Ghost responded to every demand its driver required—
accelerating, shifting, and braking. The new slicks stuck to the track. The
Ghost quickly began passing again, passing everywhere—on the straights,
on the inside of the turns, and even on the outside of the turns. The old car
and its driver had hit their stride again and the crowd took notice, once
again cheering each time number 49 screamed past.

Tullius didn't know it, but his competitors were experiencing difficulty.
A Mustang had fallen out of second place with transmission trouble. After a
40-second pit stop for dry tires, the mustard yellow Mustang began to handle much better and had taken its fallen brother's place in second. The red
white and blue Javelin still led until lap 32, when he pitted and a Mustang
took the lead.

All the while, the Gray Ghost snaked its way through the field, gaining
steadily on the leaders, slowly recovering from the interminable pit stop. On
lap 38, the Mustang in front pitted again and the patriotic Javelin regained
the lead, followed by another Javelin who'd crept up from fourth in the
starting grid. But on lap 45, one of its tires blew. The Javelin bounced off
the track and hit a guardrail. He was finished for the day.

Those relatively few spectators whose eyes weren't glued to the Gray
Ghost were watching the two leaders—the red, white and blue Javelin in
first and the yellow Mustang in second. The Javelin's pit crew flashed him a
chalkboard signal: +20. Donahue had a 20-second lead on Follmer in the
yellow Mustang. But the driver was struggling—he'd lost his front brakes. A
few laps later they flashed another signal: +16. Then another: +15. The
next sign, however, was encouraging for Donahue in the patriotic Javelin:
"*Fulm Smoke*." Indeed, the Mustang in second was spewing white smoke.
To make matters worse, the Mustang had lost a header pipe, which was
costing him 75 precious horsepower.

Nonetheless, on the 56th lap, the Mustang passed the red, white and blue Javelin and moved into first. The Mustang's white smoke had diminished significantly. The Javelin still had no front brakes and was tiptoeing around the track as a result. Meanwhile, the Gray Ghost thundered on with full horsepower, fresh wide slicks on all four corners, and four good brakes, weaving its way through the pack toward the two leaders.

By lap 60, the sun was shining and the Ghost was back among the leaders in seventh place. With only 15 laps remaining, Tullius pressed the old sedan harder.

On the 70th circuit, he had moved the Ghost into sixth and was still closing on the two handicapped leaders. On lap 72 he moved into fifth place, motivating some of the crowd to get to their feet, willing their old gray underdog on. Despite its driver's best efforts, the Ghost couldn't catch the limping leaders. Tullius had run out of time.

At the end of the 75th lap, the Ghost crossed the finish line in fifth place, behind three Mustangs—in first, third and fourth respectively—and the patriotic Javelin in second. The Ghost earned two points for Pontiac toward the manufacturer's championship.

Chapter 28

"WE'RE AN AMATEUR team and we make amateur pit stops. That will change by the next race," said a relaxed Tullius to the throng of reporters encircling him as he stood by the Ghost in pit road after the race. "We only had one jack and one impact wrench to change all four tires. I'm convinced that if we'd had a 40- or 50-second pit stop for gas and tires like the other guys, we'd have been around to challenge for first at the finish line."

~~~~

On the way home to Detroit, Herb Adams sat in the passenger seat of his Suburban while Tom Goad drove, towing the Ghost. The next race on the Trans-Am circuit was in two weeks in Edmonton, Alberta, Canada. Adams dug through the glove box, looking for a map of Canada. He found it and spread it out over his lap. Edmonton was well north of Montana—north even of Calgary—and it looked to be about 5,000 miles from Detroit. This race would require the team to spend six precious vacation days, maybe more. Each of them only had 14 vacation days total, and some of it was already spent.

Adams folded up the rumpled map. Forget it. Too far and too expensive. They'd focus on the race after Edmonton—Donnybrooke Speedway, in Brainerd, Minnesota, on the Fourth of July. Smack in the middle of Minnesota and closer to home. The break would give the team four weeks to make some modifications to the Ghost's chassis, modifications that he'd wanted to implement for a few weeks now. Improvement on pit crew equipment, too, like more jacks and some impact wrenches.

~~~~

Back home after work the following week, Adams glanced out his open garage door at the front yard. Bright yellow dandelion flowers dotted the shaggy lawn. The Trans/Action team was gathered around the Ghost. "Hey guys. I got something to tell you."

The men stopped working and looked at Adams, wiping their hands on shop rags.

"First, let me congratulate you all again for the showing at Mid-Ohio. Sure, we could have done better, but we still finished fifth out of a field of 35 and brought home $1,900 in winnings. That's gonna help on expenses. We also earned Pontiac two points in the season standings. Good job everybody." Adams turned his attention to the Ghost and held up the latest edition of the to-do list. "Now, back to the business at hand. We got some wheelspin coming off the corners, gentlemen. I noticed it last week and Tullius could feel it. We're definitely losing some time as a result—maybe even a full second on each lap." Adams looked at Joe Brady. "Let's tweak the rear suspension geometry, Joe. We gotta balance it out better, too— more weight in the back and less in the front. Let's move the battery in the trunk and lighten up the front end somehow. And move the engine back a little."

Joe Brady nodded, studying the Ghost. He yawned. "*Jeez*, I'm tired …"

"No time for sleep …" said Adams, patting the young engineer on the back.

"I know, I know," smiled Joe.

Tom Nell rubbed his chin. "Herb, Jeff and I have been talking about the engine. We're a little nervous about the oil pressure, so we're thinking maybe a change would help." Nell looked around the garage at an audience of skeptical faces. "Well, uh, changing to a dry sump for engine lube. We could put in a new oil pan, a little one. The stock pump could do the scavenging and another external belt-driven pump could supply the pressure. Nice pressure."

"Yeah," added Jeff Young. "A single element pump. We store the oil in a tank—fourteen quarts or so—between the firewall and a fender wall. Probably the right front, and we'll just add the lines, tank, and filters."

"I'll make the lines and tank," offered Dutch.

Adams studied the two engine men. "Can you do it in three weeks? We're skipping Edmonton on June 20—too damn far away—but we got Donnybrooke on the Fourth of July."

Nell and Young looked at Dutch, who took a deliberate drag on his cigarette before nodding slightly and slowly exhaling a thin plume of smoke.

"Okay. Do it," said Adams. "And don't forget to move the engine back a few inches. We really need better balance."

Adams shifted his attention to Tom Goad. "Tom, we need some more jacks. We're all set on impact wrenches. The day after Mid-Ohio, a sales guy from a big tool company called me. Said he'd heard about the race—maybe he saw our pit stop, I don't know—anyway, he offered to donate two fancy new impact wrenches to us. I took him up on it. Don't want any more pit stops like that last one ... *God* ..."

A few of the guys groaned at the thought.

"Okay, I'll get the jacks," said Goad. "Consider it done."

Adams pointed to the shoebox on the corner workbench, "And don't forget to file the receipts for everything you buy. We've had money coming in, but our budget is still tight. That's it, then. We got the plan, now let's execute." Adams taped his list to the windshield.

~~~~

Tom Nell sat at his Pontiac Motor desk, eating a baloney sandwich, studying an engine blueprint, when he felt a presence at his open office door. Nell looked up from the drawing at his boss. Herb looked different. Serious. Concerned.

"Tom, we got a problem ... a big one," Adams said with a frown. He walked into the office, closing the door behind him, and took a seat.

Nell cocked his head, squinting. "Yeah, I figured. You don't look so good. What's a matter?"

Adams blinked rapidly and swallowed hard. "Well, it seems the brass thinks we ripped off the parts from Pontiac Motor Division for the Ghost—*stole* 'em. Seems they got a complaint from someone—"

"*Stole?* They think we *stole* the parts?" asked Nell, now also blinking in disbelief. "Who the hell told 'em that? *Liar!* We bought 'em all!" Nell stood up, saying, "I want to know *who!*"

"One of our competitors."

"Which one?" asked Nell through gritted teeth.

"I don't know, Tom. They wouldn't say. But anyway, that isn't the worst of it. The Division says if we don't give 'em receipts for all the Ghost's parts ..." Adams' voice trailed off as he looked out the window.

"What? What if we don't?" asked Nell, staring at his boss and sinking back into his chair.

Adams looked back at Nell. "Uh ... well ... we're *fired*. All of us."

The men silently contemplated the situation, stunned.

Nell broke the silence, "Well, we got 'em—the receipts I mean—don't we? In that shoebox in the garage. Where you told us to put 'em. Sure we do, we've all been careful about that, right?"

Adams raised his eyebrows, "I hope so. We got two hours before I have to present them and defend us. Let's go find out."

"Only two hours?"

"Yeah. Let's go. *Now.*"

A half-eaten baloney sandwich fell absently onto the blueprint.

~~~~

Later that afternoon, Nell and Adams sat in Adams office, pale and shaken, the precious shoebox between them. The box was stuffed with dozens of short, narrow strips of white paper.

Adams leaned back in his chair. "Well, at least they believed us—"

"What's not to believe? We bought all the stuff and here's the proof!" he said pointing at the shoebox. "It's a good thing you were constantly on our backs—I mean, constantly reminding us about the receipts. Who could have accused us of such a thing anyway? Do you think it's just someone who's jealous of all the attention we've been getting? Were they serious about firing us?"

Adams was downcast. "Listen, if they're of a mind to *can* us, they'll *can* us, regardless of these receipts."

Tom Nell scratched the back of his head. "Yeah, they would ..."

Adams' eyes narrowed. "I'm only guessing here, but I suspect we've got a very jealous competitor. A guy who's pissed at our car's success and all the attention we've been getting."

"Yeah," agreed Nell. "Can't beat us on the track so they resort to lies."

Adams shrugged his shoulders. "Well, it's over now. Back to work."

~~~~

Adams stared blankly out the open garage door at a large clump of crabgrass encroaching on his driveway. He turned and looked around the garage at his team. "Gentlemen, we got trouble."

"What trouble—Pontiac management again?" spat Dutch.

"No, no. Not that. It's the Suburban. It's, well, it's got a blown engine," Adams shrugged. "And we got to get the car to Minnesota in two days."

Silence filled the garage as the team contemplated the predicament.

"How bad?" asked Nell. "Maybe we can fix it."

Adams shook his head slowly. "Afraid not ... it's bad. Needs a complete overhaul."

More silence. Nell's eyes narrowed as he stared at the ground. He rubbed his chin slowly. "I got it ... my station wagon." The heads swiveled in his direction. "It's got a hitch. And a Chevy small block V8."

~~~~

The following evening after work, the Ghost perched on its trailer and rolled westward, creeping along in the right lane of Interstate 94 between Detroit and Chicago toward Brainerd, Minnesota, towed by a station wagon. The trailer's tongue leaned heavily on the wagon's low hitch ball, bucking and swaying at every crack and seam in the superhighway's pavement. The wagon's front end pointed at a weird angle above the horizon as the sunken rear levered it up under the Ghost's weight. The wagon's rear tires nearly touched the wheel wells and its rear bumper drooped perilously close to the ground.

The Trans/Action Team, after bouncing and grinding for 20 hours from Detroit, had spent a short night at a Brainerd motel and was now on their way to the track with the bucking Ghost in tow. Despite the poorly marked entrance on Birchdale Road, the team found their way to the paddock and pulled to a stop on pit road. Adams eased out of the wagon and immediately heard an unseen, booming, voice over the public address system.

"And here it is ladies and gentlemen ... *the Gray Ghost!* Yes, this is the car we've been waiting for at Donnybrooke—the storied *car number 49 ...* the *1964 GTO ...*"

A small crowd of people began closing toward them. Adams cursed quietly. He ordered the crew to unload the car and heard a voice from the crowd ask, "You ready for tech check-out?"

Adams recognized the man as a Trans-Am official. "Yeah," Adams responded. "But let's clear out the crowd here ..."

"There she is," continued the track announcer, "the former *grocery shopper* turned Trans-Am racer."

Adams squinted at the announcer's booth and shot a quizzical look at the race official. Adams was met with a shrug. The race official calmly backed the crowd away from the car and began his deliberate inspection of the Ghost.

Adams looked nervously around for his driver. In the past, Tullius had been present for the inspections. Adams was sure that Tullius' contacts and stellar reputation among the racing officials had helped give the car credibility. With Tullius as the driver, the officials knew car 49 wasn't just another amateur entry. But Tullius wasn't here. He was nowhere around.

The announcer read the Ghost's finishing places at the first three races of the year.

Adams swallowed hard at the sudden lump in his throat, trying hard to conceal his worry from the small throng of onlookers. He busied himself writing a to-do list.

The announcer described the history of the Ghost and its makers.

A few minutes later, the inspector gave the Ghost the okay to race. A wave of relief washed over Adams.

"And now, ladies and gentlemen, the Gray Ghost will take some practice laps!"

Adams cheeks flushed. Practice laps? With no driver? Adams scratched his head, wincing at this new predicament. He turned to the crew, jerking his thumb from the car to the trailer, "Load her back on." The crew looked at each other awkwardly. "You heard me, gentlemen …"

The crew shrugged and began loading the car back onto the trailer.

The announcer's tone changed, "Uh … the Gray Ghost is … uh …"

"Hey, why you leavin'?" asked a voice from the crowd.

"We got no driver—I mean, our driver's not here yet. We'll be back."

The announcer's booming voice went silent. Adams looked up at the booth. A man up there appeared very animated, waving his arms behind the booth's glass, shouting something. "Let's get outta here—quick," muttered Adams.

~~~~

A few hours later, the Trans/Action team, with its car in tow behind the grunting, sagging station wagon, rolled back into pit road. With great relief, Adams spotted Bob Tullius talking to a reporter.

Another reporter hurried up to Adams and handed him a newspaper. "It's the latest edition," said the reporter, fumbling with a note pad. "Look at the sports section," said the reporter urgently.

Adams fumbled through the paper to the sports section and saw a photograph of the Ghost under the headline that read, *"Grocery-shopper GTO is Trans-Am fans' hero."* The caption under the photo read, *Bob Tullius in the Pontiac GTO, a "gray ghost from the past."* Adams read:

No matter who wins the Trans-Am sedan series championship this year, the season's sensation already is a seven-year-old Pontiac GTO.

The car is an independent entry and unlike any independent entry ever run in the Trans-Am, it's fast and rugged enough to run on even terms with expensively backed Mustangs, Camaros and Javelins.

Six Pontiac Motor Division engineers, who wanted to see the Pontiac nameplate back in racing, are responsible for the project.

GROCERY SHOPPER

Long before the Trans-Am season opened, they contacted Bob Tullius of Falls Church about driving the car. Bob flew to Detroit to see the car and agreed to drive it. The whole deal was kept secret and wasn't revealed until a few days before the first Trans-Am.

The GTO was the personal car of 31-year-old Bob Adams, who manages the team.

Bob Adams? Adams snorted and read on.

It had 85,000 miles on the speedometer when preparations for the Trans-Am campaign were started. Mrs. Adams had been using it for grocery shopping.

The other five Pontiac engineers and their team assignments: Jeff Young, 27, engine and powertrain; Ted Lambiris, 31, fuel system and body; Tom Nell, drivetrain (shared with Young); Joe Brady, 25, chassis and component systems; Tom Goad, 38, transportation, plus race scoring and timing.

ON A SHOESTRING

All six of the engineers are performance enthusiasts as well. Nell aptly describes their purpose: "It's to show everyone, including ourselves, that a Pontiac can be made competitive using the ideas and concepts (and wrench twisting) of a group of desk engineers."

With no factory or outside assistance whatever, the "team" is a shoestring operation competing against $50,000 cars with unlimited backing.

In the season's opening Trans-Am at Lime Rock Park, Conn., the GTO rocketed to instant fame before 20,000 rain-drenched fans. Before the race was half over, it was the unquestioned crowd favorite.

Unable to qualify because of last-minute engine troubles, Tullius had to start last in the 32-car field. It took him less than 40 laps over the twisting 1.5-mile course to sweep thru the field and into second place behind ... a Javelin which had gotten away to a long lead.

With the cheers of the crowd spurring him on, Tullius stayed in second place—ahead of all the other Javelins, Mustangs and Camaros—until he pitted seven laps from the finish with his overheated engine seized.

There was no question about the Pontiac's competitiveness—it was as fast as any car in the race except ... one and handled superbly.

Since then, the GTO has been a top contender everywhere except at Edmonton, Canada, last weekend. The "team" couldn't afford that 5,000 mile trip.

This "ghost from the past" will be shooting for its initial Trans-Am victory at Minnesota's Donnybrooke road course Sunday. Tullius, a multiple SCCA national champion and a veteran of 11 years of racing, will be at his best over tight Donnybrooke—whether it rains or shines.

And the Minnesota fans are going to love that No. 49 GTO.

Adams smiled. "Mind if I keep this?" he asked the reporter.

"No, not at all," said the reporter. "Just gimme an interview ..."

Chapter 29

BOB TULLIUS FLIPPED toggle switches, snapped the Ghost's key into the ignition with his right thumb and forefinger, twisted it forward and the big machine rumbled and shook to life in the pit.

Adams looked in the window at his driver. "We modified it since the last race. Lightened up the front end, put a battery in the trunk to balance it a little. Also, the engine now has a dry sump with two pumps—should help the oil pressure. And we moved the whole engine to the rear a little for better balance."

"Yeah, okay, okay ... but the hood's still cockeyed," said Tullius, looking ahead impatiently. He glanced at the shrugging Adams.

"Let's see how she runs out here," said Adams.

Tom Nell scrambled up next to Adams and looked urgently at Tullius, saying, "Don't forget to check the oil pressure ..."

Tullius furrowed his eyebrows at Nell, gave a small salute to Adams, eased the Ghost into first gear and rolled onto the track for his practice runs. The sky began to spit rain.

Tullius remembered Donnybrooke and began to soak up its details from behind the wheel. The main straight ran east-west, and since the track was run clockwise, the cars would run this straight in a westward direction until the first turn—a 60-degree right hander. Turn one was unusual for road tracks because it was banked. Tullius planned to take it flat out during the race, despite the fact that it narrowed from the wide straight. Turn two was flat—to the right and unbanked—but with a wider radius, about 80 degrees, than turn one. This was another sweeper that could probably be taken with his foot on the floor. Not every car could do it, but the Ghost's suspension and big tires were likely up to it. The g-forces would be tough, though. This hard, right, flat turn would test the new dry sump system in the engine. He resolved to gas it on the next circuit. Following turn two, the Ghost cruised onto another straight in third gear. Ahead of it was turn three, which was another right turn—but this time, 130 degrees—followed by a short straight that led to the left-bending, 100-degree, turn four. This was the first turn of the northeast-heading ubiquitous "Esses" or chicane, composed also of the 90-degree right-hand turn five and 90-degree left-hand turn six. Each of the three Esses curves had progressively longer straight sections after them. The front of each of these turns was slightly widened, which would help in maneuvering, but taking the wide part into turn six caused the Ghost to peak too early in the turn. Tullius made a mental note to avoid this in the future.

The Ghost rumbled around the left hand, 45-degree turn seven and dove almost immediately into the right hand, 75-degree turn eight. It was clear to Tullius that a late apex was required in turn seven in order to properly set up for the closely following turn eight, and he had hit it right on. The Ghost swung out of turn eight into a short straight heading east, and barreled faster into the 60-degree, right hand turn nine under a bridge. Hitting the apex too early here and at high speed would result in an unpleasant meeting with the bridge abutment.

Tullius made another mental note.

Tullius felt no wheel spin through the Esses. The straight following turn nine headed southeast and at the end of it was a wide, 120-degree turn to the right that led back to the front straight: the longest on the track. He felt some wheel spin, but not much. Tullius threw the stick into fourth gear and stomped on the gas. The Ghost roared with delight as it accelerated past the starter's stand and the pits on the right.

Whatever these guys did to the car since the last race, they did it right. The Ghost felt better than ever.

~~~~

While Tullius continued his practice runs, a grinning Ted Lambiris handed Adams another newspaper folded open to the sports section. "Dig this!" said the Greek excitedly.

"*'64 Pontiac is Trans-Am darling*" read the headline. Adams shook his head in mild disbelief as he read:

> *The favorite to win Sunday's GBX Trans-Am auto race at Donnybrooke Speedway will be … someone driving a sleek Javelin, Mustang or Camaro.*
>
> *But the favorite of the crowd will be a chubby gray 1964 Pontiac Tempest. Against all the 1970 and 1971 race-prepared pony cars, a 1964 Tempest looks awkwardly out of place. It is the classic underdog.*
>
> *But as a competing driver said, "It's embarrassing to have that thing go so fast."*

Chubby? Adams scanned the remainder of the article, which recounted the Ghost's familiar history as Sandi's 80,000-mile family car and its performance at Mid-Ohio:

> *The car had been called the 'Silver Bullet' sarcastically at first, perhaps. But then the Trans-Am series started and people stopped laughing at the Tempest …*
>
> *Observers calculated that, with a normal half-minute pit stop, Tullius would have either finished second or won the race …*

Adams looked at the four impact wrenches and four floor jacks next to the trailer. Bring on a change of weather now, he thought. Bring it on.

~~~~

"I got an idea," said Joe Brady to his boss a moment later. "Tullius says he's a little loose coming off the corners. Let's see if we can't get a little more anti-squat by modifying the rear end some."

Adams nodded, "I thought I saw some traction loss. Joe, Dutch," Adams motioned to the two men and all three crawled on their backs under the Ghost's rear end for a conference.

"Yeah, here," said Joe, pointing to an axle bracket. "Let's raise the upper control arm pivot—we drill a hole in each of the axle brackets—the castings—right about *here* and put the upper control arms in 'em."

"Okay." said Adams, thinking and examining the Ghost's underbelly at close range. "Yeah, geometry change ... suspension ... yeah, that'll help anti-squat."

Dutch stared mutely at the bracket, thinking.

Moments later the Greek walked, smiling, toward the team's rental truck to fetch the oxygen and acetylene tanks. A crew member from another pit crew walked passed him in the opposite direction, effortlessly pushing a large, professional-looking, heavy duty cart carrying big oxygen and acetylene tanks, a welding torch and miscellaneous welding gear. The Greek stopped to watch the passing crewmember. The smile faded from the Greek's face. He turned to the Trans/Action rental truck and slowly walked toward it.

Opening the rear overhead door, he stared at the massive tanks before taking a deep breath and exhaling slowly. He gently heaved the heavy oxygen and acetylene tanks toward him, grunting, until they hung over the edge of the tailgate. The Greek turned around, squatted, and spread his legs slightly. Placing a hand over each shoulder, the Greek grabbed the front of each tank, easing them onto his shoulders. He took two deep, rapid breaths and stood up with a quick, low, grunt. Carrying the heavy burden, he walked deliberately toward the Ghost, taking short, deep breaths with each step, concentrating on his balance. A bead of sweat streamed from his forehead and down his nose as he soldiered on toward the Ghost. Out of the corner of his eye, the Greek spotted another welding cart servicing a pony car. He cursed quietly, stumbling toward the Ghost and dripping sweat, before finally arriving at his destination. Squatting down, the Greek eased the weighty tanks from his shoulders, sliding them down his back onto the ground next to the Ghost.

The Greek slowly straightened his aching body, groaning quietly as he stood up, arching his sore back.

Adams caught his eye. "Okay?"

The Greek drew a deep breath. "No sweat, man."

~~~~

A few hours later, Tom Nell, Harry Quackenboss, and Dutch Scheppleman watched the Ghost roar around the track. A professionally uniformed member of another pit crew strolled over. "Nice day, huh?"

Nell looked at him, "Yeah …"

"Hey, you really got a Pontiac 303 in that GTO?"

"Yep."

The crewmember paused. "How's yer horsepower?"

"463.8 last time I checked on the dyno."

"463.8." The crewmember raised his eyebrows. "Dynomometer?"

Nell squinted at the track, "Yeah. *Computerized.*"

Another pause. "Well, we know …" the crewmember looked around furtively, "you're the *skunk works* for Pontiac." He cast a knowing smirk. "I mean how else could ya build a machine like that?"

Nell arched an eyebrow, "Ya think so?"

The crewmember laughed.

The three Pontiac men stared solemnly back in unison.

The crewmember's chuckle quickly petered out. His grin faded as he took in the expressions of the Pontiac team members.

"Uh … anyways … what kind of rods you runnin'?"

"Carrillos—special ones," responded Nell flatly.

"Special?"

"Oh, yeah. *Special.*"

"What ya mean?"

Nell shifted his stance, his eyes darting left and right. "Can't tell ya. *Secret.* All's I can say is that's one fine-tuned, tricked-out, old hunk a *Dee-troit* iron."

The man studied Nell's face. Nell remained expressionless, crossed his hairy, sinewy arms and watched the Ghost scream past pit row.

Quackenboss and Dutch seriously studied the speeding car, biting their respective lips.

"Well, she really goes ... See ya," said the man, watching the gray blur.

"Yeah ..."

The man turned and began walking back to his pit.

Nell, Quackenboss, and Dutch exchanged brief, strained glances, struggling to contain their laughter.

~~~~

After the practice rounds, Tullius told the crew that the modifications to the rear end helped the car coming out of the corners. Later in the day, the Ghost qualified with a typically respectable time that placed it in the front third of the pack for the next day's race.

Herb Adams studied a single typewritten page entitled "Entry List. GBX Trans-American Sedan Race. Donnybrooke International Speedway, July 4, 1971." Thirty-seven drivers and cars were listed. All but one—car number 49—was a late model Camaro, Mustang, or Javelin.

A moment later, a reporter, interviewing Adams, asked whether Herb thought making a racecar from a Tempest was funny.

Adams narrowed his eyes at the reporter, "No more funny than making a race car out of a *Javelin* ..."

~~~~

Independence Day, 1971 greeted Donnybrooke International Speedway with bright sunshine and periodic, frenetic pops of firecrackers from under the grandstands. Soon after, pit row roared to life with another sound: the collective thunder of 31 racecars as the crowd filed in to take their seats in the grandstands.

Thankfully, thought Herb Adams, the press was not swarming over the Ghost as in the previous two races. They seemed to be giving the pony cars as much attention as they gave the Ghost. For Adams, this was a welcome change. The distractions were not as great and the chances for misquotes were reduced. Perhaps the Ghost's novelty was wearing off, he mused. Regardless, they didn't come here to yap and grin to the press. They had come to race.

~~~~

Moments later, Bob Tullius fired up the Ghost and rolled onto the Donnybrooke track for the parade lap. The loudspeaker introduced the field, car by car, as they slowly rounded the course in order. The applause grew much louder at the introduction of car 49. Hundreds of spectators stood up, applauding Tullius and his old gray machine. Two homemade signs hung on the fence reading, "*Go GTO*" and "*Gray Ghost # 49!*"

The Greek waved back at the crowd from the Ghost's pit area with his hand in the air, "Thank you! Thank you!" he shouted thorough a beaming smile. Harry Quackenboss rolled his eyes, slapping a mosquito on his neck.

"Aw, *shut up*, Greek," said Tom Nell, wiping his strong, greasy hands with a shop towel. "They ain't cheerin' for *you* ..."

Lambiris shot a glance in Nell's direction. "Sure they are—cheerin' for *all* of us!" He turned his attention back to the adoring crowd, "Thank you!" he continued, now waving both arms.

"Christ ..." muttered Nell, shaking his head at Joe.

"Who needs a PR guy when you got the Greek?" grinned Joe Brady.

~~~~

A few minutes later the green flag waved and the cars broke formation, accelerating in a deafening ruckus across the starting line and toward turn one. Tullius took the 60-degree banked bend at full throttle and passed a pony car. He pressed the Ghost into the flat turn two with his foot on the floor. The g-force threw him hard into the door as he gassed the car around the right turn, but he passed another pony car midway through. Tullius forced himself to glance at the oil pressure gauge just after he passed the pony car. It was good. Nell would be happy—the dry twin sump system was working. After turn two, the Ghost accelerated onto the straight toward turn three, the sharper bend to the right. Tullius downshifted gently, rounded the bend and careened southward into the Esses as he rapidly shifted into fourth.

Tullius negotiated the Esses expertly, passed another pony car and gassed it around the remaining turns in the back of the track. He rounded turn nine, shifted into fourth and stood on the pedal close behind a Mustang. Then he downshifted, dove into turn ten, rounded it hard, and accelerated briefly before simultaneously shifting back into fourth. Neck and neck, the two cars screamed past pit row and the cheering crowd on the main straight. They crossed the start-finish line and began the second circuit.

The Ghost passed the Mustang through the Esses, continuing its assault of the field of pony cars. But after a few more circuits around the track, a loud noise emanated from the rear end, with a simultaneous loss of power and control. And the rear end seemed to have dropped. Tullius cursed and headed to pit road. He limped to a stop, urgently hollering to the pit crew about the problem in the rear end. Adams and Joe, fearing the worst, immediately ran to the rear of the car and scooted under the Ghost on their backs. A moment later they slowly slid out from under.

Dutch saw the look on their faces and needed no explanation. "Axle bracket busted," he said flatly with a cigarette dangling from the side of his mouth.

Joe sat up, astonished. "You sure?"

"Yeah," said Dutch flatly.

"How'd you ... I mean, how'd you *know*?" asked Joe.

Adams stepped in to explain, "Yeah, well when we drilled the new holes to fix the anti-squat problem, we ... ah ... well ... we ...."

"Drilled 'em in the wrong goddamn place," said Dutch hoarsely.

Donnybrooke was over for the Gray Ghost.

~~~~

The Trans/Action crew, slapping mosquitoes, looked dejectedly at their car on pit road. The rain fell heavier and the pony cars ripped around the damp track, spewing noise and misty exhaust.

"Joe," said Adams to the young engineer.

Brady turned his pained face to Adams. "I'm sorry, Herb," Joe shook his head dejectedly. "*Man ...*"

Adams wrapped his arm around Joe's shoulder. "Forget it. We had a problem—loose coming off the corners. You had an idea to fix it. It was a good idea. I okayed it. Then it became *our* idea. It didn't work. Don't blame yourself, now. We're a team. We win together, we lose together, understand?"

Joe exhaled slowly, "yeah ..."

Adams reached into his pocket, pulled out his wallet, removed a wad of bills and gave them to Joe. "Here. It's from the kitty. Now go out and buy some beer, a *lot* of beer, and bring it back here. We'll watch the race. All of us, *together.*"

Half an hour later the sounds of popping beer bottles punctuated the noise of the passing pony cars.

Chapter 30

THE 20-HOUR TRIP home to Detroit from Brainerd, Minnesota was a long one for the Trans/Action Team. They came away from Donnybrooke with a measly 50 dollars and no points to show for their effort. The Ghost only managed to complete ten laps—its worst showing yet. Their only consolation was that two other top cars also failed to finish, after completing only 15 and 20 laps respectively. The patriotic Javelin won again, very closely followed by his teammate. Collectively, the two Javelin guys won $7,000, and the first place guy earned nine points for AMC at Donnybrooke.

Herb sat in the passenger seat studying the race schedule for the remainder of the season. As Tom Goad drove, Adams looked up from the schedule, gazing through the station wagon's bug-spattered windshield at the highway rushing past. A familiar voice from the car radio excitedly announced that preparations were being made for baseball's All-Star game on July 13th at Detroit's Tiger Stadium. Adams switched it off abruptly.

With no pressing work or race deadlines, these drives were good times to strategize. The team was exhausted and emotionally flat after failing to finish. But that was only temporary. The next race was scheduled at Road America in Elkhart Lake, Wisconsin, on July 17—only two weeks away. Elkhart Lake. Adams winced as the image of that crumpled blue and white Firebird flashed across his mind.

He quickly turned around and looked through the rear hatch window at the reassuring Ghost, bucking on the trailer behind them. They'd fix the Suburban, but they'd skip Elkhart Lake. Too tired and broke.

They'd concentrate on St. Jovite in Quebec on August first. St. Jovite was a beautiful course at the foot of Mont-Tremblant in Canada's Laurentian Mountains. Then they'd go to Watkins Glen in New York, another pretty course, albeit a long haul from Motown. After that, they'd close out the season on September 6th at MIS, the Michigan International Speedway, in the Irish Hills west of Detroit, close to home. Home track advantage. That would be nice. They'd have to skip the last two races of the season at Riverside California on October 3rd and Laguna Seca in Monterey on October 16th. That was *way* too far to haul the car, even once, and particularly on Goad's rickety trailer. And way too expensive. Anyway, by that time, they'd all have long since blown their vacation days.

~~~~

On the evening of Tuesday, July 13th, Adams listened to the corner radio in the garage call the play-by-play at the All-Star game from nearby Tiger Stadium as the Trans-Action members tinkered with the Ghost.

> *It's the bottom of the third ... and the American League Manager has sent the Oakland A's outfielder to the plate to pinch hit before this record attendance of 53,559 ... The left handed outfielder is in his fourth season as a major leaguer ... the pitcher has two strikes on him ... he gets the sign ... here's the windup ... and the pitch ... he swings ... oh my ... it's a long shot headed to right center field ... still going ... headed over the roof ... still going ... it's gone! The ball hit the light tower, ladies and gentlemen ... the huge light tower on top of the second deck in right center field! The ball's bounced back onto the field now ... oh ... I don't believe I have ever seen a ball hit that hard! That ball would have gone over 500 feet! Only eight players have ever hit a ball over the roof here at Tiger Stadium ...*

The engineers continued working.

~~~~

While the Trans/Action crew worked back home in Detroit and sulked about their results at Donnybrooke, word came late on July 17ᵗʰ that the patriotic Javelin had won again at Elkhart Lake. He beat a Mustang to the finish line by 2.1 seconds. Another $4,000 and nine more points for AMC. They had now won four out of seven races. The red, white and blue Javelin seemed invincible.

~~~~

Ten days later in his Pontiac office, Herb Adams took a bite of baloney sandwich while he read the newspaper's latest batch of bad news.

"Hey boss ..."

Adams looked up at the smiling face of Jeff Young.

"Hey," Young continued. "I met a guy at the Pontiac Airport last week. He's got a Cessna 310," Young held his hands up, twirling his index fingers. "Ya know, twin engines. Anyway, he's a race fan, so I told him about us and he said he'd *heard* about us! He knows about the *Gray Ghost*, man!"

Adams scratched his head, "So what?"

"Oh—so I told him we wanted to go to St. Jovite, but it's a 20-hour drive. A real drag. So he says, 'Hey, I'll fly you guys in my Cessna!' For *free*, man! We just buy the gas—that's it!"

Adams arched his eyebrows and looked out the window, "... free ..."

"*Yeah*, man! Gas won't be much, and we'll get there in no time—couple hours. We could even leave Friday after work."

Adams narrowed his eyes and nodded, "How many seats? Six?"

"Yeah—including the pilot. And I'll sit in the right chair—ya know, co-pilot."

"This guy's a real pilot? I mean, he knows what he's doing?"

Young shot an indignant look at his boss. "He's got a *Cessna 310, man!* Hell *yeah*, he knows what he's doing!"

Adams stared expressionless at the indignant face for a moment, testing Young.

Young stared back, furrowed brow and wide-eyed. He hunched his shoulders, holding up the palms of his hands, "He's good, man … IFR and twin engine rated … I mean he's experienced. It's groovy, man."

A slow grin cracked across Adams face. "Yeah, okay. I'll drive the Suburban with Harry and anybody else who wants to stay on the ground. The rest of you guys can … uh … *fly*."

~~~~

The next day, Adams squinted at a blueprint covering his desk. The ringing phone interrupted him. "Herb Adams …" he said into the receiver.

"Hi—it's Tullius."

"*Hey!* How's things in Falls Church?"

"Busy, man. In fact, that's why I'm calling. I got to drive for Group 44 on the 17th. Isn't that the day of the Trans-Am at St. Jovite?"

"Yeah … it is."

"Sorry, man. Group 44 is my priority. That's *my* team. Anyway, I can still make Watkins Glen August 15th and Michigan on September 6th. You're not goin' to Riverside or Laguna Seca, right?"

"Right—too far away. I'll see if I can get somebody to drive in Quebec. No problem. Hell, maybe I'll drive myself."

"Oh, Sandi will *love* that."

"Yeah," said Adams through a smile. "Hey, don't worry about St. Jovite. Listen, you've done a great job for us this year and we appreciate it—thanks."

"My pleasure. That's a good car you put together. But it ain't over yet—maybe we'll win at Watkins Glen. And we got home field advantage at MIS. Good luck in Canada."

"Okay. Any suggestions on who to drive?"

"Ah … no. Just ask around the track when you get there. There's bound to be somebody with a busted ride or something."

"No sweat. We'll find him."

~~~~

Adams surveyed his front lawn from the open garage. Dandelions dotted the unkempt grass. The mass of crabgrass at the driveway's edge had easily doubled in size, sprouting seedpods. Adams shrugged and turned. "All right, gentlemen. I have an idea," Adams said loudly in the garage. The talking trailed off and heads turned toward him. "We got too much vibration, and I believe at least part of it's from the exhaust configuration. So I got a couple nice big four inch exhaust pipes here," Adams said, pointing to two 10-foot long, four-inch diameter thick stainless steel tubes on the floor. "Let's yank these little side pipes and slap these monsters on."

The crew grinned approvingly. "Better horsepower, too" said Young.

"Yeah—pipe 'em right out the rear to the bumper."

Nell winced, "But what about the noise? I mean, *damn!*"

Adams shrugged, "No Trans-Am rule against noise … not *technically*."

~~~~

The following day, Adams methodically examined the huge new gaping silver pipes jutting from the rear of the Ghost's rear bumper. He walked around the driver's side and slid into the Ghost's seat, gripped the key, deliberately slid it into the ignition and warned his crew, "Here we go …" Nell and Young covered their ears. Adams started the engine.

An earsplitting thunder erupted from the new big twin pipes, spewing out the open garage, and reverberating through the neighborhood like a bomb blast. Adams winced hard, ducking and hunching his shoulders involuntarily. *Jesus*, what a noise!

~~~~

Two weeks later, Herb Adams and his passengers in the newly repaired Suburban, Harry Quackenboss and Sandi Adams, hauled the Ghost eastward along a dark Canadian highway on the 20-hour journey from Pontiac to St. Jovite, Quebec—northeast of Ottawa, northwest of Montreal, and a long way from Motown. It is very French-Canadian, which, as far as the Trans-Action guys were concerned, really meant that although the people spoke English, many did so reluctantly and even resentfully. Most of the

Trans-Action guys knew this from personal experience—and none of them spoke a word of French. No matter, thought Herb Adams; they had come to race, not socialize with the locals. Race toot sweet.

They had left suburban Detroit after work on Thursday and it was now midnight. Adams glanced in the side view mirror and saw something unusual in the light of the car behind him: smoke. Smoke from the trailer? He looked again. Definitely smoke, and a lot of it and getting worse. "Damn," he remarked calmly. Adams hit the right turn signal and brake simultaneously and began easing over to the shoulder.

Harry, from the front passenger seat, looked at his chief. "What?"

"Wheel bearing on the trailer."

Harry shot a look into the side view mirror and saw the gray-white smoke billowing from the trailer's wheel. He rubbed his red eyes and looked back over his left shoulder through the rear window of the Suburban, vainly hoping the mirror was playing tricks on them. The bad news was confirmed. Smoke. "Oh Christ," he muttered.

Sandi, lying half asleep in the second row seats, felt them slowing. "Are we there?" she asked groggily.

"No," responded Adams curtly.

Sandi sat up, scratching her thick, tousled hair. "Something wrong?" she asked more alertly.

"Yeah, sweetie. We got a problem with the trailer ... the wheel." A quick analysis of the smoking wheel by the two engineers revealed that the wheel hub was seriously shot, thanks to a wheel bearing that went bad from lack of lubrication. This was problem enough in daylight, in the United States. But it was dark, in Canada, with semi-trucks barreling past them at 65 miles an hour. And tomorrow was practice and qualifying day, and they had no driver.

Harry squatted to examine the wheel. "Need a new hub and bearing," he shouted above the windy blast of a passing 18-wheeler.

Adams squatted next to him. "And maybe a new thread for the axle stub," he said, wincing. The two engineers jacked up the trailer and disconnected it from the Suburban. They quickly removed the wheel and their fears were confirmed: the stub did indeed require re-threading.

How in *hell* are we going to fix this in time? Adams thought. Another big rig bore down on them. Adams slowly shook his head, looking at his partner. "So much for the glamour of racing," he said, wiping his greasy hands. He stared back at the wheel and stub, studying them. "Well, let's go find a hub, a bearing, and somethin' to re-thread the stub."

They looked at the Ghost. The old racecar sat helpless and dark on the crippled trailer, parked on a narrow shoulder. Another semi-truck roared toward them and skimmed past the Ghost, buffeting the engineers. The unthinkable crossed Adams' mind: what if the next one *hit* the trailer? He glanced at Harry's face. Harry too, was clearly worried.

Harry said, "We've got no choice, Herb. We've gotta leave it." Harry put his arm on Adams' shoulder. "Half of racing is—"

"—just showing up for the race," Adams interrupted. Adams already knew it, but it was good to hear confirmation from Harry's measured, calm, professional, almost intellectual voice. It was good to feel his reassuring presence. Adams took a deep breath. "Yeah. Let's go, quick."

The engineers and Sandi drove off in the Suburban, leaving the dark Ghost to the night. Within an hour they had procured a new wheel hub and bearing from an all-night garage near the highway. But how to re-thread the stub? They stopped at another garage, an old one, with its lights on. They peered inside the cramped, cluttered, office and saw an old man, his feet propped on an ancient wooden desk, asleep in a beaten-up chair. As Adams opened the squeaking office door, squinting under the blinding, flickering, fluorescent lights, the tinkle of a bell sounded from the top of the door. He stepped onto the greasy tiled floor.

The old man opened one eye, then another. "*Huh?* Wah ya want?"

"Uh ... well ... sorry Mister," muttered Adams.

The old man sat up in the creaking chair, rubbing his wrinkled eyes. "Reg'ler or ethyl?"

"Oh, we don't need gas."

"Ay?"

Adams spoke up, "No gas—we don't need any gas."

"Don't need no gas?"

"No. No gas. We need—"

"Well, what ya want then?" the old man interrupted. He stood up, slowly and skeptically eyeing this young man and the taller young guy behind him.

"We got a busted trailer on the highway and—"

"Trusted trailer?" The old man rubbed the gray stubble on his chin with a quivering hand.

"No—a *BUSTED* trailer."

"Oh … busted," he grunted.

"Yeah. Wheel bearing went out and—"

"What's a matter with yer trailer?"

"Wheel bearing burned up and—"

"Wheel bearing?"

"Yes. A wheel bearing. And now we need—"

"Oh, I got some bearings," said the old man, lowering his guard. "Out in the garage here."

"No, no—we don't need a bearing. We already got—"

The old man squinted at Adams. "Thought ya said yer bearing burned up!"

"Yes, it did, but we already got a new one. Now we need a tool—"

"Well what the *hell* ya asking me fer then?" The old man paused. "Hey, you ain't from around these parts is ya? I mean ya talk kinda funny. You a *Yankee?*"

"Well, yes. But we need a hub threading—"

"*Ha!* Thought so. Yer kinda pushy, just like a Yank."

Adams looked at Harry in frustration, then over his shoulder at Sandi, rubbing her eyes back in safety of the Suburban. He glanced at his watch: 3:05 a.m. Harry stepped up alongside Adams. "We don't mean to be pushy," he shouted. "We just need some help."

"No need to holler, big fella. Whatcha need? I know it ain't no bearing."

"Ah, nope. Just something to re-thread an axle stub."

"Re-tread a axle stump?" The old man scratched his mottled, balding, head.

"No," said Harry patiently. "A *tool* to re-thread our axle stub … *re-thread axle stub.*"

"Oh hell! I got that! Out here in the garage! Bring yer trailer in an' I'll fix it fer ya."

Harry sighed. "We can't," he said loudly. "It's stuck out on the shoulder of the highway."

"Oh. Oh yeah, too bad." The old man sagged back into his chair.

Harry and Adams glanced at each other. They couldn't give up now. Adams spoke up again, "We were towing a race car—"

"Pace car?"

"No—*race* car, *race* car. On our way to St. Jovite for the Trans-Am race Sunday. We need to fix ... to chase the correct threads ..."

The old man's face brightened as he stood up with surprising spryness. "You fellas *racers?*" he asked eagerly through a growing grin.

Adams grinned back, "Yeah. We're the engineers and pit crew."

"Racers." The old man paused. "I used to do some racin' meself." He looked at his shoes, mumbling to himself, and then looked up eagerly at the two young racing Yanks, squinting though decades of weathered wrinkles. "Well, why doesn't ya just *borrow* me threadin' tool?"

At 6:00 a.m., the Ghost and its trailer were back on the road to St. Jovite through a thickening fog.

~~~~

An hour later, Tom Nell climbed up the few steps on the Cessna's stairway, hunched down, and entered the plane parked on the tarmac at the Oakland Executive Airport in Pontiac, Michigan. Jeff Young grinned widely back at him from the right seat. The pilot focused on the myriad lights and switches in cockpit, occasionally turning and flipping them. Nell glanced toward the rear. *This thing is a flying cigar tube* ... Nell slowly took one of the four available seats in the back of the tube and fastened his seatbelt as Joe Brady squeezed down the narrow, short aisle and eased himself into the seat across from Nell.

Joe and Nell exchanged brief, nervous glances.

Dutch and the Greek settled in the seats ahead as Nell looked out the window at another twin-engine plane. It was white with red stripes along the fuselage. The pilot stood up and walked hunched over to the stairs leading down to the tarmac. Pointing to the red and white twin-engine plane, the pilot said, "He's goin' to St. Jovite, too." The pilot pulled up the hinged stairs and snapped them into the fuselage. He threw a latch, locked the door, and smiled at the passengers, "Welcome aboard. Fasten your seat belts, please."

The engines began to grind the propellers around slowly and twin streams of blue-gray exhaust spewed rearward from them. As the propellers noisily spun faster, the passengers shook with harmonic vibrations. The engines began to whine. The plane began to move. A grin creased the Greek's face. Tom Nell tugged his seatbelt tighter. They taxied, bouncing to the runway and were soon airborne, headed east-northeast in the early morning overcast sky.

~~~~

An hour later, the Suburban, towing the Ghost, approached St. Jovite. "We gotta find the airport," said Adams, rubbing his weary eyes from behind the Suburban's steering wheel. Adams blinked through the windshield, "Look at this *fog*."

Harry fumbled with a map in the passenger seat. "We're close …"

At the same time, in the Cessna, Jeff Young peered out the cockpit window, vainly searching for the runway through the morning fog. "We're close …"

The Cessna had been circling for 35 minutes, searching for the airport. As the plane slowly descended through the pea soup, Joe Brady squinted out his little oval window. The clouds were beginning to look greenish. He blinked hard. A mottled black and white object went quickly past, silhouetted through the fog and against the green. Then another … *"COWS! Oh Christ … Cows! And we're on top of 'em!"*

The passengers' heads quickly swiveled, wide-eyed, to the port side as the Cessna immediately lurched upward. Dutch cursed, tightening his belt again. The Greek chuckled over his shoulder, "Where's a chute when you need it, man?"

"Wind sock," said Young calmly, pointing out the cockpit window. "And there's our red and white twin engine buddy we saw at the Pontiac airport on the ground over there."

Five minutes later the Cessna rolled to a stop at the end of a grass landing strip. They taxied, bouncing violently on the ground, toward the red and white plane. The pilot cut the engines and dropped the steps. The Greek bounded out of the plane, spread his arms, looked to the sky, took a deep breath of the damp, gray, thick air and slowly exhaled, "*Ahhhhh* ... Canada!" The remaining passengers slowly wobbled down the stairs into the Canadian fog.

"Greek? Tom?" called a familiar voice through the mist.

"Herb!" responded Nell. "We made it!"

The team greeted each other, exchanging stories of their respective journeys. "All right," said Adams. "Let's get to the track, find a driver and qualify." He looked around at the heads. "Uh ... now we got a couple too many passengers here for the Suburban to handle."

"Well, what we gonna do?" asked the Greek.

Adams flashed a sly grin, scratched the top of his head, and looked at the Ghost on the trailer.

Nell and the Greek looked at each other with arched eyebrows.

"The track's not far," offered Adams apologetically.

Moments later the Suburban, filled with passengers, crawled through the fog towing the tarp-covered Ghost with its own two passengers.

~~~~

The Trans-Am Series featured two distinct car classes: the bigger American pony cars with their corresponding larger engines that were over two liters in displacement, and the smaller, mostly European and Japanese cars with their under two liter engines. The races were run on the same days— generally Sundays—and there were plenty of good drivers in each class. As he looked through bleary eyes over the St. Jovite course under the clearing mid-morning fog, Adams' challenge now was to find one of those good, albeit currently unemployed, drivers who would drive the Ghost.

Tomorrow was the race. They also needed a hotel, but that could wait. Sandi would look for a place to stay.

Adams glanced to his left and a saw the familiar face of a young driver down pit road, a redhead. He just couldn't place the name. Adams looked away, imploring his memory to recall. *Rusty!* Rusty *Jowett!* That was it. He had a real good year in '69 driving a Camaro for Chevy. The two men made eye contact. Adams waved, Rusty smiled, and they began walking toward each other.

"Herb Adams! Father of the Pontiac Trans Am!" The men shook hands and briefly made small talk, when Jowett casually, innocently, revealed he was looking for a car to drive.

"Hey, we need a driver *today*. I know you got a real good record."

Jowett looked pleasantly surprised. "What about your driver—Bob Tullius isn't it?"

"He can't make it."

Jowett looked over Adams' shoulder at a dirty, gray sedan sporting number 49 in pit row. It wasn't a pony car. It was big and old. An early GTO. This was the underdog car he'd heard about everywhere. This thing was tearing up the Trans-Am tracks. A wide grin broke out under Rusty Jowett's red mop. His eyes darted back to Adams. "*I'll* drive for ya!"

~~~~

St. Jovite, or Le Circuit Mont Tremblant as they liked to call it around here, was a relatively hilly, 6.25 mile track, bordered on the west by Lake Moore and on the east by La Diable River—the Devil River. A hilly, curvy track made up a sweeping north loop, a sharper south loop, and another loop to the west, where pit lane, the control tower, and paddock were located. It was a beautiful track in beautiful country. Ninety miles northwest of Montreal, the track was built in the shadow of the Laurentian Mountains in 1964.

Jowett was familiar with Trans-Am racing, having driven a Camaro for Chevrolet during the 1969 season and finishing in the top ten nine times, including a third place result at Watkins Glen. Another one of those top ten finishes that season was here at St. Jovite, where he finished fifth.

The sky began to drip a steady rain.

Jowett settled into the Ghost and turned the key. The Trans/Action crew covered their ears. The deafening noise startled Rusty. "*Jesus ...*" he mouthed to Adams.

Adams grinned at him, saying something inaudible. Nearly all the heads up and down pit road, and those in the stands, stared in the direction of car 49.

Jowett gently engaged first gear and pressed the gas. The Ghost roared slowly out of pit road and onto the track. Off to the left, at about eleven o'clock and way up in the distance, Jowett could see treeless ski runs carved into the mountain. They were unmistakable, even in summer. He slowly gassed the Ghost and eased into second gear as he approached the first two turns, which was really one turn—a big sweeper to the right that rose in the middle and quickly flattened out before entering turn three, a nice down-shifting right bend with a quick view of La Diable. This was immediately followed by turn four, a more than ninety-degree left that was itself followed by turn five—a hard ninety-degree right. These were known as the Esses, and the raucous Ghost stayed glued to the track, ripping and roaring coolly around them.

Jowett, pleased with the slick-handling GTO, allowed himself a slight smile. A short, flat straightaway then led into turn six, a left-bending eighty-degree curve that flowed into the first leg of the south loop, which was a descending straightaway that took Jowett and his big gray machine into turn seven, a right ninety-degree turn immediately followed by a slight leftward bend in an otherwise straight section. This allowed Jowett to shift into third easily before encountering turn eight, a U-shaped right that led into turn seven, a section much better known as the "Hump." The Hump was, as the name implies, a rise in the track; but at its summit the Hump bent slightly to the left, then dropped and poured the cars into the longest straight on the track.

Jowett smoothly shifted the old GTO into fourth and squeezed the gas to the floor. The Ghost, responding with characteristic immediacy, rocketed down the Hump, accelerating fast with an earsplitting thunder before roaring into a downshift and turning hard right into turn ten, a seventy-degree flat turn that almost instantly met the right bending, ninety-degree turn eleven. This low-lying area was known as the Gulch. The track now rose slightly as Jowett and the Ghost tore up toward the ninety-degree left turn twelve, better known as Bridge Turn, so-named because a concrete arch spanned it, allowing spectator access to the infield. The track now led into an area called the Kink—officially turn thirteen—that bent slightly to the right, spilled into a short straight, and reached turn 14, called Namerow, a hairpin right that led, via the gently left sweeping turn 15, back to where Jowett started with the ski runs in the distance.

Jowett was exhilarated. Herb Adams was right. Hell, even the press reports were correct. This old thing could *move*.

~~~~

Standing between Joe Brady and Dutch, Adams critically eyed the GTO as Jowett exited the car grinning as he removed his helmet.

"*Man*," said Jowett. "Kinda noisy, but that beats walkin'!"

Tom Nell quickly approached, "How was the oil pressure?"

"Oil pressure? Oh ... well, I ..."

"Well, check it next time would ya?" Nell eagerly stuck his head through the window, peering intently at the gauges.

"How's it feel?" asked Adams.

"Good," said Jowett, eager to change the subject. "I mean *real* good. Handling and horses both, yeah. Maybe a little traction loss under hard acceleration, but ..." Jowett looked at the Ghost admiringly.

~~~~

An hour later, Sandi approached her husband. "Honey?" she asked.

Adams, examining the Ghost's new rear-end modification and wiping his hands with a shop rag turned to his wife, "Yeah?"

"Bad news. I can't find a motel or hotel with any vacancy."

Adams stopped wiping his hands. "*Nothing?*"

"I've looked everywhere. They're all booked. Maybe it's because I don't speak French, but I don't think so. I mean, I've got Canadian money."

Adams shook his head slowly. "Ya know, the actual *racing* part of this is *easy* compared to the logistics and other stuff. Did you check with the track office? Maybe they have some ideas."

"Okay, I'll check." Sandi pecked her husband on the cheek and walked off in the direction of the office.

A short while later she returned. "Herb, the track office has a suggestion, but—"

"What—what suggestion?" Adams rubbed his burning, sleep-deprived eyes.

"Well, they have a list of families with houses. People who rent out rooms. Like a bed and breakfast, I guess."

"Families? In *houses?*"

"That's it. Nothing else available. Anyway, it's more like bed and breakfasts, like I said. Maybe it'll even be fun. I reserved rooms in three houses for all of us."

Adams scratched his head, "A bunch of Detroit gearheads spread out in French-Canadian bed and breakfasts ... *God.*"

~~~~

That evening, the Trans/Action team settled into their rooms in their respective houses. The host families were very friendly and seemed to appreciate the engineers' rudimentary efforts at French. With directions—in English—from one of the host family wives, the team soon found a nearby restaurant. They were seated together at a big table and were quickly greeted by a buxom young waitress wearing a close-fitting top and mini-skirt typical of young Quebec women.

"*Bonsoir!*" she said through a wide smile in a perky young voice. "*Bienvenu.*" She began distributing menus.

"Uh ... bone jer," stammered Adams. "Uh, do you speak *English?*" he asked imploringly.

"*Ahh, yes!* I am sorry. Good evening. May I bring you a drink?" she responded in a beautiful accent.

Adams broke into a big smile. The Americans quickly ordered beer—Canadian of course—and began squinting at the foreign menu as the cute waitress bounced off to fetch the brew. The Greek watched her high heels walk off before finally directing his attention to the menu. "What in hell," he muttered. "It's all in *French!*" The other guys whispered profanities, scratching their heads and rubbing their chins at the menus.

"*Man*, we been here a day and I'm already sick of this French. Why can't they speak *American* like the rest of us?" complained Dutch seriously, looking desperately at the menu. "I'm *hungry*." The engineers nodded, grumbling in agreement.

"Oh, you guys," said Sandi. "It's not *that* difficult. Look, see where it says *poulet*? That's chicken. And see *boeuf*? That's beef. And *porc*—that's pork, I think …"

"Yeah? Well where's it say *hamburger and fries*? They gotta have *french* fries," demanded the Greek.

"Ted, don't be silly," Sandi said. "They have fish. See, right here— *poisson*." She pointed at the menu.

"*Poison?* I don't want no poison. I'm too young to—" the Greek was distracted by the return of the waitress with a tray full of beer. "Oh! *Merci! Merci!*" he sputtered through a big, sudden grin as she leaned over the table and placed a large beer in front of him. "Uh … *Bon! Bon!*" he stammered.

She flashed the Greek a smile, "*De rien. Il n'y à pas de quoi.*"

He nodded emphatically, "Yeah. I mean *oui!*" Without taking his eyes off of her, the Greek took a huge gulp of the cold ale, "*Merci*," he whispered admiringly.

After another round of beer and some ribbing of the Greek for his newfound fluency, the group ordered their meals and, with the exception of Sandi, wolfed it down and ordered one last round of beer. They paid for their respective portions of the check, pulling from their wallets handfuls of colored paper money bearing the Queen's face. They littered the middle of the table with the money before standing up to leave.

"*Au revoir!*" said the passing waitress. "*Merci.* Please come again!"

"*Au revoir, di la petit poo-say!*" blurted the Greek.

Sandi's eyes widened in her blushing face. The waitress looked puzzled. Sandi looked apologetically at the waitress and said, "He is trying, but his French is *misérable, oui?*" The men cleared their throats and sniggered. The waitress smiled.

"*Okay*, Romeo. Time to *split*," said Adams, unable to contain his laughter. He grabbed Lambiris by the elbow and led him to the door, "*Toot sweet …*"

~~~~

On August 1, 1971, St Jovite, Quebec, woke to a beautiful day. It was Sunday, the day of the seventh race in the season's Trans-Am series: the Players Quebec Trans-Am Event. During the practice rounds, the crew watched their gray machine growl around the track. But then it slowed unexpectedly.

Jowett returned slowly to pit road, coasting to a stop.

"Engine sounds funny. Feels funny, too. Rough," he said to Nell and Young from the cockpit.

Nell and Young immediately popped the hood and craned their heads into the hot engine compartment. A few minutes later Nell, wiping his greasy, thick, hands with a shop rag, announced the diagnosis to Adams. "Bad cylinder head, boss. Got to replace it."

Adams glanced at his watch, "Hurry, man … race soon …"

Nell nodded silently.

The Ghost was pushed over to the wall, near an overhanging bleacher. Nell and Young furiously dug into the engine with their hand tools. After a few minutes, as he was about to remove the bad cylinder head, Nell heard voices whispering above them. He looked up into a sea of faces staring down at them from the stands. Many broke into smiles.

"*Right on man*," whispered one of them.

"*Go Gray Ghost!*" said another in a French accent.

Nell shot them a quick grin before re-focusing on the engine. He and Young soon had the bad cylinder head out, replaced by the new head. Nell slammed down the hood, "Let's *go!*" Jowett scrambled into the Ghost as Young connected the hood pins.

"*Oui—Gray Ghost!*" hollered a voice from the growing murmuring above them.

The engine turned over and a familiar earsplitting blast erupted from the gaping tailpipes. The crowd above recoiled in delight, cheering wildly. Nell and Young shook greasy hands with each other, smiling broadly.

Adams glanced at his watch and sighed ... just in time. The cars rumbled onto the track for the start. As the green flag waved, Rusty Jowett gunned the Ghost which responded with its customary piercing, guttural, urgency. The riotous noise from its huge tailpipes could easily be heard over the entire pack of young pony cars.

Jowett passed one pony car on the first lap and another two on the second. At lap six, two cars had already retired—a Mustang and a Camaro. By the tenth lap, the thundering Ghost had moved up considerably through the field and Jowett and the Ghost were hungry for more. But then Jowett heard a loud noise from under the hood and the Ghost immediately lost almost all its power. A plume of smoke trailed from the suddenly muted exhaust.

Jowett cursed loudly as he nursed the Ghost into pit road. The three faces of Adams, Nell and Young stared urgently into the cockpit at the shrugging Jowett.

"No power," muttered Jowett as the engineers rushed to the hood, popped the pins, flung open the hood and squinted, coughing, into the smoking hot engine compartment. The engine went silent. Adams, Nell and Young withdrew from the blinding smoke, cursing and waving their hands.

"Turn it over," hollered Nell to Jowett.

Jowett twisted the key hard. The engine refused to respond.

Nell and Young exchanged furrowed-brow glances. Nell shook his head at the smoldering motor, "Con rod, I bet. I mean I hate to say it but—"

"Yeah ... connecting rod," agreed Young reluctantly.

~~~~

Two and a half hours later, the patriotic Javelin was again crowned the winner and its driver was awarded a kiss on the cheek by the beautiful, well-endowed, blonde "Player's Girl" along with a $4,000 check. After just 11 laps, the Trans/Action Team went home with $100, zero points for Pontiac, and not even a wink or a smile from the Player's Girl. At the conclusion of the winner's circle ceremony, Tom Nell stood over the Ghost's open hood disgustedly examining the two pieces of a busted connecting rod in his greasy hands. Adams patted him on the back, smiling. "Consolation prize …"

~~~~

An hour later, Tom Nell and The Greek sat bouncing in the tarpaulin-shrouded dimness of the Ghost on its trailer, headed back to the landing strip. Nell sat in the driver's seat, his arms crossed and his face straight.

"Here," said the squatting Greek, handing Nell a cold can of beer, "make ya feel better."

Nell took the beer and looked at his teammate. "Thanks, Ted." Nell popped the can, spewing some foam across the interior of the windshield. The Greek popped another and held his jostling can up near Nell's can.

"To next time … to *Watkins Glen!*" said the Greek through a grin. The men gently, slowly, knocked their cans together.

Nell snorted and allowed himself a smile. "To Watkins Glen …" They each took a long gulp.

Young, Nell, the Greek, Dutch and Brady soon squeezed into the Cessna with the pilot and waved goodbye through the little oval windows to Adams, Sandi and Harry in the Suburban. As the plane's engines began to turn over, the Greek handed out cold beer to the other three passengers. The cans were soon emptied and another round was distributed, then another. By the time the little Cessna landed in Pontiac, the cans were filled with another kind of yellow liquid, and the Ghost's broken connecting rod had been forgotten.

Chapter 31

HERB SAT AT his Pontiac desk on Monday morning, thinking and staring at his stuffed inbox. He was beginning to think that the Javelin and company were so good they really didn't go as fast as they *could* at the races—only as fast as they *needed* to win, just fast enough to beat everyone else. Adams couldn't prove this; it was only a hunch, but a hunch based on a few years of racing experience and on watching the patriotic Javelin all season. The Ghost had hung with it at the first Lime Rock race, but the Javelin had won the last three—no, four—races. In contrast, the Ghost had finished a grand total of 21 laps in the last three races. Adams recollected the finishing order of the first seven races of the season. AMC had amassed an incredible 55 points, mostly thanks to that single Javelin, although another one had picked up four points for AMC at Bryar, when the favorite failed to finish—a rare DNF. By contrast, the Ghost had won a grand total of *five* points for Pontiac over the same period.

Adams took a gulp of Diet Coke and winced. Maybe this hadn't been such a good idea. After a good start, nearly finishing second in the first race, followed by two consecutive top five finishes, the Trans/Action team had recently stumbled. They had skipped two of the last five races and hadn't even *finished* the three they'd actually started. Morale was down. Maybe this idea of competing against the professionals and the factories and their money and seemingly endless resources was unrealistic. Adams rested his elbows on the desk and slumped his tired, aching forehead into his cupped hands. All the sacrifice. The lost sleep. The lost money—their own money. The blown vacations. The lost time. The lost effort ...

"*Hey!*" Tom Nell poked his head through the open doorway of Adams' office, "Watkins Glen in two weeks! We're gonna *kick ass!*"

~~~~

"Hey guys," said Adams, his raised voice reverberating slightly over the parked Ghost in the garage. The team members hushed and began rubbing bloodshot eyes and sipping steaming coffee. "Next race is Watkins Glen, upstate New York. A long way from Pontiac. And this time, we got no airplane to get us there. The pilot can't make it. So we all got to take some vacation days and drive. The good news is Tullius can make it; he'll drive for us at Watkins Glen. I want an advance crew to split early—Wednesday after work—with the car to give Tullius some practice time. Tom, Jeff, Dutch and Greek—can you make it?"

Three of the four heads nodded. The Greek scratched his head, "I gotta ... uh ... a date with the wife Wednesday. It's kind of a big deal. Then we got another thing Thursday night," he said sheepishly. "And we only got one car," he said slowly, "So I can't drive it to Watkins Glen because my wife would be stranded." His eyes began darting around, a grin spread across his face. "But I can *ride!*"

"Ride?" asked Adams.

"*Yeah*, man," said the Greek excitedly, nodding his head. "My bike—my *motorcycle*, man!"

Someone snorted in disbelief.

Adams raised his eyebrows at the Greek. "All the way to upstate New York?"

"*Right on*, man, no sweat! I'll leave Friday afternoon."

"Okay Greek," Adams shrugged. "Just get there in one piece, man. I'll leave after work Thursday with the rest of the crew. We'll drive right through the night." Adams looked around the garage. "All right. I got something else to say. I'm not much for speeches, but, well, we had some rough luck lately, but we're gonna turn it around next weekend at Watkins Glen. We know Tullius can do it. We know the car can do it. And most of all, we know *we* can do it." Adams paused, quickly surveying the garage to ensure the gravity of his message was being received properly. He had their attention. "We damn near beat Donahue at Lime Rock," he continued. "Why? Because we came to race. We finished fourth at Byar, even without a third gear. How? Because we came to race. We finished fourth at Mid-Ohio with a single jack in the pit ... because we came to *race*. We've since solved all the problems that kept us from winning those races and the troubles that kept us from finishing at Donnybrooke and Mont Tremblant. We ain't given up yet and we ain't *gonna* give up."

"Hell *no!*" muttered a gruff voice from the corner. The eyes of Trans/Action were riveted on their leader, their heads nodding in agreement.

"That's right," said Adams, pointing at the Ghost. "We've invested way too much time, money and effort into this machine to quit now. We're in a lull, that's all, and we're gonna pull out of it. Now we're not gonna confuse effort with results. *Results* are what count in racing. Despite our effort, our results—lately anyway—well, they *suck*. We all know that. So, are we gonna quit?"

The heads slowly shook from left to right and back again.

"That's *right*. We're *not* gonna quit. We're gonna get *results*." Adams thumped his fist on his chest, "We come to *race*."

Dutch slapped his open palm hard on the hood of the Ghost, "*Goddamn right!*"

Adams' eyes narrowed. "Now there's only two more races in the season for us—Watkins Glen and MIS. Watkins Glen is a whole new course this year, so since nobody knows it yet, it ain't nobody's home track now. But MIS? That's right here in our backyard. MIS is *our* track." He held the to-do list high in the air. "We gonna *race* 'em?"

Heads nodded and someone mumbled, "Yeah ..."

"*I CAN'T HEAR YOU!*"

"*YES!*" the team shouted in unison.

"*WHY?*" shouted Adams, a grin creeping across his face.

"*WE COME TO* **RACE!**"

~~~~

Watkins Glen was the unlikely brainchild of a Cornell law student in 1948, four years after the founding of the Sports Car Club of America. The law student was fortunate enough to be the son of a man who owned a summer house on Seneca Lake, one of upstate New York's beautiful Finger Lakes, near the little town of Watkins Glen. While still in law school, he designed a 6.6-mile European style road racing course through and around the village, over asphalt, cement, gravel, and dirt roads. On October 2, 1948, the SCCA held its first race in Watkins Glen on the course.

Over the years, the Watkins Glen course changed—first to a temporary course southwest of town in 1953, and then to a 2.3-mile permanent course in 1956. 1957 marked the 10th Watkins Glen Grand Prix and, notably, NASCAR's first race at the Glen as the Grand National Division, later known as the Winston Cup. In 1971 more turns were added to the track; it was on this new course that the eighth Trans-Am race of 1971 was scheduled on August 15th.

Chapter 32

A CANADIAN BORDER patrol officer in Windsor, Ontario, waved on an American car after asking some perfunctory questions and glanced across the wide, shimmering river at the Detroit skyline. A loud motorcycle rumbled to a stop in front of him, idling angrily. "Purpose in entering Canada?" The officer casually dropped his eyes from the skyline to the motorcycle, and the sight stopped him cold. The rider wore a leather jacket with a large chain over his left shoulder, draped diagonally across his chest, around his right hip, and up across his back. Spying the chain he slowly asked, "Why are you carrying that weapon?"

"Weapon?" asked the rider.

"The chain, eh?" said the guard flatly, pointing at the rider's chest.

"Oh, that's for security. It's not a weapon."

"Security?"

"Yeah, ya know—for lockin' up the bike when it's parked."

The guard studied the motorcycle, unconvinced. It sported a sissy bar with a tattered duffel bag strapped to it. "What is your purpose in entering Canada?"

"I'm going to a race."

"A race?"

"Yeah—a car race. Trans-Am. I'm part of the race crew."

"Race crew? And where is this ... *race?*"

"Watkins Glen."

The officer narrowed his eyes.

"New York," offered the rider. "Watkins Glen, New York. I'm just taking the 401 highway through here because it's closer than going down through Ohio."

"Where you coming from?"

A wave of emotional heat washed over the rider. He was unprepared for this grilling. "Uh, Pontiac. I work for the Pontiac Motor Division and—" His leather jacket trapped the rider's rapidly rising body temperature. It was making him hot. The rider clicked his bike into neutral with his left toe and unzipped his leather jacket, revealing a conservative white dress shirt and striped tie. "I just left from work. It's quicker to come through Ontario to get to upstate New York. I—"

"Oh, I never saw a motorcycle rider with a shirt and tie."

"Well, I just came from work, see."

The officer scanned the bike again as the skepticism melted from his face. He chuckled. "Good luck, eh?"

~~~~

The advance team, towing car 49, arrived at the Glen on the morning of practice day. Friday the 13th.

"Here," said Bob Tullius to Tom Nell, handing Nell a stack of new, neatly folded shirts. They were white, with horizontal blue stripes. "For the team to wear in the pit, during the race."

Nell, in the Watkins Glen sunshine, squinted at the stack of shirts. "For us? Thanks ... but how come?"

The driver shrugged, "Thought ya might like 'em, ya know."

Nell furrowed his brow at the shirts.

"Well," continued Tullius, "all the other teams have uniforms, so ..."

Nell smiled at the driver. "Thanks."

"Yer welcome." Tullius eyed the Ghost. "Now let's see how the old goat can do on the new Glen." Tullius donned his helmet, settled into the familiar seat, and turned the key. A thunderous blast erupted from below the rear bumper. Tullius' eyes widened as he mouthed an obscenity.

"Oh," hollered Nell at the driver. "We put new *pipes* on her!" The GTO bellowed, shaking itself awake. The Trans/Action team watched their old gray car blur past in an earsplitting moment. Each grinned with great satisfaction.

~~~~

In late evening, as the crew was making a few minor chassis adjustments to the Ghost, the Greek walked with a large, empty gas can to the track's gas station, smiling and greeting everyone he passed. No other pit team members were in sight. Alone, he filled the can with racing fuel, ambled back to the Ghost, and poured the contents of his can into the Ghost's empty tank, saving a small amount for his covert Coke bottle. He looked up and down pit road. Since he'd been at the track, he had not seen any other teams fill up their tanks with gas from the track's gas station. These pros were so fancy, they brought their own gas to the races. The Greek shook his head.

Tullius took the Ghost out again. On the second circuit, he heard a loud clang from the engine compartment and the Ghost lost nearly all its power. Tullius nursed the GTO back to pit road, trailing a plume of smoke.

"Blown engine," he said flatly, exiting the car. "I know it this time."

Tom Nell winced. "Oil pressure?"

"None," responded Tullius, deliberately shaking his head. "This time, I actually had time to look, Tom."

Nell cursed sharply under his breath.

"Let's pop the hood," said Jeff Young.

Young and Nell peered into the engine compartment, not waiting for the residual smoke to clear, and began coughing, waving their hands over the smoldering motor.

Five minutes later, Nell and Young were still attempting to diagnose the problem. "Gentlemen," said Nell dejectedly, "we gotta pull the engine. It's burned up. I think it needs a rebuild. It's something bad … rod bearings knocked out, maybe. Or blown head gasket … busted piston rings … I don't know … burned valve—exhaust probably … maybe even a hole in a piston head." Nell squinted at his smoking engine, shaking his head. "*Damn.*"

"Well, drop in the back-up motor," said the Greek urgently.

"Yeah … won't take long," agreed Young.

Nell and Young soon had the dead engine out of the Ghost, replaced by the back-up. The Greek poured more gas into the tank. Tullius twisted the key again and rolled car 49 back onto the track. After two laps, the new engine began to make strange noises and smoke began billowing from the exhaust again. Tullius let up on the gas and carefully guided the smoking Ghost back to the pit, filled with cursing crewmembers.

Nell and Young popped the hood again, vainly squinting through the smoke at their second engine. "What the *hell*, man?" coughed Young, frustrated.

Nell shook his head deliberately. This couldn't be an engine problem, not again. This had to be caused by an external element. *Gas?* Nell lurched out of the engine compartment, looking from side to side, "Ted? Hey *Ted!*"

"Yeah, what?" responded the Greek.

"Where'd you get the gas?"

"From the track." He pointed in the direction of the track depot. "Over there."

"So you bought the gas from the track?"

"Yeah …"

Nell picked up a shop towel, wiping his sinewy hands. He looked at Young, who nodded knowingly at him.

"What's up?" asked the Greek.

"Bad gas, I think. But we won't know 'till we pull it," said Nell solemnly.

"Bad gas from the *track?* How the *hell* …"

Nell raised his eyebrows and shrugged, "That's what it looks like to me."

The Greek looked at Young in disbelief and exhaled slowly, re-focusing on solving the problem. "We got qualifying tomorrow. We got time to rebuild an engine?" he asked Nell.

Nell glanced at the sun, now orange in the hazy air and hanging above the horizon. Herb Adams' face flashed across his mind's eye. He thought of the season's early successes and more recent disappointments at Donnybrooke and Mont Tremblant. He didn't want to be disappointed again, but an engine rebuild would take hours—maybe all night, depending on the damage. Yet he was *sure* he and Young, with help from Dutch and the Greek, could pull it off.

Adams wouldn't be here until late that night. What would Herb do if he were here? Hell, this was *Watkins Glen*. Only one more race after this. They'd busted their butts to get this far.

Nell glanced at Young, who was slowly rubbing the back of his hand across his lips. Young looked back at his engine partner with narrowing eyes, clenched teeth, and a sly grin. As he wiped his thick hands with a shop towel, Nell nodded his head slowly and looked into the eyes of his team-mate. "*We come to race ...*"

~~~~

The wounded Ghost was loaded back onto the trailer and the crew set out to search for an all-night gas station where they could perform the major mechanical surgery required to rebuild a Pontiac 303 racing engine. They found it: Frank's Esso, a three-bay garage. After hearing their story, Frank himself gave them the use of the center bay.

Eight hours later, at 2:20 a.m. Saturday, Herb Adams and the remaining members of the Trans/Action team rolled down a hill into the town of Watkins Glen. Adams drove while the crew slept. The lights from a small Esso gas station stood out in the darkness and attracted his attention. As they approached the station, Adams glanced through the open garage and did a double take. "Oh, *Christ!*"

"Wha ..." asked a roused voice from the back seat. "Whassa madder ..."

Adams hit the brakes and turned the car hard toward the gas station. The rocking woke his passengers. "We got trouble with the car ..."

~~~~

Two hours later, Nell and Young leaned back out of the Ghost's engine compartment, stretched, and rubbed their aching backs. A chorus of crickets and frogs chirped and croaked in the damp, still, cool moonlight. Adams handed Young an open, cold, bottle of malt liquor from the nearby cooler. Young wiped his hands, looking at the car. "It was definitely the fuel, Herb." He grabbed the bottle and took a long gulp.

Adams handed Nell a bottle. Nell took it appreciatively, nodding in agreement, "And we got it from the track. Don't know if it was low octane, or contaminants, or what, man. Just know it was bad shit." He shot his boss a disgusted look, "*Bad shit ...*"

"Whatever it was, it caused one *hell* of a detonation problem," said Joe, shaking his head at the motor.

Adams listened to the buggy, reptilian chorus emanating from the darkness beyond the open garage.

"Blew a head gasket in the first engine and got a scored cylinder in the back-up," said Nell. "Anyway, we drained that bad shit, cobbled together one good engine from two bad ones, and the Greek went out and found some decent fuel—"

"Yeah," interrupted the Greek. "Sunoco 260 from a station down there," he pointed into the darkness. "Frank, the owner of this joint recommended it—he uses it in his race car."

Adams shook his head, grinning in slow admiration of his crew.

"Hey," Young grinned back, "*we come to race.*"

Tom Nell winked at his boss, "Okay, Herb. You get the honors. Fire it up."

Adams slowly dropped into the driver's seat and turned the ignition. The new engine's bellow ripped a huge audible hole through the silky fabric of the sleepy Watkins Glen night.

As the engine settled to idle, Nell took a large screwdriver and placed the blade end on the idling engine. He bent down, pressing his ear against the screwdriver's handle, and shut his eyes for a few seconds. He nodded, stood up, and handed the screwdriver to Young, who repeated the process himself.

"Yeah ..." said Young a few moments later. "Cool, man."

Nell shut the hood and he and Young attached the hood pins. "Let's take her for a spin," said Nell to Adams over the growling Ghost. "I want to put some time on this engine ... want to *feel* it, just to make sure. Tell you what, I'll drive the Ghost and you follow with the headlights. Just like back in the neighborhood."

Adams grinned. "Let's go."

Nell and Young climbed into the Ghost, Nell in the driver's seat, Young crouched on the bare floor formerly occupied by the Tempest's back seat. Nell eased the Ghost into gear and gingerly pressed the gas. The Ghost's roar split the dark silence like twin rolling thunderclaps from the gaping exhaust pipes. The car began rumbling across the gas station's lot, down the street, up the hill, and onto the highway. Adams' headlights from behind provided little help. Once on the highway, Nell very slowly shifted into second. The engine responded with an approving growl as the Ghost crept through the still night. Nell pressed the gas closer to the floor, eased up, shifted into third, and hit the gas harder. The engine raucously responded as the Ghost accelerated fast. Nell shifted into fourth.

"No problem with the engine," shouted Nell to his passenger, squinting at the road ahead. "But I can't see too good."

"Slow down," said Young urgently, "Pull in here, to the right, and turn around." The Ghost made a hard right, braking onto a narrow dirt road with thick woods on either side. There was a large sign at the intersection, but no one could make it out in the dark. Adams stopped on the shoulder, waiting for the Ghost to turn around. The Ghost growled, guttural and noisy, creeping along the black, washboard road.

"Nowhere to turn around," muttered Nell, squinting vainly into the dark ahead. "We got no reverse gear." They passed a small path on the left, then another on the right. Smoke from burning wood wafted by in the damp air. The faint moonlight showed the road widening as they approached a turn, and large, box-shaped objects of some kind were in clearings just off the road. A pickup truck was parked in one clearing, then another, then a Suburban. The orange, flickering, glow of a small fire came from another clearing.

"Where the *hell* are we," asked Young over the engine's rumble, his voice shaking from the road's washboard vibrations.

Suddenly, a small light pierced the dark, flashing across the engineers' faces. A flashlight, coming from the woods. A nearby voice in a sharp tone hollered something incomprehensible. Another light flicked on in the woods as the Ghost lumbered past, then another angry voice and more lights.

"Uh … I … I think we're …" stammered Nell, "… uh … pissing off some people. *Hang on!*" Nell shifted into second and gunned the Ghost.

The racecar emitted a deafening roar through a rooster-tail of dirt, gravel, and stones. The Ghost fishtailed down the road, which quickly met an intersection with another dirt road—big enough to turn around. Nell rammed the brake to the floor and snapped the wheel to the right, spinning the Ghost around in a 180-degree arc, billowing a crescent-shaped cloud of dust and stones. Young tumbled into the door.

"*Christ*," muttered Nell as he gassed the Ghost, again piercing the tranquil night with its throaty, rowdy roar. The Ghost screamed back up the narrow, dirt road, bouncing its passengers violently as it fishtailed over the washboard. It accelerated hard past the little lights, pickups, and some fist-shaking men in pajamas and underwear. A beer can sailed across the windshield, spewing its foaming contents wildly across the car. Nell continued gunning it until finally skidding to a stop at the intersection of the highway and the dirt road, where Adams waited with his headlights.

The engineers sat, staring ahead, in the vibrating Ghost, breathing hard. Nell hit a switch and the windshield wipers smeared the beer foam across the glass. He looked over his shoulder at the passenger in the rear, "*That* was an exciting test drive."

Young rubbed his bruised arm. "Well, glad to see our engine passed the test, but what the hell *was* that place?" he asked, befuddled. They heard a whistle from Adams.

Adams grinned, pointing to the big sign at the intersection faintly illuminated by his dim headlights, "Take a look."

Nell read it aloud: "*Welcome to Watkins Glen Campground.*"

~~~~

A few hours later, in the morning sun, Herb Adams looked blearily at the Day-Glo red cover of the race program. It almost hurt his eyes. *THE GLEN* it read in big block letters. *August 14-15.* "You don't look so good," said Bob Tullius, staring at Adams in the morning Watkins Glen sun.

Adams rubbed his eyes, sighed heavily, and scratched the stubble on his chin. "Just reading about you and Group 44," said Adams, pointing at the program.

"And it took a lot out of you, apparently."

"No, no. Had a long night," Adams said to the driver through a smiling yawn. "But we—I mean Nell and Young—they did it. They rebuilt the engine. She's ready to go."

Tullius looked at the GTO, scratching the top of his head, silently appreciating the tremendous all-night effort expended in fixing the engine. "Ain't racing glamorous?" grinned Tullius, glancing sideways at Adams.

Adams grunted, rubbing the back of his neck. "Just get in and qualify, and get us near the front."

Chuckling quietly, Tullius donned his helmet and settled into the Ghost. "Hey," he said, pointing at the program and grinning. "Keep reading—toward the middle." Tullius turned over the engine and rumbled the GTO down pit road onto the track, joining the glinting stream of new pony cars.

Adams quickly flipped through the program until he saw it—a black and white photo of the Ghost. The headline shouted: *The Gray Ghost Rides Again!* Adams grinned.

Tullius shows the Pontiac's heels to one of the American Racing Associate's Javelins at Lime Rock read the caption under the photo. Another Ghost photo appeared at the bottom of the page. *Fans at Mid-Ohio cheer the Gray Ghost on as Tullius streaks into a turn* the caption read. On the opposite page was the broadly smiling face of Tullius. At the bottom of the page appeared the Ghost rounding a wet corner ahead of car #16, which was spinning out. *#16 slides through a turn the wrong way, but the sure-footed Tempest had no problem.* Adams chuckled out loud.

~~~~

After a few nervous, jostling, warm-up laps, the green flag waved and 31 race cars emitted a collective roar over Watkins Glen as they accelerated hard over the start/finish line and rocketed toward the ninety. A few laps later, Tullius had once again qualified the Ghost respectably near the front of the pack for tomorrow's race, easily in position to contend for the win and the $4,000 that came with it.

The engineers did their job and the driver did his. Adams, Nell and Young, relieved with the engine's performance, quietly congratulated each other.

~~~~

Sunday morning brought sunshine and an air of excitement to the Glen. The pony car pit crews worked busily on their shiny new machines as fans ogled them. But, like every race since Lime Rock, it was old car number 49 that attracted the most attention. Tullius took it around the track slowly a few times to get a better feel for the new track.

"How's the oil pressure?" asked Nell eagerly as Tullius rolled the Ghost to a stop in pit road.

"Oh, *Christ*, Tom. You and your oil pressure!"

Nell looked at Young, puzzled.

"*Engineers*," muttered Tullius under his breath.

"But we gotta know," insisted Nell.

"Yeah, yeah, but he's tryin' to get the lay of the track. I mean, that's what he's focused on. If the engine *sounds* good and the car goes, well, ya know …"

Nell raised an eyebrow, rubbed his chin, and shook his head, muttering, "*Drivers*." He popped the hood and peered into the Ghost's engine compartment and sensed heat—too much heat. He gingerly, quickly, touched the engine's valve cover with the tips of his fingers. "*Damn!*" he whispered loudly, shaking the burn from his fingertips. "She's overheating, Jeff."

Young leaned into the engine compartment with his open palms facing the motor. He recoiled rapidly, "*Oooh* … yeah, man."

Nell studied the engine earnestly, rubbing his burned fingertips. He glanced at his watch. "It's gotta be a cooling system leak. No time to fix whatever the root of the problem is—not even time to *find* it. Even if it's only a pinhole leak, we need a quick fix. BarsLeak!"

A look or recognition swept over Young's face, "Yeah! BarsLeak, man!" He turned, ran toward the toolbox, and quickly returned with a small can of fluid. "Got some! Here!" he said, thrusting the can to Nell.

Nell placed a shop rag over the radiator cap and slowly eased it open. Searing steam shot furiously from beneath the cap like a geyser as Nell jerked his hand away. When the steam subsided moments later, Nell gingerly removed the cap, opened the can of BarsLeak and slowly poured it into the radiator. "There, that oughta do it. *Maybe*." Nell turned to Young, "Got any more? Just in case?"

"No, man. That's it."

"We better find some. I got a feeling ..."

They closed the hood. Car 49 crept deafeningly out of pit road and into the starting grid, when Tom Nell heard a faint chant from the grandstands behind him.

"Gray Ghost ... Gray Ghost ..."

Nell turned, squinting into the stands, wiping his greasy hands with a shop cloth. A group of college kids, most of whom held beer bottles, were bobbing their heads up and down, chanting louder, *"Gray Ghost ... Gray Ghost ..."* Nell, smiling broadly at them, raised the dirty shop rag high in his clenched, muscular fist. The group roared their approval.

~~~~

Moments later, the green flag waved over a Watkins Glen field of 29 roaring pony cars and one old GTO, signaling the start of the season's eighth Trans-Am race. It was a grueling 90-lap race in the August heat. As the race wore on, a number of the cars retired for various reasons, including a top driver after only 15 laps in his Camaro.

Tom Nell focused intently on the Ghost. "Look what the cat dragged in," said a voice behind him. He turned to a beaming Greek holding an armful of BarsLeak cans.

At lap 30, the Ghost rolled into pit road, smoking slightly from under the hood. As Nell poured gas into the tank, Young and Joe Brady popped the hood, fumbled with the scorching radiator cap, and gurgled two more cans of BarsLeak into the radiator.

"Gray Ghost! ... Gray Ghost!" chanted the college kids loudly from the stands.

Young rammed the cap back on, twisted it hard, and slammed down the hood. He rapidly attached one hood pin while Joe attached the other. A split second after the two crewmembers had moved to the side, Adams furiously waved on Tullius. The Ghost's Pontiac 303 spewed piercing hot thunder from the gaping maws of its twin tailpipes, audibly dominating the entire track as it screeched from the pit in a cloud of white rubber smoke.

"*Damn!*" hollered an incredulous voice from the silenced crowd.

In lap 53 another Mustang retired, but Tullius and the Ghost thundered on, attacking the undulating Glen and the pony cars alike, encroaching upon the leaders and passing most others. At lap 60, Tullius quickly pulled his smoldering old car into the pit again; and again, the crew swung into action, filling the tank with gas and the geyser-like radiator with BarsLeak as the crowd chanted even louder for the Ghost. Adams waved on Tullius and the Ghost peeled out of the pit, emitting another deafening snarl, taking aim at the field of pony cars once more.

Yet another Mustang retired after 80 laps. Once again, it became a race within a race—a battle between the red, white, and blue Javelin and the aggressive Mustang. The two pony cars lapped every other car in the field, including the smoking Ghost. When the checkered flag fell, the Javelin again crossed the finish line first, followed 26 seconds later by the Mustang. Another Mustang finished a lap later in third place. In all, 17 cars completed the race.

The hot Ghost finished in 15th place, 23 laps behind the winner.

~~~~

The post-race mood among the Trans/Action pit crew was ambivalent. To Herb Adams, Watkins Glen was a success; for the first time since June 6, car 49 had finished a race. Pontiac received zero points for this effort, but the team was rewarded with $350 in winnings, and more importantly, renewed confidence. The team had proven itself again. They were eager to race back home in Michigan.

The car had also proven itself again. It was mechanically sound, almost, and ready for its final race of the season on its home track. Maybe its last race.

Chapter 33

HERB ADAMS SAT at his kitchen table on a bright Saturday morning in late August 1971, holding a mechanical pencil, staring at a blank pad of paper. He glanced at the back yard for inspiration. Despite the wild, long, grass, the dandelions were clearly taking over, winning the suburban horticultural war. He had to cut the damn grass ...

He had to do something else, too. He knew it had to be done, because this was a business about winning. He didn't want to do it because, although he'd never admit it to anyone, he'd grown fond of the old Ghost. Adams picked up a small black and white photograph of car 49 from the table. It was more than just a racecar now. More than just sheet metal, rubber, chrome, glass and one hell of a chassis and engine.

It was the bloody knuckles, the sweaty brows and the busted gears. It was also the greasy hands, the bad jokes, and the cheap beer that lubricated the guys who created it.

It was the dead neighborhood dog, the backslapping after beating the hotshot drivers and keeping up with the patriot Javelin at Lime Rock's downpour.

It was the unexpected tidal wave of press attention that followed and the new moniker—the *Gray Ghost*.

It was taking fourth at Bryar and fifth at Mid-Ohio before the wildly cheering crowds.

Kicking the asses of countless factory teams.

It was leering at the French-Canadian chicks in mini-skirts and yapping in pig-French.

It was a defogger made of freshly drained beer cans.

It was duct tape and BarsLeak.

All-nighters, three-two beer, blown vacations, busted connecting rods, bad gas and drained bank accounts.

It was the incredible effort put forth by his guys to compete with big factory, big money racers.

It was an escape from the war news, runaway inflation, and the politics of work.

And the siren song of racing spewed from its exhaust pipes.

Man, it was *fun*.

But now, this had to be done. No room for emotion. Anyway, this wasn't about the car; it was about the people who made and raced the car. Adams took a gulp of Diet Coke, winced, and gingerly placed his pencil to the paper:

TRANS ACTION TEMPEST, lack of sponsor money prevents running the Western Trans-Am races. The car plus spares will be for sale after M.I.S. on Sept. 6. Serious inquiries only.

At the end, Adams added "Trans Action," his address and telephone number. He read over the draft classified newspaper ad. This couldn't be the end of their racing.

He gazed out the window at his green backyard and began to think. If they could build a new car from the ground up it would undoubtedly be more competitive than the Ghost. They could build the entire chassis and drivetrain themselves, and not be saddled with all the stock stuff. It would be more than merely customizing, it would be *creating*. That guy in Southern California did it—Max Balchowski. Balchowski and his wife built a car from scratch and raced the factory prepared Ferarris and Maseratis. Ol' Yeller, they called it. If they could do it, so could we. All we'd need is a body. A Firebird, perhaps. Yeah, a late model Firebird body on our own hand-built racing chassis, right from the ground up. Then we could *really* compete. Hell, we could *win*. Beat the pros, beat the factories, beat the money. And wins would attract more sponsors. The team would be up to it. They'd understand about the Ghost. Nobody races the same car for more than two seasons anyway.

Adams tossed the pencil on the table, leaned back in his chair, and whispered to himself, "Yeah, a *Firebird* ..."

~~~~

Later that afternoon, Adams took a drive to a nearby junkyard, "just for kicks," he told a quizzical Sandi as he pecked her a goodbye kiss on the cheek. Adams creaked open the door to the junkyard's office, a small cinderblock structure with a cracked, dirty window. Stale cigarette smoke permeated the hot, dank room. Near a wooden desk sat a grizzled man holding a girly magazine in front of his face, his dirty boots propped up on an old drab green and silver aluminum desk. Adams shut the creaking door with a thud.

The man lowered the magazine slightly, eyeing Adams over the top.

"Hi," said Adams, his eyebrows raised.

The man grunted, raising his magazine to cover his face. The local newspaper rested on his desk with a headline announcing that a U.S. Army Lieutenant's sentence had been cut to 20 years. Another headline shouted that a federal parole board had denied parole to former Teamster leader and Detroiter James Hoffa.

"Uh ... you work here?" asked Adams, scratching his head.

The man continued his intent, silent study of the magazine.

Adams cleared his throat. "I'm looking for a car ..." No response. Adams looked around the dim room. "Good articles in there, huh?"

"Wha?" The man reluctantly closed the magazine, plunked his feet to the floor, and sat up in his chair.

"I'm looking for a car."

"We only got busted ones here, fella," he snorted.

"Yeah, well actually, I'm looking for a body."

"Body? *Got a few here!*" the man held up the magazine, laughing hoarsely.

Adams smiled thinly, "How about a Firebird? A late model Pontiac Firebird."

Recovering from his self-induced fit of humor, the man said, "Firebird?" He cocked his head. "Yeah, we got some a dem."

"I'm looking for a late model—a fairly new one. Maybe a Trans Am."

The man looked out the smudged, mud-flecked window. "Uh, yeah. We got a new one." He looked back at Adams, "Not too banged up, but enough for da *in*surance company ta total da sucker. Wanna see it?"

"Sure."

"Okay. Folla me." The man arched his back, wincing, and stood up slowly. He walked in a hunch to the door, creaked it open, stepped into the junkyard dirt and began leading Herb into a jungle of twisted metal, broken glass and bald rubber. A few minutes later, he stopped. "Here she is."

Adams' experienced eyes darted over a late model Firebird Trans Am—1972 by the look of it. A Pontiac Firebird Trans Am. A wave of memories washed over Herb Adams. Flared fenders, chrome-bordered split front grill. Big scoop jutting rearward from the hood. Big spoiler on the rear deck. This was one of his babies.

The car was a dirty black. The windshield sported a big spider-web-like crack on the driver's side. Minute flecks of what appeared to be mud were spattered across the spider web. Adams leaned closer, squinting; they didn't really look like mud. He scratched at one of them. Smooth. These flecks were on the interior. He leaned inside the open driver's side window and looked through the spider-webbed windshield. The flecks were clearly on the interior. Adams studied them briefly—hundreds of minute specs of deep red, almost black—spattered across the fractured glass. He quickly scanned the interior. The steering column had collapsed under violent impact. Adams knew the reason: the driver's torso had rammed into it.

A big, crusty, dark red stain lay on the seat. Adams swallowed hard. "*Jesus,*" he whispered. He slowly removed his head from the car and looked sideways at the junkyard man, who shrugged. Adams took a deep breath and blinked deliberately. He exhaled, refocusing on his task. Adams lay down alongside the car on his back, pulled a flashlight from his pocket, and slid in the dirt under the car. The front suspension was clearly shot, but the sub-frame looked intact. Adams glanced around the underbody for another few moments, studying the sub-frame. Not bent. Nothing wrong with it. He slowly extricated himself from under the wreck and stood, brushing the dirt and mud from his back.

It *was* a wreck. Even so, it was a muscular, good-looking car. He was proud of it. Adams felt a brief pang of sorrow for the car and its driver, as a father looking at a sick child. So many memories.

Pushing away the emotion, Adams again forced his mind back to the business of objectively evaluating the car. The body appeared in great shape. A large blob of black oil had puddled under the front end. Adams walked around the Trans Am, studying the body. No major dents, not even any dings. He scratched his head. "What ya want for it?"

"Oh ... well, it's in great shape, ain't it?"

"Except for the shot front end, the busted windshield, blood, collapsed steering column and God knows what else."

The dealer was puzzled. How did this guy know so much? "Yeah, but otherwise ..."

Adams shot the man a skeptical glance. "The insurance company totaled it. It's in a junkyard."

"I prefer da term *'automobile recamation facility,'*" said the dealer indignantly, straightening his shirt collar and dirty, worn sleeve cuffs.

Adams rolled his eyes. "Well, ain't the only busted Firebird in town. Now, whaddya want for it?"

The man furrowed his brow, squinting and rubbing his thin lips with a calloused index finger as he studied the broken Pontiac. "Only $750," he blurted at last.

Adams physically recoiled. "*What?*"

"Well, uh—"

"Seven-fifty? This is not even worth talking about." Adams turned and began to walk.

"Hey, wait!" said the man sputtering after him. "Wait ... how about somethin' less?"

Adams continued to walk. "Something? Something like what?"

"Well, hell. I mean ain't *you* supposed to say how much now?"

Adams snorted. "Me? Not when you start out in left field. See ya." Adams turned and began to walk again.

The dealer looked back at the Firebird, then wheeled around and sprinted up to Adams, huffing. "Okay, okay. Ya drive a hard bargain. How 'bout five hunderd?"

Adams stopped. "Way too much bread, man. Anyway, all I need is the body."

"Well gimme a *offer*."

"I'm not offering you anything." Adams resumed his walk to the parking lot.

"What? Ya want dis car or not? I mean, come on, fella!" said the dealer, standing amid his sea of wreckage.

Adams, chuckling quietly, continued to walk, shook his head, and waved his hands in the air.

The dealer cursed and began trudging toward the sanctuary of his magazines.

~~~~

Herb sat at the middle of the cafeteria table at Pontiac Motor Division's headquarters surrounded by most of the Trans/Action team. He swallowed a last bite of sandwich, took a swig of diet pop, and spoke. "Hey guys. I got something important." The engineers hushed.

He hesitated. How was he going to tell these guys they should dump the Ghost and start over? Maybe he should start with something else.

"What? What's a matter Herb?" asked the Greek in a concerned voice.

"Well," Adams looked quickly around at the faces staring at him. "Now, uh, we got a problem with SCCA." Squinting eyes and furrowed brows silently responded.

"What problem?" asked Dutch gruffly.

"Well, SCCA wasn't very impressed with our new tailpipes."

"Why?" asked a voice.

"Well, they told me the pipes made the car too, uh ..."

"What? Too *what*?"

Adams winced. "Too *distracting* to the competitors."

"*Distracting*?" asked the number of voices in unison. "What the hell?" blurted another voice.

"Hey—that's what they told me. Too noisy. Too loud. Illegal." Adams shrugged.

Dutch cursed loudly.

"Well, listen. SCCA runs the show," said Adams calmly. "They set the rules. If we don't put the pipes back the way they were, we're gonna get DQ'd for the next race."

The team grumbled.

"We can do it, and we will do it," Adams said firmly. "Hey guys," continued Adams. "I got something else." The men quieted. "The Ghost has been a great machine, but I think we all know it can only take us so far against the competition we're facing. I mean, we've wrung every bit of juice anyone could get outta the old goat." A few nodded. "So I got an idea ... for next year," he paused again.

"What? What idea?" someone asked.

Adams loosened his tie. "Well, we learned a lot about racing this year, and it would be a shame just to let it go, just walk away from it all. So I think we should race again next year. And I got an idea, but it's gonna take a lot of work and money. All over again." Adams' eyes darted around the table, gauging the response. He received only their continued collectively stone-faced attention. "Okay, then. Well ... I propose we ... uh ... *sell* the Ghost and build a new Trans-Am car—a Firebird—from the ground up." The engineers stared in silence. Adams, with raised eyebrows, looked around the table, desperately searching for a response, any response. He continued, "It's nothing that hasn't been done before. There's a guy in southern California—Max Balchowski—ten or twelve years ago he and his wife—*his wife*—built a car from scratch in their garage and raced it against the factory Maseratis and Ferraris out there. They called it Ol' Yeller II or somethin'. It was ugly as hell, but man it *went*. I hear they got the parts from junkyards—all kinds of parts from Fords, Jags, Pontiacs, and dropped a Buick nailhead V8 in it."

"Buick?" asked someone in disgust.

"Yeah," continued Adams. "Probably because it had small valves and you could rev the bejeezus out of it. Anyway, they got a garage called Hollywood Motors. I suspect it was a skunk works for Buick, but none of the Buick guys I know will admit it, even now. Anyway, this Ol' Yeller did pretty good against the Europeans." Adams looked gingerly around the table. "So anyway, if a guy and his *wife* can do it there, I figure *we* can do it here."

Tom Nell began to grin.

"I'm in, goddamn it!" shouted Dutch.

Some people at a neighboring table looked disapprovingly over their shoulders at the engineers and the grizzled machinist.

"Me too!" hollered the Greek, stabbing a fist in the air, "*Sonofabitch!*"

Adams, through a broad smile, said, "Hey, hey, keep it down ..."

All but Joe Brady soon voiced their enthusiastic support. "Okay. I found this cherry '72 Firebird in the junkyard. The guy already offered to sell it to me for $500, even though he started at $750. I figure I can get him lower, don't know how much. Now, let's start peddling the Ghost before MIS."

~~~~

At the end of the workday, Tom Nell sat in Adams' office, talking to his boss about the GTO and the new Firebird. "I know a guy who might be interested in buying the Ghost," said Nell. "An old college buddy, Lou Spoerl. Turns out he's a Pontiac dealer in Cumberland, Maryland, and he likes to race—ya know, amateur racing. I'll call him."

"Good," responded Adams.

"Young and I are going to have the backup engine done for MIS. It's almost ready now."

"All right. We'll keep one of 'em for next year, drop it in the new car. I got Goad and Dutch working on a big box to stick on the front of the trailer. We can carry the backup engine and our own damn gas in it." Adams winked at Nell. "No more all-nighter rebuilds. The Greek's got a few 55-gallon drums. He's going out to that refinery by Metro Airport to get some good gas."

Joe Brady knocked sheepishly on the open door. "Hey, guys," he winced, rubbing the back of his neck. "I've got something to tell you. I had one helluva good time racing with you guys. Learned a lot, too. I mean, you guys are the two best automotive engineers I ever met."

Adams interrupted, "You gotta go to graduate school soon. We know that. We knew that at the beginning. You go, you helped us tremendously, Joe. You're a heads-up guy and we appreciate all your help."

"Thanks. Hey, you guys should do real well with a scratch-built Firebird. I'll be following you in the papers. How about a Trans Am? I mean, they named it after the race."

Nell and Adams smiled at each other.

"What's so funny?"

"Herb did all the product development work on the Trans Am Firebird," said Nell. "Back in '67. Herb was in advanced design, making prototypes."

Joe looked, eyebrows raised, at Adams, "So you're the *father* of the Pontiac Firebird Trans Am?"

Adams shrugged, "Well ..."

"Well nothing. Tell him, Herbie," said Tom Nell proudly.

"Okay," said Adams reluctantly. "See, DeLorean knew the Camaro Z28 was coming from Chevy, so he told my boss to have me develop a high performance Firebird. He wanted a six-banger, so we put a shaker hood on it with a big air cleaner sticking out. It was fast. But then we tried a V8. Built six of them in '68. They went like all hell and were the basis for the Firebird Trans Am, which was launched in '69 and a half. The chief engineer thought they'd never sell, and for good reason: a Trans Am cost six thousand dollars, which was twice as much as a regular Firebird. But man, they could move," said Adams through an expanding smile.

"Yeah," said Nell. "Still can. The irony is that the Firebird Trans Am never competed in the racing series it was named after."

"Well, maybe we can remedy that little problem next year." Adams stood and extended his hand. "Anyway, thanks Joe."

The men shook hands as Tom Nell stood and said, "Yeah. You gotta lot of potential, kid." Nell and Joe shook hands. "But you aren't leaving until after MIS are ya?" grinned Nell, tightening his grip.

Joe, with no intention of missing the Ghost's last Trans-Am race, squeezed back and grinned, "What if I am?"

Nell set his jaw, grinning broadly up at Joe, "Well, maybe I'd have to change your mind." Nell continued to close his vise-like grip.

"*Yeow!*" protested Joe, wincing at his crumpling hand. "Yeah, yeah, I'll be at MIS!"

Chapter 34

IN 1967, A Detroit developer with a passion for racing hired the designer of Daytona to lay out a banked oval in the Irish Hills west of Detroit. He then tasked a legendary Formula One driver to design a road course in and around the oval. They broke ground on September 28, 1967, and during the next 365 days, two-and-a-half million yards of dirt were carved out of a small piece of the Irish Hills to create a big, 18-degree D-shaped oval and the road course. They called it the Michigan International Speedway. The first MIS event was held on October 13, 1968, and the driver was awarded $20,088. Three years later, MIS hosted the ninth race in the 1971 Trans-Am season—the 70-lap Wolverine Trans-Am. And the Gray Ghost appeared.

~~~~

Bob Tullius flipped the toggles, twisted the key and pushed a button, and the big GTO growled and rumbled to life in the MIS pit road. Friday, September 3, 1971, was a dry, sunny day in the Irish Hills and Tullius meant to take full advantage of the opportunity to test the old goat one last time. According to the map, the track had 15 turns and was run counter-clockwise. Pit road was a straight shortcut under the bowed front straight, a huge, sweeping left that formed the deep front of the "D" in the oval track. Upon exiting pit road, the road course made a hard left, then another left before spilling into the ubiquitous Esses—a rapid right-left combination followed by a sweeping right that led into a long straight. Tullius smoothly shifted the Ghost into fourth, squeezed the gas to the floor, and was quickly pinned into the seatback as the Ghost rocketed down this straight, crossing the back straight of the oval at a 90-degree angle. He eased off, rounded the next two right turns, and gassed it into turn eight—a big left sweeper. He rounded the next few turns around the bottom of the track and began weaving his way back up four gentle turns in a right-left-right-left combination. At the apex of the last turn, he quickly eased the Hurst stick shift into fourth and gently stood on the gas as the Ghost entered the longest straight of the track, heading back toward the oval's infield. The old car thundered up the straight as it re-entered the oval's infield. Tullius glanced at the tachometer. The red needle clocked past the 5,000 RPM mark as the Ghost screamed over the warm asphalt. Near the end of the straight, Tullius glanced again at the tachometer before easing off. He braked and blipped into third as he rounded the last turn and entered the only part of the road course on the oval track—the mammoth sweeping left that made up the bulge in the oval's "D" shape. He shifted back into fourth and squeezed the gas again, flashing a 130 mph grin at his pit crew.

Saturday was qualifying day in the Irish Hills. After the Ghost was tuned to its driver's liking, Tullius rolled car number 49 slowly down pit road and joined 39 glinting pony cars streaming onto the track for qualifying. Someone had put a yellow pylon in the grass at the front of the first turn: a turn-in marker. The number six patriot Javelin tore around the track, followed closely by its nemesis, the number 15 Mustang. Near the end, Milt Minter in his Javelin pressed the leaders closely from behind. He was followed by a group of four Mustangs and a Camaro. Then came the Ghost.

Tullius smoothly, aggressively raced the Ghost through the wild qualifying traffic, passing two-thirds of the smaller, newer pony cars at will. But the transition from the infield to the straight was rough. The Ghost bounced hard, triggering a little red light on the dashboard. Tullius ignored it, pressing the old machine hard.

Car 49 crossed the line in tenth place at an average qualifying speed of 92.844 miles per hour. The officials clocked Tullius' qualifying circuit at 1:55.936. The patriotic Javelin did it in 1:49.934 and got the pole with an average speed of 97.884 mph. He was followed by a Mustang in second place. The Ghost qualified in tenth place, followed by 30 others.

As Tullius rolled into pit road, he glanced at the dashboard. The little red light continued to glow and the oil pressure gauge read "low." He rolled to a stop before the smiling crew, shaking his head. "Trouble, boys." He looked at Nell, "Low oil pressure, Tom—and this little red light ..."

Nell cursed quietly, ran to the front of the car and popped the hood immediately. Young hurried up alongside and asked earnestly, "What's happenin' man?"

Nell peered hard into the engine compartment, "Low pressure and the red light." Tullius pulled off his helmet and joined them at the engine. "When did the pressure drop and the light come on?" Nell asked urgently.

Tullius rubbed his chin for a moment. "At the transition—*yeah*—at the transition from the infield to the straight. It was rough. Bounced like hell, man."

The engine men winced vainly at the hot engine. "Start it up," said Nell flatly as he turned and walked to the tool chest. As he removed a large screwdriver from a drawer, Tullius twisted the key in the Ghost's ignition. Nell gingerly placed the screwdriver's blade on the engine block and slowly put his right ear against the screwdriver's handle, his eyes closed. "*Ohhhh* ..." Nell muttered slowly. He moved the screwdriver to another place on the engine block and repeated the procedure. "*Damn.*" He stood up, handing the screwdriver to Young. "Take a listen."

Young put the screwdriver on the engine block and eased his ear to the screwdriver's butt. He winced, "Oh *no* ..." He moved the screwdriver, closed his eyes, and bit his lip. "Oh *man*! We got trouble." He stood up and looked solemnly at Nell, who nodded silently.

"What? What trouble?" asked Adams, looking at Nell.

"Uh, well, sounds to me like multiple problems, Herb. I hear possible problems with the crankshaft and bearings." Adams looked at Young for confirmation.

"Yeah," said Young reluctantly. "And maybe some bad conn rods."

"Some?" asked Adams.

"More than one, I think. We won't know until we—"

"Yeah," interrupted Adams. "Until you pull it apart and take a look."

Nell shrugged. Adams put his hand over his mouth, staring at the engine, shaking his head. "Not again."

~~~~

With the Sunday morning sun at his back, Bob Tullius scanned the clear Michigan horizon from pit road, disappointed. No rain coming, not even a cloud. He wasn't sure of the reason, but the old goat could go in the rain—really go. Maybe it was the big tires, maybe the balance, or perhaps some engineering magic Herb and his team of gearheads laid on it. Whatever it was, with a little water on the track he knew he could win in car 49.

Tullius looked at the old car and a thin smile crept over his lips. Water was good. The Ghost was good. But the Ghost could run in the dry, too. This was its last chance, the Ghost's last chance to prove it could beat the big boys.

~~~~

In the early afternoon, Bob Tullius walked deliberately toward car 49, focusing on the coming race, blankly studying his shoes. Someone nearby cleared his throat. Tullius walked on, concentrating. Someone else coughed loudly as he approached the Ghost. Tullius, his concentration broken, looked in the direction of the cougher. His eyes met an unexpected sight: the seven-member Trans/Action crew, standing at attention next to the Ghost with their hands behind their backs, wearing matching shirts, white with horizontal blue stripes. Tullius blinked hard at the grinning engineers before erupting into laughter.

Moments later, Tullius entered the Ghost, stuck the worn key into the ignition and, for the last time, twisted it. The big machine's characteristic guttural roar spewed audibly across pit road. "We dropped a new engine in last night. Now, go get 'em, Bob," said Adams over the thumping engine. The driver winked at him, took a deep breath, and the Ghost began rumbling down pit road to the track.

The 40 cars took their positions in the grid, slowly coursing around the track in two undulating and impatient rows, side by side. The fifth car back, in the outside row, was visibly different—big, dull gray, and old. Directly in front of it was the sparkling number 3 Mustang, and to its left was a shiny new Camaro.

The starter waved the green flag furiously, and the collective roar of 40 racecars erupted across the Irish Hills. During the first frantic circuit, Tullius attacked the course, passing a Camaro and a Mustang. At the start of the second lap, a Mustang had the lead, followed closely by five pony cars and Tullius.

Two pit stops later, the leaders had completed 50 laps. The patriotic Javelin had the lead followed by a Mustang, a Javelin, and Milt Minter in another Javelin. Two pony cars were behind them, battling for fifth, with 20 laps to go. As the race wore on, the favored Javelin gradually stretched its lead and at the finish, beat the Mustang by 38 seconds. Another Javelin finished a lap later, and two laps later came Milt Minter in fourth. Fifty-one seconds later the big GTO rumbled over the line. In its last Trans-Am race, the Ghost performed flawlessly, finishing fifth, earning a respectable two points for Pontiac and nineteen hundred dollars for the Trans/Action team.

~~~~

"Congratulations," said a voice from behind Herb Adams. Adams turned his attention from the team's efforts in loading the Ghost onto Goad's trailer and saw the smiling, vaguely familiar face of a Trans-Am race official.

"Thanks," responded Adams, "we did okay."

The man snorted. "Okay? Just okay? Your '64 GTO here just whipped 35 fancy new pony cars. I'd say that's better than just *okay*." Adams shrugged. "Anyway, the crowd loved it. Look forward to seein' ya in California in a month, October 3rd."

"Oh, we're not going to Riverside," said Adams.

The man's smile dropped from his face, replaced by a stunned look. "What? You're not going?" The man furrowed his brow, "*How come?*"

"Too far. Too much money." Adams re-directed his attention to the car, carefully watching the Ghost being loaded onto the trailer.

"Too far? But ya *gotta*! I mean the crowds *love* ya. They *love* the Gray Ghost."

Adams scratched his head, "Yeah, but they don't pay the way—not for us anyway. My guys are tight on vacation time, too. It's been a long season, man."

"Oh look, man—only two more races. Maybe you'll win! Riverside, it's not that far."

Adams continued his focus on the team's loading effort as they chained the Ghost onto the trailer. Adams said deliberately, "Well, it ain't close to here. We're from Detroit."

"I know, but ..." a mildly frantic look grew over the official's face. "Look, I'll be blunt. Trans-Am wants you out there because the Ghost helps fill the stands."

Adams looked at the official. "We'd like to go, but like I said, we don't have the money or the vacation time to spend a week in California. We'd have to make a trip there and back. Can't do it." Adams smiled, "Maybe if Trans-Am or SCCA wants to pay our expenses ..."

"Oh, *man*, can't do that. Policy, ya know, and we'd catch *hell* from your competitors."

Adams shrugged, squinting back at the Ghost. "We got no factory support and our budget is all blown to hell."

The man grimaced at his shoes.

"But maybe we'll be back next year with a new car. I mean *newer* car, and a refilled piggy bank and plenty of vacation time."

The man looked up hopefully, "That's outta sight!"

Chapter 35

ADAMS SHUT THE creaking door behind him with a dull thud and looked across the dank room at the grizzled man's open mouth, slowly inhaling and exhaling stinking breath across yellowed teeth under a bent nose and closed eyes. The man slept in his chair, feet propped on the old desk in the clammy cinderblock room.

"Hey," Adams said. No response. Adams took a step forward and raised his voice, "*Hey!*" The regular breathing continued. Adams approached the desk, "*HEY!*" The man twitched, quickly resuming his slumber. Finally, Adams grabbed the man's dirty boot and shook it. "*HEY! WAKE UP, MAN!*"

The man's eyes flashed wide open, "*Wha ...?*" Blinking rapidly, he focused on Adams.

Adams leaned over the desk, "Remember me?"

The man's feet thunked to the floor and he sat up, rubbing his red eyes with the heel of a dirty, calloused hand. "Whatcha yellin' fer?"

"Listen, I'll give you $200 for it—the Firebird."

"Da what?" asked the man, struggling to clear the cobwebs.

"The *Firebird*, man. I'm the guy who wants the Trans Am, remember?"

The man squinted at Adams and a look of recognition dawned across his stubbled face. "Oh yeah. Da Firebird. Yeah ..." The man looked out the broken window, grinning. "What makes ya think I still got it?"

"I just saw it a minute ago, and it ain't lookin' any better. Now, you want to do a deal or not?"

The man's stubbled grin faded quickly. "Two hundred, ya say? That ain't no deal. Can't let dat nice bird go for nuthin' under four."

"It's junk, man. That's why it's here." The man shrugged. "Okay, two-fifty," said Adams.

"Three-fifty."

Adams paused. "Three hundred or I walk … *again.*"

The man yawned, squinted out the window, and cocked his head. "Deal," he said with resignation.

~~~~

A week later, the Trans/Action team stood in Adams' garage after work, staring silently at the lifeless, broken Firebird Trans Am that had taken the place of the Gray Ghost. "Gentlemen, we've had a good week for deals," said Adams. A few eyes darted at Adams before dejectedly settling again on the busted black hulk before them. "A Pontiac dealer from Maryland—Tom's college fraternity buddy Spoerl—bought the Ghost. He's paying $2,500 for it, and he's coming to pick it up next week. And we got this baby," smiled Adams at the Firebird.

Someone sighed.

Tom Nell raised his eyebrows at the crippled machine and scratched his head deliberately. Dutch quietly grunted a curse.

Adams' widening eyes scanned the faces. "Hey, hey, we can do this. Remember, all we need is the sheet metal—the body, the control arms, and the sub-frame. SCCA requires those as stock stuff. We're making the rest ourselves, our way."

Silence. The Greek wrinkled his nose at the dirty wreck, rubbing the back of his neck. Someone farted in the corner.

Adams bit his lip. "Listen, the Ghost was a good car. But if you do what you did, you get what you got. And the Ghost didn't get us any wins." He pointed at the Firebird. "If we do this one right, we'll have a very, very good car. I mean a car like that Javelin this year. Nothin's gonna beat us!" Adams nervously rubbed his forefinger across his lips in the silence.

Tom Nell nodded. "Yeah." He squinted at the broken car. "We can do it." His twinkling eyes slowly scanned the faces in the garage. "Let's get the body off …"

~~~~

Under the dim, smoky light of the Gridiron Bar on Woodward Avenue in Pontiac, Adams' team sat eating lunch. The local newspaper lay sprawled across the Formica table, sporting a front page headline about six KKK members who had been arrested in Pontiac for bombing ten local school buses; school integration protesters were suspected. Glancing at the paper, Adams sighed and turned to his team.

"Listen, Tom. Jeff, you too," said Adams to his engine men. "I got an idea for the exhaust. A nice, smooth exhaust flow." Nell shot his boss a skeptical look. "Really. It'll improve the horsepower, but it'll be a lot of work."

Dutch squinted, curious. "What?"

"Well, the firing order in an eight cylinder, with the odd numbered cylinders on one side of the block and the even on the other, is uh … let me think … 1-8-4-3-6-5-7-2. Right?"

Dutch cocked his head and arched an eyebrow, "Yeah. So what?"

"Typical twin headers give no regard to firing order, so the sequencing of the exhaust is uneven relative to each 360 degree rotation of the crankshaft."

"Speak English, professor," uttered Dutch flatly.

Adams paused, thinking. "Okay. The crankshaft goes 270 degrees, a cylinder spits out the exhaust, then it goes only another 90 degrees before another cylinder spits out some more exhaust. As a result, you get two or even three cylinders exhausting through the same pipe at about the same time. The exhaust pipe—the headers—can't handle that kind of sudden pressure. There's just not enough room for all the exhaust to vent, so some of it backs up in the cylinders before rushing out. That pressure inhibits the cylinder from moving freely. And immediately after, no exhaust at all is flowing through that pipe while another pipe is backing up with exhaust. That's why you hear the *bangety-bang* of typically exhausted engines. It's a rough sound, and it's inefficient. The backed-up exhaust robs the engine of horsepower and torque. But some engines are different. Actually, it's not really the engines that are different, it's the way they're exhausted. Their headers are configured so that the fumes from the cylinders take turns exhausting out the pipes. For every 180 degree rotation of the crankshaft, one cylinder—and only one—exhausts through the pipes, so they don't compete for the same, limited space in the same narrow exhaust pipe. The firing order agrees with the exhaust pipes, see? The result is a nice smooth flow of exhaust, and more power because there's no exhaust backup."

The confusion on Dutch's face melted into understanding. "Yeah, I see. Smooth exhaust flow. It'll improve the horsepower."

Adams grinned at his sandwich and took a bite. Young and Nell glanced at each other.

"That's gonna require one hell of a lot of work, gentlemen," said Nell. Young nodded silently.

"Yeah," acknowledged Adams. "We'll have to weave the headers under and around the oil pan. We'll have to fit, re-fit, and fit them again, piece it together from scratch. Very complicated, 180 degree headers. That's what they're called." He nodded. "I'll fabricate, fit, and install them."

"Which means we'll have to drop the engine in and yank it back out a hundred times," said Nell deliberately.

"We can do it," Adams said through a mouthful of olive loaf on rye. "It'll be worth it."

Nell nodded slowly and took a long gulp of pop. "*Yeah*. No one else is gonna do it, too much work. We'll have a competitive advantage."

"Yep. Okay," said Adams. "Now, about the chassis. We need a nice light frame and a lot of torsional stiffness in the chassis, and the stock Firebird is front heavy. I'm thinking we acid dip the entire sub frame to get weight off it, and we reinforce it with gussets. We're also gonna de-camber the rear axle, just like on the Ghost. And move the engine back for better front-to-rear balance. We'll make a bigger space in the cockpit for the transmission, if necessary."

"Aren't there rules or somethin' against that? Moving the trannie into the cockpit?" asked the Greek.

"No. I checked the Trans-Am and SCCA books. Nothing prohibits it." Adams cocked his head slightly at the ceiling and winced, "Not exactly …"

~~~~

The following Saturday afternoon, the Trans/Action crew stood in Herb Adams' driveway, staring ambivalently at the Ghost on Lou Spoerl's trailer. Adams and Tom Nell shook Spoerl's hand before he slowly, matter-of-factly, towed the Ghost down the crabgrass-lined driveway, onto the street, and out of sight.

Dutch glanced at Adams' lawn, now an agrarian mosaic of overgrown fescue, bright yellow dandelions, and sprawling patches of crabgrass. The shrubs in front of the house sprouted long, uneven tentacles. On the house, paint peeled from a window shutter. A maple sapling sprouted from a second story gutter.

Dutch stared at the wrecked Firebird in the garage and took a long, slow breath. He lit a cigarette and rubbed his eye with the heel of his hand, exhaling slowly. "Man, I need a beer."

Chapter 36

"HARRY," SAID ADAMS, studying the rear end of the Firebird. "Joe Brady's back at school."

"Yes," said Quackenboss, shrugging his broad shoulders. "MBA," he said with a hint of reverence.

"Anyway, we're without his services for this project so we're gonna need your help more than ever on this suspension."

"You got it," Harry beamed.

"Good. Listen, we're gonna de-camber the rear axle again, just like the Ghost. Only one degree or so, but since nobody else does it, it'll give us an edge on the competition. I'm convinced that the de-cambered axle on the Ghost really helped us last season."

"Oh, yes," responded Harry professionally. "I'll take care of it."

"Okay. We got leaf springs back here, unlike the Ghost. If we raise the front of the leafs, we'll get more anti-squat."

Quackenboss shook his head slowly. "But we've only got about three-quarters of an inch to do it. I checked."

Adams squinted, his eyes darting around the garage.

"What?" asked Harry. "What are you thinking?"

Adams quickly dropped to one knee, looking under the bare frame at the front of the leaf springs. His head darted up at the top of the frame. "A tower ..."

"Pardon me?"

"A tower—a little tower. We build a tower, a six- or eight-inch high box, cut a hole in the floorboard and make a box around it in the interior of the car, and put the suspension point up in it."

Harry glanced at the frame as recognition of the concept dawned across his face, "Build little towers over the front end of each of the rear leafs, raise the leaf up in there and attach it ..."

"Yeah. Better anti-squat. It'll lower the rear end, too. Tullius will be able to gas it sooner coming out of the corners."

Harry suddenly squinted. "What about the rules?"

"SCCA only says we have to keep the basic configuration the same. Nothin' stops us from moving the suspension points." Harry grinned his approval. "And let's replace the stock rubber bushings on the front of the leafs, too, with mono-balls."

"Yeah," replied Harry. "Steel on steel bearings that ... articulate."

"Articulate." Adams grinned slyly, "Right on, man. And on the rear of the leafs, let's put some longer shackles. That'll drop it a little more and also help with anti-squat."

Harry nodded, "Indeed."

"Speaking of stock rubber bushings, we got 'em on the front end, too," said Adams, pointing to the front of the chassis. "That's gonna give us too much deflexion. I mean the front end'll be moving all over the place in the races if we leave the rubber on."

"How about some nylon sleeves instead?" offered Harry, walking to the front end, studying the offending bushings with an intellectual glare. "The front end will stick better."

"Yeah, do it." Adams studied a front-end spindle. "Ya know, if we move the spindles here up on the knuckle—"

"It'll drop the front end," interrupted Harry.

"I like the way you think, man," said Adams through a smile.

"Hey, how about the stabilizer bars? The stock front bar here is too small. We need about a one-and-a-quarter incher. Conventional wisdom says we use pogo sticks on the joint links, but I like—"

"Heims," interrupted Adams. "Just like on the Ghost. Heim joint links will give us better handling than pogos." Harry nodded deliberately, his lips pursed. Adams glanced at the rear end. "We need this car as neutral as possible—no understeer, no oversteer. I mean, I don't want Tullius holler-ing about being loose in the corners. So, let's get three rear stabilizer bars. That way we can tune this baby to be neutral depending on track conditions and other set-up variables. We'll have a small bar of about three-quarters of an inch or so diameter, a medium of about seven-eighths, and a bigger one at one inch. We can swap 'em out at practice until we're neutral."

"Good idea."

"One more thing. The factory bolted the body to the sub-frame with rubber mounts. When we put the body back on, let's ditch the rubber and bolt it right to the sub-frame. That'll lower it some more."

Harry flashed his teeth. "Ya know, man, I kinda like the way *you* think, too."

~~~~

Adams and Tom Nell stood at the front of the stripped Firebird's chassis, staring at the gaping emptiness of the engine compartment. "Jeff can't join us this year, Tom."

"So I hear."

The two men glanced glumly at each other.

"We got two 303 engines already built—400s de-stroked with dry sumps, Holley four barrel double pumpers," said Nell. "Ya know, I been thinking about your fancy 180 degree headers."

"I'll weave them around."

"Yeah, but you'll have to do it *under* the oil pan, Herb. I mean, there's gonna be no room anywhere else ..."

Adams shrugged.

Nell continued. "I'm not trying to talk you out of it, but there may not be enough room for the pipes with the oil pan in the way. Anyway, I got an idea. Since we'll have a dry sump, we can cut away part of the oil pan to make room for the headers, if necessary."

Adams nodded silently. "And we got some extra help." Adams shot him a puzzled look. "Don Haller—the engine mechanic from work. We can handle the engine job."

"The experimental engine build-up guy?"

Nell nodded, "Yeah. He's good."

"Yeah, I know him—UAW guy. He's good." Adams pointed at the chassis. "Anyway, this thing is real front-end heavy."

"You ought to know," responded Nell slyly.

"Yeah … well, when you drop the 303 in here, you gotta back it way up, right up near the firewall. I want good balance on this car, just like—"

"The Ghost," interrupted Nell, nodding. "Yeah. We'll drop it in way back." He squinted, pointing at the firewall, "but we'll have to make a bigger opening there for the transmission."

"Fine—do it. And we need a nice 50-50 balance between front and rear. I mean the center of gravity right in the middle. We gotta do something else, too." Adams turned around, facing the bumper that lay on the garage floor. "I'm gonna take the brackets and mounts off of this thing and bolt it right onto the fenders. Save some weight and help with the balance. Who needs bumpers that actually work, anyway?"

Chapter 37

THE BLACK ROTARY telephone on Adams' desk rang, rudely rattling the early morning office silence. Adams stabbed his hand at the receiver, absently placing it alongside his head, "Pontiac Special Projects. Adams speaking," he muttered flatly.

"Hey!" said a familiar voice. "Hear you got a new car."

"Bob?"

"Yeah. Ya know—your *driver.*"

Adams snorted, smiling into the phone. "Yeah, man, we got a new car. Firebird. *Trans Am.*"

"Oh. I hear you know a thing or two about them," said Tullius through an obvious smile. "Hoppin' it up good, I bet."

Adams nodded. "It's gonna blow your mind ..."

"Can't wait to get behind the wheel."

"Good. You're gonna like it, I think."

"Yeah, but before that, I gotta go to Bangkok."

"Bangkok ... *Thailand?*"

"Yeah, man. *Bangkok.* But I'm not going until January."

Adams paused. "Why Bangkok? I mean, maybe you didn't hear about this *war* goin' on around there? Viet Cong ... *bad guys* ..."

"Well, there's this ... ahhh ... there's this ..."

"This what? What're you talkin' about?"

"Ahh ... well, she's—"

"Oh—a *chick!*" interrupted Adams.

Tullius paused, "Uh, yeah …"

"Must be one *hell* of a chick for you to go halfway around the world to a *war zone*, man."

Another pause, "Yeah. A honey."

"What's she doing in *Bangkok, Thailand,* of all places?"

"Schoolteacher. Teaching English to school kids." Adams grunted. "I'll be back in plenty of time to break in the 'Bird."

Adams exhaled slowly through pursed lips, "Okay, man. Be careful."

~~~~

A few weeks later, the Trans/Action crew worked in Adams' garage. Herb stepped out of his house into the garage. "Hey guys," shouted Adams through the cold, dry air "I hear we have a problem." The garage fell silent. All heads turned to Adams as he shut the door behind him. "I hear Tullius is hurt—hurt badly."

"What track?" asked an urgent voice.

Adams shook his head, "Not on a track. In Bangkok."

Stunned silence ensued. "*Thailand?*" asked another voice.

"Yeah. Bangkok, Thailand. He's hurt bad, I hear."

More silence.

"He … he didn't get himself an M-16 and go shootin' up the *Viet Cong,* did he?" asked the Greek. "I heard some stories from some paratrooper buddies about the Viet Cong."

"No, no … nothing like that. A traffic accident. *Bad* one."

More silence while the garage contemplated this news. "So our driver—our *racecar* driver—got hurt in a *traffic accident?*"

~~~~

A month later, Adams picked up the ringing telephone in his office. "Pontiac Special—"

"Yeah, I know. *Special Projects,*" croaked a vaguely familiar voice.

Adams squinted. "Bob?"

"I ain't dead yet."

"What *happened*, man? Where are you? We heard you got creamed in a traffic accident in Bangkok. You okay?"

"Yeah, well … it seems I can get around a racetrack lickety-split, but can't seem to remember they drive on the *other* side of the road in Thailand. So anyway, I got clobbered by a car—run over, man. I was a pedestrian, crossing the street. Looked the wrong way. Broke my left leg in five places and busted a shoulder, too."

Adams winced. "When did you get back?"

"Well, spent two weeks in a Bangkok hospital, then I managed to hitch a ride on a U.S. military C141 thanks to being an Air Force veteran. That took another two weeks, hopscotching home. And ya know, there ain't no first class in a C141. Every time we hit some turbulence, it kinda, well, *hurt* a little. Anyway, been back in the States taking it easy for a few days now."

Adams paused. "You okay now?"

"Better, but far from 100 percent. In fact, that's why I'm calling."

"What you mean?"

"Well, I'm in the hospital here. They won't spring me for a few months."

"*Months?*"

"Yeah, man. I'm lucky to be alive."

Adams blinked rapidly, taking in the significance of the words. Tullius was not prone to exaggeration. This was the truth.

"Anyway," Tullius continued, "even after the sawbones here cut me loose, it's gonna be a long time before I drive again. I was really looking forward to driving the new 'Bird for you this summer but—"

"Oh, don't worry about that, man, just get better. Just get better."

~~~~

Under harsh fluorescent light, the Trans Action team sat huddled around the Pontiac Motor Division cafeteria table. "So it's true. Tullius got run over in Thailand," muttered Tom Nell through a baloney sandwich.

"Yeah, *creamed*. I mean, *damn*," said Adams. The men stared in unison at their cold cuts, soda cans and lukewarm coffee. "Anyway," continued Adams, "he says he'll be okay, but not for a long time. A very long time."

The men darted nervous looks at each other.

"So … we need a new driver," said Nell.

Adams snapped a pretzel in half. "Bingo."

"Who?" asked an urgent voice.

Adams popped half of the pretzel in his mouth, chewing deliberately. "I got an idea."

~~~~

"Yes, Mrs. Heath," said the service manager into the telephone. "Your car should be ready any time now. I'll check for you now … please hold." He stabbed the red hold button with a nervous index finger, slammed the receiver onto his desk and stormed out into the garage. Quickly spying the yellow VW Bug, he ran past a row of German cars toward the mechanic standing near the Bug. "*Done?*" he barked at the grease monkey.

The mechanic, wearing a dirty white shop coat and wiping his hands with a shop rag examined the Bug. "*Ja, ist gut,*" said the mechanic.

The manager ran back to the office, speared the flashing button on the telephone with his stiff finger, and slapped the receiver to his ear. "Mrs. Heath? Uh, your car is ready. Yes ten minutes will be fine."

A short time later, the service manager held out a set of car keys. "Here you are Mrs. Heath. Thank you for—"

"It's about time. I waited all day …" Her voice trailed off as a man in a dirty white shop coat approached them. He was eating potato chips from a large, rumpled bag. His eyes were bloodshot, his hair was a mess, and he sported a two- or three-day-old beard. "Who is *that* man?" she asked the manager.

"Well," the manager winced, scratching his head, "he's the mechanic who repaired your car."

The mechanic smiled at her, ambling to a stop.

She studied the mechanic critically. "And is everything all right with my little yellow baby?"

"Ja, ja," responded the mechanic. "Iz *goot,*" he said, chewing a chip.

"Oh! Well, thank you," she said with sudden pleasure in her voice. "Or, should I say, *danke?* I'm sure it was worth the wait," she said approvingly, smiling broadly now at the mechanic. "Good German engineering needs good German maintenance and repair."

The mechanic smiled again, "Iz *goot*."

Mrs. Heath, still grinning, gracefully entered the Bug, started the motor and drove off, waving gleefully.

"What the hell was that?" asked the service manager, squinting at the mechanic.

"What?" asked the squinting mechanic, holding a fistful of chips.

"The fake German accent, and those *potato chips*." He looked at the yellow Bug driving off in the distance. "Well, never mind. It worked, so I'm hip." He studied the mechanic's narrow, red eyes. "You gettin' enough sleep?"

"Hey boss!" a voice shouted from the office. "Phone call!" The service manager trotted to his office and picked up the receiver as the mechanic watched, munching chips.

"Yeah," said the manager into the phone, looking at the mechanic, "he works here. I'm hip. Just a minute, I'll get him." The manager waved the mechanic to the office.

The mechanic leisurely approached, and the manager thrust the phone at his grimy chest. "For me?" asked the mechanic, spraying crumbs from his mouth.

"Yeah. Says his name is Herb Allen, or Adams, or something. Hey, no more personal calls at work, okay? And get rid of the potato chips, for Christ's sake."

The mechanic swallowed a mouthful of chips. He dropped a handful of them back into the bag, wiped his greasy hand on his dirty shop coat, and took the phone from his boss. Pressing the phone to his ear the mechanic spoke, "Milt Minter ..."

Chapter 38

A DRY, BITING Saturday morning wind blew across Detroit from
the northeast, carrying countless swirling bits of red, orange, and yellow
from the shedding trees. The crispy leaves, like an autumnal kaleidoscope,
blanketed the Adams' front lawn concealing a weed-choked suburban jungle. In the relative shelter of his garage, Herb Adams grunted on his back
under the gutted Firebird. The shell of a car rested on jack stands, its open
hood revealing a newly mated engine and massive transmission. The two
had been installed so far toward the rear of the engine compartment that a
large hole had been cut through the firewall into the cockpit, to accommodate the transmission, nearly half of which was visible from the interior.
The car's four thin stock tires had been removed and were lying forgotten
on the floor.

Tom Nell, wiping his greasy, calloused hands with a shop rag, scanned
a newspaper on the corner workbench. The headline screamed about labor
leader George Meany's demand that Congress take control of the economy
from President Nixon. Another article announced the U.S. House of
Representatives had just passed something called the Equal Rights
Amendment. But some tiny print in the corner caught Nell's eye. "Hey
Herbie," he said, leaning into the paper, "says here some guy in Utah set a
snowmobile speed record—140.6 miles an hour." He absently dropped the
shop rag on the workbench. "On a snowmobile, 140 … *damn* …"

Adams scooted out from under the car, holding two bits of steel tub-
ing in each hand. He stood up, placed the tubes on the workbench,

scratched his head and took a gulp of warm, flat Diet Coke from a grimy, dented can. After a hard swallow, Adams squinted at the Firebird and said, "If we can't beat a Mormon on a snowmobile ..."

Nell raised a wry eyebrow over his shoulder at his boss. "How's the fitting of the crossover headers going?"

"Slow, but I'm getting there. Where's Dutch? Hey, Dutch."

The machinist dropped his cigarette, ground it underfoot and ambled over. Adams pointed at the interior section of the transmission. "We need to fabricate a tunnel running right down the middle here, past the driver's seat, over the transmission to cover it and the hole there in the firewall. SCCA maybe won't like it, but there's no rule against it."

Dutch studied the problem for a moment, then nodded. "Yep. Easy."

Adams looked at Nell and pointed to the Firebird's steering wheel through the open driver's side window. "This stock's got a twenty-two to one ratio. We need a manual sixteen to one ratio. See if you can find that guy at Saginaw who sold Joe the steering system we used in the Ghost last year."

Nell nodded. The image of a huge, mid-Michigan complex of GM's pale blue factories on Interstate 75 flashed across his mind. He'd driven past it a hundred times on the way to northern Michigan. "Saginaw Steering Gear," he said quietly. "I'll call Joe and ask him for a name and number."

"Look at these," said Adams disgustedly, pointing at the exposed rear drum brakes. Nell winced, shaking his head silently. Adams continued, "And up here." he pointed at the front brakes, "calipers, but only two pistons. We need four piston calipers and discs, on all four corners."

"Corvette brakes," said Nell.

Adams nodded. "Big ones, just like last year." He turned and kicked a tire on the floor. "And we'll do something else like last year." Nell squinted sideways at his boss. Adams continued. "Maybe our tire sponsor can make us some cantilevered tires. More overhang. More road contact." Adams rubbed his chin absently. "We'll need 18-inch wheels to accommodate them, and even then they'll hang over the outside and inside rims ... very sticky."

"Yeah, but everyone runs them," said Nell with a furrowed brow. Adams flashed a sardonic grin. Recognition dawned across Nell's face, "But not on the front!"

"Right, engine man."

Nell patted a front fender, "Stock fenders will be too narrow to handle huge gumballs like that."

"We'll flare the fenders, just like the Ghost. I'll do it. Cut and weld 'em. Heat 'em and beat 'em."

Nell grinned, "Another tank."

Adams opened the driver's side door, crouched down, and peered into the interior. "I'll fabricate a roll cage."

"Great. Now all we need is a driver to steer this rocket."

Adams shot a sideways look at Nell.

"Don't tell me you already got one," said Nell.

Adams nodded, unable to conceal his obvious delight. "A good one, Tom. Milt Minter."

Tom Nell let out a loud, exuberant hoot.

~~~~

In the following weeks, the falling leaves gave way to falling snow in suburban Detroit.

On the evening of Monday, November 15, 1971, Adams' garage was filled with clanking tools and activity. Herb Adams slid out on his back from under the Firebird while grasping two small, curved, steel tubes. He stood up quickly, set them on the workbench, and abruptly snapped off the radio with its stream of bad news, muttering indecipherably.

Harry Quackenboss sensed the frustration. "Politics or the headers?"

"Screw politics," answered Adams. "It's fitting these headers. *Man.*"

The Greek shouted from across the garage, "Hey, boss, I got the fuel cell done."

Adams rubbed his eyes with the heels of his hands. "Good. Now help Harry on the rear end."

"It'll be worth it, all the fitting. You know it will," whispered Harry to Adams.

Adams exhaled slowly, wiping a congealing mix of blood and grime from his knuckles with a shop rag. "Keep tellin' me that ..."

~~~~

Five weeks later, on a Thursday evening two days before Christmas, Tom Nell watched as Adams fiddled and grunted on his back under the front end of the Firebird, only vaguely aware of the war protest rock song spewing from the radio in the corner of the garage. The song ended and a throaty radio voice spoke, *"Today, perhaps in the spirit of the season, President Nixon commuted the sentence of Teamsters' leader Jimmy Hoffa. Separately, GM began its previously announced recall of 6.7 million Chevrolets."*

"Oh yeah!" said a voice from under the engine. "They fit!" Adams slid out from under the car and pumped his fist in the air.

"Progress on the headers?" asked Nell.

Adams stood up, nodding, "Two of 'em, finally. But remember that offer you made a while back about chopping off some of the oil pan to accommodate the headers? Well, I'm taking you up on it. You were right—too cramped down there for all the headers. All the snaking and weaving in Bombay couldn't fit 'em in there without a little more room."

"Okay. Where do you want to cut?"

The door from the house opened and Sandi poked her head into the garage, "Tom—Marilyn's on the phone." Nell's eyes darted at his watch. He cursed under his breath.

"Maybe tomorrow," offered Adams.

~~~~

The evening of January 5, 1972, found the Trans Am team busy again in Adams' garage. Two sets of dirty, blue jeaned legs protruded from beneath the Firebird. Welding smoke emanated from the bottom of the engine compartment, shrouding the garage in a blue-gray haze. The hissing welding torch fell silent and muffled voices came from under the car.

"Okay under there?" asked Adams.

Dutch and Nell slid out from under the car.

"Yeah," said Dutch, lying on his back.

"He cut the oil pan," grunted Nell, standing up. "More room for your headers. Take a look."

Adams grabbed a handful of short header tubes from the workbench and slid under the car on his back. He took a quick look, fumbled with the tubes and emitted a short whoop.

Nell looked at Dutch, "I think that means we did good."

Adams shot out from under the car, beaming. "They fit! All of 'em. Oh, man—we're almost there, gentlemen. Good work." He jumped to his feet. "Hell of a lot of work, but these headers are gonna pay off ..."

~~~~

Two and a half weeks later, Tom Nell sat in the Trans Am's driver's seat looking intently at Adams through the windshield. His fingers twitched near the key protruding from the ignition in the steering column.

Dutch creaked open the garage door and bitingly cold, dry air flooded the garage. Adams stood at the front bumper, gripping an adjustable end wrench in one hand. He nodded at Nell. For an instant, the garage fell silent, except for the radio: *"In other war news, yesterday's American body count was ..."*

Nell deliberately twisted the key and the car's engine jumped to life, audibly swamping the little radio. An unexpected resonance flowed from the Trans Am's tailpipes. The engineers had heard this tone before, but not from a Pontiac. Not even from a Trans-Am race car. This was smooth. It was pure ... harmonic.

Nell let it idle, a broad smile creeping across his face. He caught Adams' twinkling eye. Nell raised his eyebrows, and nodded short and quick. Adams nodded slowly back, mouthing, "Yeah."

Nell goosed the accelerator. The engine's tuned purr grew instantly to a melodic roar before settling back to a silky smooth idle. The engineers grinned at each other.

Still holding the wrench, Adams looked at Nell and slowly swept his hands together and upward. Nell closed his eyes and squeezed very slowly on the gas. The engine again responded immediately, emitting a beautifully tuned mechanical note, smoothly rising in pitch as Nell eased the accelerator to the floor. A constant, acoustically perfect roar sang out in the wide-open garage door and cascaded across the frigid neighborhood in a gear-head symphony.

The engineers basked in the siren sound of the mechanical orchestra. Adams raised his face to the ceiling and closed his eyes, focusing on the audible smorgasbord, smiling broadly with his arms outstretched, twitching the wrench rhythmically. Nell continued the mechanical refrain for a few glorious seconds before easing off the gas and letting the engine settle to its soft, smoothly tuned idle.

A widely grinning Adams opened his eyes, looked at Nell, and drew his free hand across his throat in a cutting action. Nell switched off the ignition.

"God*damn!*" muttered Dutch through the ensuing silence. "We got us a ... a ... *Ferrari!*"

Adams carefully opened the hood and beamed with great satisfaction at the warm, iron orchestra resting quietly now in the engine compartment. A beautiful engine with a beautiful voice.

~~~~

Three months later, Adams stood next to young Jim in the garage examining the low-slung, dirty black Firebird.

"Wow," muttered Jim. "This thing even *looks* fast."

"Yeah. Hey, have you applied to college yet?"

Jim's eyes quickly crawled over the car. The fenders had been flared to accommodate fat black tires on all four corners, just like last year. "What?" Jim answered blankly.

"College. You going? In order to be a real engineer, you have to get an engineering degree."

The car's signature scoop protruded uncharacteristically high from the hood. "How come the scoop is sticking up so high?" asked Jim.

"We dropped the body around the engine, and the entire chassis. Called a shaker hood. Hey, how about college? You want to be an engineer or not?"

"What?" Jim looked up briefly from his intense study. "Oh ... yeah. I'm applying. I hear college is outta sight, man. Good parties." He peered into the interior. "Hey, why the big tunnel through the middle?"

"We pushed the engine back—way back—for better balance. That meant pushing part of the transmission back into the cockpit," responded Adams. "Listen, are you going to apply to the engineering school?"

Jim examined the vacant rear of the interior, "What are these little metal box things sticking up back here?"

Adams smiled patiently. "We jacked up the rear end. Suspension points are in there. We call them towers. Hey, what about engineering school?"

Jim glanced at Adams. "What? Oh yeah. I want to be a mechanical engineering major, like you." Jim refocused his attention on the car.

"Ya don't say. You think you'll like it?" persisted Adams.

"Hey, can I pop the hood?"

"Answer the question."

"Oh, yeah, sorry ..." muttered the young man, tearing his lusting young eyes from the car. "But I'm like ... motivated, too."

"Motivated?"

A sheepish grin grew across Jim's fresh, unwrinkled face. "Well, I'm as patriotic as the next guy, but I'm really just a gearhead. Maybe a junior gearhead, but ..."

Adams cocked his head quizzically.

"What I mean is ... the war ... I ... I just," Jim shrugged his shoulders.

A wave of understanding swept across Adams' face. "I see. You go to school, you—"

"Avoid the draft," finished Jim.

Adams grinned and patted the young man on the back.

Chapter 39

"JA?" THE VOICE croaked through the phone.

"This is Herb Adams calling for Milt Minter." The voice didn't sound quite right. It sounded old, tired. "Milt Minter?"

"Ja."

"Oh. How you doing, Milt?"

"Gut. You?"

"Fine. What's with the fake German accent?"

"Oh yeah," said Minter, shifting back to his natural, Midwestern dialect. "The customers at the VW dealership seem to like it, but sometimes I forget I don't need it when I'm talking to my buddies."

Adams snorted. "Anyway, we got our first race soon. May 6th at Lime Rock. You can make it, right? You're our driver. Trans Am ..."

"Yep."

"Okay. Lime Rock, Connecticut. You know it—you raced there, right?"

"Oh, yeah. I know it."

"Good. See you there, right? We got a nice car. Firebird Trans Am."

"Good. I got a motorhome."

"Motorhome. Okay. Warm up on May 4th, qualifying on May 5th, race on May 6th. First race of the season, so you need to get a feel for the car. Get there Friday, if you can. It'll be your first time in the car. Okay?"

"Yep ... May."

"Yes. May 4th. Be there May 4th if you can. Or May 5th. Race on Sunday, May 6th."

"Yep …"

Adams slowly drew the receiver away from his ear and briefly studied it. "You okay, Milt?"

"Yep … Okay. You okay?"

"Uh, yeah. See you May 4th?"

"Okay."

"Okay. See ya."

Adams gingerly returned the receiver to its cradle, squinting at the phone and rubbing his chin hard. Maybe getting Milt to drive for them was a mistake, but Minter in his Javelin beat them last year at MIS. Minter finished fourth, 53 seconds ahead of Tullius in the Ghost. Only the big guys finished ahead of him. Milt was a guy with a proven driving record. A winner with incredible talent.

Adams scratched the back of his neck and drew a long breath. Maybe Milt was just hanging around the German car guys too much at the dealership. Yes, that was it. He'd be all right.

~~~~

May 4th, warm up day. Herb stood next to his team's glinting black Firebird—number 96—parked in Lime Rock's pit road, studying a race committee sheet in Connecticut's late morning sun. The names of many of the expected drivers were familiar, but some were conspicuously absent. So the rumor was true; American Motors had pulled the Trans-Am racing plug. Ford too. They wouldn't be sponsoring any cars this year. Bad news for racing, but not for us, thought Adams. He glanced at his watch. If only Milt would show up.

A few hours later, Tom Nell shook his head at his watch and looked at Adams. "No Minter. Unbelievable." Nell gritted his teeth, absently balled his hands into fists and squeezed hard as he glanced at the driver from a competing team slide behind the wheel. His mind raced, seeking a practical solution to this new emergency. Finding none, he cursed Minter. "All this work we've done to get here, man, and our new driver doesn't show. So, what now?"

Adams squinted at the track, seething with anger about the absent Minter, but attempting to project an image of control. He took a deep breath and exhaled slowly. "I'll take her for a spin. Meantime, see if you can find a driver looking for a ride. Somebody good. And find him fast. Screw Minter, we can't wait."

Nell nodded, his eyes already darting around pit road.

Adams eased into the Firebird and slipped on the helmet. He stepped on the clutch, shifted the Hurst stick into neutral, and twisted the key. A familiar, silky, pure mechanical note flowed from the tailpipes. This was comforting, hearing the car come alive. He was alone for a moment and took advantage of it, cursing loudly at Minter and slamming the outside of his fist against the steering wheel. Adams glanced in the rearview mirror, seething. The entire five man crew on the car behind him had stopped their work and was staring at the black Firebird's rear end.

Adams shifted into first and eased off the clutch. *Take a good look boys, and get used to that view,* thought Adams, now grinning. *You got trouble.*

After a few moderately cautious warm-up laps around the Lime Rock track, Adams pulled into pit road, stopping next to Tom Nell and another guy. They may not have a driver, but they sure had a car.

"Look what the cat dragged in!" beamed Nell, pointing to the other man. Adams shot a bewildered look at both of them before exiting the Firebird and pulling off his helmet. Nell said, "Herb, this is—"

"Tony DeLorenzo," interrupted Adams through a widening smile.

DeLorenzo nodded as he shook Adams' hand. "Hear ya need a driver for this sweet-sounding baby." Tony DeLorenzo was one of the best drivers on the circuit. In the '71 season he'd driven a Mustang for Ford and had a number of top five finishes, including a second place finish here at Lime Rock and fourth place finish at Mid-Ohio, just ahead of Tullius and the Ghost.

Adams remembered that race in particular. "You and your 'Stang beat us here a year ago."

"Yeah, but you and your old goat got all the attention," DeLorenzo said, shaking his head. "Never saw anything like it."

Adams also remembered DeLorenzo's third place finish at Donnybrooke and fifth place at Elkhart Lake. He handed DeLorenzo the helmet. "Well, maybe we can help get you some attention this year. Welcome to the team." Adams felt a huge weight lifted from his shoulders. Minter was instantly forgotten.

DeLorenzo quickly slid into the car, donned the helmet, and turned over the engine. The exhaust pipes emitted the familiar silky-smooth tune. Still in neutral, DeLorenzo quickly gassed the throttle. The engine sang. Incredulous, DeLorenzo lifted his foot from the gas and stared at the dashboard. Slack jawed, he looked at the engineers. "How ... I mean ... what ... hey, you got a *legal* engine in here?"

Nell and Adams grinned at each other.

"I don't want to get my hopes up here only to be DQ'd, now," said the new driver.

"It's legal," said Adams, glancing quickly up and down pit road and leaning toward the window. "We just tuned it, like."

"Tuned it?"

"Yeah—crossover headers, 180 headers. It allows for nice, uniform exhaust. No exhaust back up. No bang-bang. It's smooth, like a—"

"*Ferrari*," DeLorenzo interrupted.

"Yeah. It'll pass tech inspection. No sweat, man."

DeLorenzo looked admiringly at the dashboard. He slipped the Hurst stick shift into first gear, lifted the clutch, and squeezed the gas pedal toward the bare floorboard, easing the black, purring machine onto the Main Straight and around the flat Big Bend. The machine lowered its shoulder into the curve, following the quickly bending track back to the left, into the Esses. The Firebird's thick, wide slicks stuck to the pavement through the snaking chicane. DeLorenzo smoothly shifted the Hurst into third gear and squeezed the accelerator quickly at the start of No Name Straight. The powerplant sang as it pinned the driver's body into the seatback. Halfway down the straightaway DeLorenzo eased up on the gas, squeezed down the clutch, flicked the Hurst into fourth gear and quickly pressed the gas pedal to the floor. A big cat-like whine instantly bellowed from the twin tailpipes of the glinting black car. DeLorenzo eased off as he approached Climbing Turn before smoothly gassing it again near the curve's apex and sling-shotting onto the Back Straight. Nimbly snapping the buttery-smooth Hurst shifter into fourth gear, he stood on the accelerator and was again pinned to the seat as the Firebird hurtled toward 130 mph. DeLorenzo grinned.

Approaching the next curve, West Bend, he hit the brake pedal hard and heel-toe downshifted again. The black machine's silky, mechanical voice quieted as the driver nailed the apex. DeLorenzo gassed it, eased off, hit the clutch, and smoothly rammed the stick into fourth before standing on the gas again. The black 'Bird soared toward the final turn—Driving Turn. He eased off the accelerator as he rounded the sweeping right bend. At the apex, he smoothly pushed the gas pedal to the floor and glanced ahead to the Main Straight. The massive engine purred its thunderous approval as a smooth exhaust plumed from the gaping tailpipes.

DeLorenzo, pinned to the seat again, guided the accelerating black rocket down the center of the straightaway as the tachometer needle swung rapidly toward the 5,000 rpm mark. The shiny black Firebird flashed past its cheering crew, its tailpipes emitting their earsplitting, smooth song. DeLorenzo chuckled from under his helmet.

~~~~

"Tech inspection ..." said a flat, unfamiliar voice from behind Herb Adams and Tom Nell the next morning. Adams lifted his eyes from the Firebird's engine compartment and looked over his shoulder at two stone-faced, middle-aged men each holding clipboards.

"Oh, yeah. Take a look," responded Adams, wiping his hands with a shop towel. Nell continued to fiddle with the engine.

One of the inspectors walked around to the side of the car, noted the number 96 on the door and studied his clipboard. He glanced at the number again, then back to his clipboard. Adams watched him intently, absently wiping his hands. "Oh—you Herb Adams? From Pontiac?"

"Yeah, that's me."

The inspector raised his eyebrows as a barely perceptible half-grin crept across his lips. The inspector's eyes darted to his partner, who also glanced up from his clipboard at Adams. He nodded in recognition. The first inspector strode toward Adams, dropped the clipboard to his side and extended his hand. "It's a pleasure to meet you, sir."

Surprised, Adams shook his hand. "Uh ... nice to meet you, too."

The other inspector, now grinning broadly, quickly extended his hand also. "An honor to meet you, Mr. Adams."

Adams furrowed his brow. "Uh ... well ... thanks," said Adams as the inspector pumped his hand enthusiastically. The two inspectors stepped back, looking admiringly at Adams in silence.

"Uh, well," said Adams, uncomfortable with the unexpected attention, "anyway, here's our car ..."

"Oh!" the inspectors uttered in unison. "Of course!" stammered one inspector. "Sorry," said the other sheepishly, "it's just that we followed you and your car last year ..."

"Yeah," said the first inspector, still grinning. "We've heard about you."

Adams wiped his hands self-consciously, "Oh, thanks. Anyway, we got this new car. Take a look."

Smiling politely, the two inspectors set about their work, circling the Firebird and making perfunctory notes on the clipboard. "Could you start it up, please?" asked the first inspector.

Adams nodded. "Hey, Tom." Nell continued to work in the engine compartment. "Tom!" repeated Adams.

"What?" responded a voice from under the hood.

"I'm starting it up. Tech inspection."

Nell reluctantly extracted himself from the engine compartment and gazed at the inspectors. "Oh ..."

The inspectors smiled and nodded at Nell, who squinted back at them wiping his hands slowly.

Adams entered the car, stepped on the clutch and twisted the key. The inspectors stood frozen for a moment at the sound of the idling car, number 96. One blinked repeatedly at his clipboard. The other simply stared slack-jawed at the open engine compartment. They gathered themselves and began muttering to each other. One of them walked around to the driver's side and spoke to Adams. "Could you gas it a little, please?" Adams flashed his teeth and squeezed the accelerator. The engine sang.

The inspector's eyes narrowed as he muttered something. Adams glanced in the rearview mirror at the other inspector, who was now staring at the car's tailpipes with wide eyes and wrinkled brows. Adams read his lips. "*Oh my God ...*"

~~~~

Race day. Herb Adams held a sheet of paper, studying familiar names on the starting grid of the "over two liter sedan" race scheduled to begin in a few minutes. Some names were unfamiliar, but a few others were not. Not surprising, thought Adams. These guys—and many others—would race for nothing if they had to, fame and money be dammed. They raced for the love of it.

"Welcome ladies and gentlemen," bellowed the loudspeaker, "to the first race of the 1972 Trans-Am racing season—the Schaefer Beer Trans-Am Race here at Lime Rock Park!" An approving roar erupted from the growing crowd. "In 131 laps, ladies and gentlemen, we will have a winner who will take home $4,000!" said the announcer.

Adams glanced up at the crowd and felt some butterflies flit through his guts. He hadn't noticed the number of fans. Glancing around the track, he quickly estimated 25,000 people. Wow. More than last year. More butterflies. Adams closed his eyes, drew a long breath, and slowly exhaled. *We've done this before.* The butterflies continued. *We've got a good driver.* He felt beads of sweat forming on his forehead. *We've got a good car and a good spot in the starting grid.*

He overheard Nell's voice. "Push it hard now, Tony, it's a good machine. You can be confident in it ..."

Adams turned to see DeLorenzo slipping into the Firebird. "Yeah," DeLorenzo responded. "I'm hip. I'll push it. Push it like hell. I got confidence ..." DeLorenzo stood on the clutch, moved the Hurst stick into neutral, turned the key and with great satisfaction listened to the powerplant purr to life beneath the shining black shaker hood. He eased the Hurst into first gear, gently lifted his left foot from the clutch, winked at his pit crew, and rolled down pit road toward the track among the growing cacophony of harsh racing car engines.

A member of a competitor's pit crew ogled the low-slung, humming car number 96 as it quietly rumbled past him. Without breaking his gaze, he tapped a team member on the arm and pointed at the Firebird's tailpipes. The team member winced, scratched the top of his head, and shook it slowly.

DeLorenzo guided his purring rocket onto the Main Straight, joining his competitors on their warm-up laps, and squeezed the gas pedal. The big black slicks slowly warmed as DeLorenzo deliberately swerved his car from side to side on the track. After a few purposeful trips around the track, DeLorenzo coasted into his allotted position on the starting grid, swallowed hard and fixed his eyes on the starter.

He barely heard the roar of the crowd over the furious clatter spewing from his competitors' engines. DeLorenzo swallowed hard again. He pressed the clutch and eased the Hurst into first gear. The rear-facing black hood scoop trembled above the idling engine, like a thoroughbred in the starting gate. The starter slowly raised the green flag.

Time stretched. Seconds became minutes. DeLorenzo eased off the clutch and began softly squeezing the accelerator with his foot, still pressing on the massive brakes with his other foot. The Firebird's nose dropped slightly as the potent black machine coiled, straining to be released. The starter held the green flag above his head, quivering. The black hood scoop shook violently now, jutting above a smooth, mechanical, impatient growl. DeLorenzo braced himself.

The starter dropped the flag.

In an instant the world became engulfed in a deafening roar as thirty race cars simultaneously snapped open their throttles. DeLorenzo mashed the gas pedal to the floor and was rammed back into his seat as his purring black animal sprang to life, accelerating down the Main Straight. He hung the Hurst into second gear and rocketed confidently around the flat Big Bend, passing two cars. He steered back to the left, into the Esses as the gumball tires glued the black car to the track. DeLorenzo smoothly shifted into third gear and squeezed the accelerator fast as he entered No Name Straight. The humming powerplant gleefully unleashed its pent-up power, ripping down the straight and passing another competitor. DeLorenzo shifted into fourth gear and gassed it hard. The familiar tiger-like growl screamed from the tailpipes until DeLorenzo eased off in his approach to Climbing Turn. He hit the apex and vaulted onto the Back Straight, stuck the Hurst shifter into fourth gear and pushed the gas pedal to the floor. The seatback pressed against his tingling spine as car 96 passed another competitor and reached 135 mph. *Only a few cars ahead of me ...*

Approaching West Bend, DeLorenzo squeezed the brake pedal and downshifted. The screaming engine quieted to a familiar purr as the car hit the apex. DeLorenzo eased the stick into fourth and tried to ram the gas pedal through the floor. Car 96 winged toward Driving Turn before DeLorenzo slowed to take the sweeping right bend. The massive slicks groaned as the Firebird rocketed around the turn. At the apex, DeLorenzo up-shifted before blistering onto the straightaway and past pit road in a sparkling, black blur. *Only 130 more like that ...*

As the race wore on, it became clear that a Javelin was the team to beat. It lapped the field twice before finishing first after 131 laps. The real race was for second, and it was fought among three cars: a Camaro, another Javelin, and a low black Firebird with DeLorenzo behind the wheel, car number 96. The Camaro took second and car 96 took third, along with $2,500 and four points for the Pontiac team.

As DeLorenzo rolled into the pit, the crew surrounded him, cheering and banging on the car with their hands. DeLorenzo slid out from behind the wheel and was immediately surrounded by the grinning crew, hopping up and down, slapping him hard on the back and shouting their appreciation. Adams approached the driver and their eyes met. "Damn," said DeLorenzo. "You'd think I just won the Indy 500 or something!"

Adams grinned. "You gotta remember, man—this morning we didn't have a driver, weren't even sure we'd race. And now we got third!"

"Yeah. Well, you got a great car here."

"Great driver, too. Thanks for taking a chance on us and at the last minute."

"Hell, I didn't take a chance. I mean, everyone knows your reputation, man. I'm just happy to help."

~~~~

On the way back to Detroit, Herb Adams sat in the passenger seat of the Suburban, poring over papers. Tom Nell was driving, the Firebird in tow on its flatbed trailer.

"Whatcha lookin' at?" asked Nell flatly.

Adams looked out the windshield, scratching his head. "We got the Bryar 200 in New Hampshire at the end of the month—May 29th—and I'm not sure we've got a driver. DeLorenzo says he can't make it."

Nell shook his head. "Still can't believe Minter didn't show. And who knows if he'll appear at Bryar. I mean his credibility is shot." Nell gritted his teeth and took a deliberate deep breath, exhaling slowly. "Anyway man, let's celebrate our third place finish and our newfound cash for a while before we worry about the next race. The car's in good shape. It did great today."

Adams looked at his teammate and allowed himself a small grin. "Yeah, maybe we can take it easy for a while."

~~~~

On Monday morning, after receiving congratulations from his co-workers, Herb Adams picked up his office phone and dialed a number. "Ja?" answered a voice on the other end of the phone.

"Milt? It's Herb Adams."

"Oh, yes."

"Uh, Milt, we missed you at the race this weekend. What happened, man?"

"Oh ... I, uh ... well ... I ..."

"What? You couldn't find the track or something?"

"Yeah."

"Really? You couldn't find the track? But you raced at Lime Rock before."

"Yeah ... well, couldn't find it this time. Sorry."

Adams eyes darted around, his head processing this information. "You let us down, man. I mean we bust our asses to prepare the car and then you don't show for the race. The guys are pissed, man."

"Sorry, man," Minter said genuinely. "I got no excuse."

"So, you still want to drive for us? DeLorenzo did a great job for us at Lime Rock."

"Hell yeah, I want to drive for you, man. I just screwed up once. I won't do it again."

Adams paused. "You sure?"

"I'm your driver. Count on it."

"OK, well how about the next race? It's at Bryar. You know— Loudon, New Hampshire."

"Yes."

"You'll be there?"

"You bet."

"You can find it okay?"

"Oh, yeah. I'll find it."

"Okay. We're counting on you."

"I won't let you down. You don't need DeLorenzo."

"Okay—see you May 27th. Race is on the 29th."

"Understood."

"At Bryar—in Loudon, New Hampshire."

"I know."

"Okay. See you then …"

"Count on it, man."

Adams cocked his head at the receiver before gingerly hanging it up.

"Hey, man," said Tom Nell, standing at the office doorway. "You all right?"

Adams shot a perplexed look at the phone. "Just had a talk with Milt."

"How come he didn't show at Lime Rock?" spat Nell through clenched teeth.

Adams scratched his chin. "Says he couldn't find it."

Nell's eyes narrowed. "But he's been there before—he's raced there."

"I know," said Adams, studying the phone.

Nell's eyes narrowed. "Well is he gonna show at Bryar?"

"He says so …"

"But what if he doesn't?"

Adams drew a long breath and exhaled slowly. "We punt again—just like last week."

Chapter 40

"HEY LOOK," SAID Adams, standing beside Nell and the Firebird in the Bryar pit. Adams beamed at the sight of the man walking toward him. "Hi Milt," said Adams enthusiastically. "Glad you could make it!"

Minter grinned back, "Yeah—I found it," he said with a hint of embarrassment. The men shook hands. Adams, relieved, slapped Minter on the back. A smiling Tom Nell dropped the newspaper and extended his hand to the new driver.

"Well, here she is," said Adams turning to the Firebird.

Minter eyed the car, nodding his approval. "Nice and low ... big front tires. How come?"

"Better grip." Minter looked at him skeptically. "Remember the GTO we ran last year?" asked Nell.

"Yeah ..."

"Well, it had big gumballs on the front, too—worked great."

Minter nodded, resuming his inspection of the car.

Adams raised the hood. "Look at the engine. We got special headers," said Nell.

Minter squinted into the engine compartment. "What's so special?"

"We—really Herb—built the exhaust system so that the firing order agrees with the exhaust pipes," explained Nell. "The exhaust fumes are not being jammed into the same tight space at once, see, so we get a nice smooth exhaust flow. And more power because there's no exhaust backup."

Minter blinked rapidly. Recognition dawned across his face. "How's it handle?"

"Give it a try," said Adams through a wide grin. "DeLorenzo took third three weeks ago at Lime Rock."

"*DeLorenzo*," grunted Minter with a scowl. He entered the car, donned his helmet and started the engine. A pure mechanical note sang from the tailpipes. Minter's eyes widened. "This pass tech inspection?"

"Yeah," said Adams, still smiling. "It's the headers—I told you."

"Yeah. Yeah. Cool pipes." Milt grinned widely at the steering wheel.

~~~~

Milt Minter remembered Bryar as a tight little road course with unbanked turns and four straightaways. It was about a mile and a half around and laid out in the shape of a molar, with two legs at the bottom and a crown at the top. Minter squeezed the clutch to the floor, eased the Hurst into first gear and purred slowly down pit road past the eyes of twenty-nine competing teams. He guided the black machine onto the main straight and gunned it. The car erupted in a fury of power, mashing Minter into the seatback. He eased off the gas, tapped the clutch, quickly hung the Hurst into third gear, and pressed the accelerator. Again the black car rocketed in a flurry of power, acceleration and smooth growl.

Minter nodded approvingly at the dashboard, grinning widely. He slowed as the track curved to the left before doubling back to the right, then to the left again. He had the feeling this car could take this chicane much faster. He eased off the gas before rounding down to the right and completing the top of the molar, the top of the track. He eased the clutch into third as he approached the long straightaway at the back of the track and gassed it. The car shot forward. Minter heel-toe shifted into fourth and stuck the gas to the floor. He felt his cheeks become slightly distorted from the acceleration as the engine sang like a baritone. Minter pressed the engine hard down the straightaway as it approached 125 mph. *OK, engine, you passed the test, but I ain't done with the rest of you, car ...*

Approaching the right hairpin at the end of the straight, Minter eased off the gas, downshifted and squeezed the brakes hard. The big slicks spewed a smoking, squealing protest as the black machine hurtled around the hairpin. *Oh, yeah ...*

Minter accelerated north toward the next hairpin—this one to the left. He rounded the turn aggressively and roared onto the short straight. He pushed the car hard into the next turn—a right bend leading to the main straightaway. He blipped the car around the last turn and gassed it hard at the apex. His face was pushed out of shape again as the Firebird sling-shotted out of the last curve onto the straight, the big wide tires leaving wisps of acrid rubber smoke to commingle with the hot, blue-gray exhaust. Car 96 rocketed past dozens of attentive eyes in pit road in a black, acoustically perfect blur. *Jesus ... This thing's a Swiss watch.*

~~~~

Herb Adams squinted at a piece of paper listing the starting grid for tomorrow's race. "Pretty good, hey?" said Nell from beside him. "We qualified in second place. We only got that Javelin ahead of us—again." Nell glanced at the track. "Minter can *drive*, man. I mean, if he can drive like that tomorrow, all is forgiven about Lime Rock."

"Well ..." said Adams.

Nell shot his boss a puzzled look. "Well what? What's a matter, Herb?"

"Nothing's the matter. It's just that I hear that Javelin has some trouble."

Nell couldn't contain his smile. "Gee—too bad. What kind of trouble?"

Adams shrugged his shoulders, "Car trouble, that's all I heard."

Nell slowly put his fingers together, forming a steeple. "So ..." he muttered, turning his attention to Adams, "we may get the pole."

Adams met his gaze and smiled.

~~~~

"Milt," said Herb Adams slowly the next morning, race day. "I got good news."

"What is it?" responded Minter as he scanned the track.

"We're on the pole."

Minter snapped his gaze from the track to Adams' eyes. "The pole?"

Adams nodded. "Yes. We're starting at the head of the pack. Hot shot's got trouble with his Javelin—he's got to start at the end of the field. So we move from second to first."

Minter grunted and jutted out his lower jaw. "Good. Nobody in my way at the start."

"But we got 95 laps—"

"Yeah, and I'm gonna make 'em quick," said the driver as he eased into the black Firebird.

Tom Nell squatted at the driver's door, looking at Minter. "Now don't forget to check the oil pressure, and—"

"Hey, how about another number?" interrupted Minter.

"What?" asked Nell.

"I don't like 96."

Nell furrowed his brows, squinted, and cocked his head slightly at the driver. "You *what?*" The other cars were starting their engines.

Adams gently put his hand on Nell's shoulder and looked at the driver. "What number you want, Milt?" asked Adams patiently.

Minter connected his chin strap and looked at Adams. "Zero."

"ZERO?" shouted Nell.

Adams squeezed Nell's shoulder. "Okay, okay—we'll change it to zero for the next race," said Adams.

Nell stood up, absently scratching his head.

"Now get out there and win," shouted Adams.

"Yeah, baby!"

~~~~

During the course of the next 95 laps at Bryar, the favorite Javelin relentlessly, methodically snaked his way through the field until he caught the black Firebird at the head of the field. Despite Milt Minter's best efforts he could not hold off the Javelin, which passed the finish line in first, followed by car 96 in second. A Camaro took third.

After the race, Minter rolled the Firebird into pit road and coasted to a stop. The crowd cheered as Minter exited the car. He waved to them before turning his attention to Adams.

"How much is second worth?" he asked Adams.

"Good race, Milt …"

"How much?"

"Uh, $3,000 I think."

"Good." Minter pulled off his helmet. "I could have won, but …"

The smile fell from Adams' face. "But *what?*"

"I didn't want to risk it."

Adams cocked his head slightly. "Why not?"

Minter shrugged. "I wanted to be sure you guys won some money— you need cash. So I didn't want to crash and get you nothing."

Adams shook his head slowly at the driver. "Yeah," he chuckled. "We need the bread, man. But next time, I want you really bookin'. Screw the money. You get me?"

Minter raised his eyebrows and a thin smile grew across his dry lips. "Okay, man."

Chapter 41

THE FIREBIRD RACING team stood in Herb Adams' garage, staring at car 96. Nell shook his head, "Herb, you really want to change the number? What's the problem with 96?"

"Yeah," agreed Dutch. "It ain't the number of the anti-Christ or nothin', for Christ's sake."

Adams looked at his shoes and held up his hands. "Listen," he said slowly. "We got a real good driver and he wants a new number."

"But *zero?*" asked a voice from the corner. "What kind of number is that for a Trans-Am car?"

Adams smiled. "So, he's a little ... different. Who cares? He got us results at Bryar, didn't he? And I'll bet he does it again this weekend at Mid-Ohio." Adams scanned the stubborn faces in his garage. "And it's not like we've got a blown engine to rebuild before now and Friday. Hell, we got *nothing* to do to the car. It's running like a charm."

"But ain't it bad luck to change the number?" asked Dutch, his nostrils spewing twin streams of cigarette smoke. "It's bad luck."

"No. Changing the name of a boat—that's bad luck, maybe. But the number of a car?"

Silence. "It's easy," Adams continued. "We pull off two decals and slap two new ones on. See, I already got them right here." Adams held up a rectangular decal with an oblong "0" in the center. He shrugged his shoulders, "Simple. And when Minter wins Mid-Ohio in a couple of days, we'll forget all about this."

~~~~

Herb Adams and Milt Minter stood next to the newly christened "0" car, studying the Mid-Ohio track in the warm, June morning.

"They fixed up the track some," said Minter flatly.

"Yeah," Adams scanned the track. "They put up more guardrails. Cut some trees that were too close to the track. Put in that hospital at the end of pit road. And laid down new asphalt."

Minter studied the black track. "New?"

"New."

Minter inhaled deeply and slowly exhaled. The men knew the significance of fresh asphalt. There was no need to discuss it. New, unseasoned asphalt is far more challenging because the tires don't grip it as well. As a result, drivers have to be more vigilant to avoid getting loose on the corners, resulting in spinouts. The problem worsened on sunny, hot days—the asphalt could become mushy and could even break up.

Marbles. There would be some sliding cars on this track. The new guardrails would be tested.

"What's the forecast for tomorrow?" asked Minter, staring down at the black hardtop.

"Sunny. Hot, 85 or so. But that's gonna help us," said Adams through a grin.

Minter shot Adams a skeptical look. "How?"

Adams glanced down the line of glinting pony cars in pit road. "We've got something they don't."

"I know, a hell of a good driver."

"I wish," Adams snorted with a grin. "But something else, too. Big tires all around."

Minter's furrowed brow gave way to a grin as he nodded. "Big *sticky* tires. Four of 'em."

Minter tested the soft, warm asphalt with this big toe, turned, and walked away from the track toward the nearest grandstand. He walked up the center aisle, stopped at the top and turned to view the track. He remembered Mid-Ohio's flat and plentiful turns, but this track would be different now with its new surface. His hawk-like eyes ran clockwise around the black strip below him, past pit road and the start/finish line on the east-west straightaway. He visualized the low-slung, black Trans Am with its mammoth tires leaving the pit to the west, following the new asphalt to a left 90-degree bend leading down a long straight to a right-left-right mish-mash they creatively called a chicane. His virtual car followed the immaculate black asphalt as the track instantly bent back to the right into a 180-degree turn to the north. Keyhole Chicane.

Nodding imperceptibly, Minter imagined driving his Trans Am, optically tracing the Keyhole carefully before following the track directly north into the long straightaway that bent slightly to the right at the halfway point where grandstands were perched. Minter's practiced eye followed his speeding imaginary car on the straight into the Esses—a snaking chicane. This would be a good place to pass the skimpy-tired competitors. He would put the big gumballs to good use here.

Minter imagined his car following the track as it spilled out of the Esses and straightened out briefly before leading east. Following the fresh asphalt, Minter's eyes directed the black car onto a 90-degree south turn, flowing to the right, then back left before entering the 180 degree right called the Carousel. He visually traced the Carousel as it joined the last straightaway. His eyes darted past the start/finish line, willing his imaginary black machine forward. He took a deep breath, closed his eyes, and slowly exhaled as the checkered flag waved furiously in his mind's eye.

~~~~

Moments later, Minter rumbled his black Trans Am around the Mid-Ohio circuit, deliberately warming up amid the skittish young pony cars on their skinny, delicate tires. Minter again took a deep breath and slowly exhaled. The Trans Am felt anxious to Minter, eager for its driver to tap the accelerator and rip into a neck-jarring blast. At the end of the Carousel, Minter granted the car's wish—he hung the Hurst rapidly into third gear and mashed the gas pedal against the sole of his right foot. The glinting, hot black machine spat a harmonious thunder from its tailpipes and screamed past the furiously waving green flag. The qualifying race was on.

The black Pontiac squealed around the big bend to the left and rocketed down the straight in fourth gear to Keyhole Chicane. Minter downshifted, shot through the chicane and swung around the Keyhole, forcing
the driver to fight the centrifugal forces that pressed him hard into the
door. Minter smoothly pressed the Hurst shifter into fourth and squeezed
the accelerator to the bare metal floor pan. The Trans Am rammed its
driver into the seatback as the engine sang along the back straight. *We must
be at 150 easy* ...

Minter lifted his foot from the gas and coasted, screaming around the
easy right bend to the next straight. He downshifted back into third,
pressed the gas and sang through the Esses, cutting the apexes hard and
close as the big tires alternately rooted themselves into the virgin black asphalt. The black car accelerated in a blur along the short straight at the top
of the track, followed it south around the bend, and Minter lightly threw the
stick into fourth as he squeezed the pedal to the floor.

The car melodiously ripped down the straightaway and bit the corner
into the Carousel. Minter downshifted, careened through the Carousel and
gently leaned on the pedal again. The car and its driver were as one. Minter
quickly guided the stick into fourth gear as car number "0" echoed its
beautiful voice flashing past pit row and the start/finish line.

"*Goddamn!*" muttered Herb Adams at his stopwatch in pit road. Minter
finished with an average speed of 84.716 miles per hour.

A few laps later Milt Minter pulled into pit road, eased himself out of
the Trans Am and into the circle of grinning pit crew engineers. Through
the little crowd Herb Adams caught Minter's eye and waved him over.

Minter held his helmet under his arm, smiling broadly at Adams. "We
got a good car."

"Yeah," agreed Adams. "Nice job out there."

~~~~

But now Adams knew they had more than a good car. They had another
good driver. Tullius was outstanding last year and now they had Minter.
Through years of experience as an automotive engineer, racecar builder,
and some time behind the wheel, Adams recognized good racecar drivers

when he saw them. They were guys who were somehow able to do what Adams himself could never seem to do—extract 100 percent of the performance potential from a racecar. They squeezed their machines so hard, they left nothing on the track but black rubber and blue smoke. These guys got beaten occasionally, but not for lack of effort or skill.

Adams didn't exactly know how they did it. It was part shifting, part acceleration, part braking, part luck, part judgment. And maybe it was just big balls. Whatever it was, only a relatively few guys really had it. Parnelli Jones had it. Adams now knew that Minter had it too—at least occasionally. These qualifying laps sure as hell proved he had it today. There was little chance anyone else would take the pole at Mid-Ohio now.

It was more than just the car. Today it was also the driver. Herb Adams knew it, he felt it. At his best, Milt Minter was a 100 percent driver.

~~~~

That evening, through bloodshot eyes, Milt Minter stood next to Herb Adams and examined the high arch of empty beer cans over a motel room door before closely examining his own can.

"You had a good day today, man," said Adams to the driver.

"Yeah, but a good car, too." Minter took a long, slow pull from his beer can. "Good speed, good feel, good sound even," he burped.

Adams studied the driver. "Yeah, it's a good car, but you get everything out of it."

Minter shrugged, admiring the beer can arch.

"I mean it, man," continued Adams without a hint of reservation. "There's lots of good cars out there. But to win, they need good drivers."

Minter squinted suspiciously at Adams and took another gulp of beer.

Adams shook his head earnestly, "Listen, some drivers are 85 percent guys, some are 95 percent guys."

Minter scratched his forehead, "What?"

Adams swirled his warm, flat beer around in the can and burped. "See, there ain't many guys who are 100 percent drivers."

Minter drained the last of his beer and walked slowly toward the arch of beer cans. "What the hell's a 100 percent driver?" he asked.

"It's a guy who gets absolutely everything from his car—he pushes it as hard as the laws of physics let him, without losing control. So he leaves nothing on the track. No wasted motion, no wasted effort, no wasted energy or speed."

Reaching over the doorway, Minter carefully placed his empty can at the top of the arch. "And no wasted beers."

~~~~

The next morning, Tom Nell stood in pit road next to the Firebird, eyes wide. "*Hey,*" he muttered urgently to Adams. "*Hey—Herb!*"

"What?" answered Adams shortly.

Nell explained a rumor he had just heard about a hot-shot driver who had flown in last night from Canada and was planning to race today in a Javelin. It was the driver who had won the first two races of the season.

"So what?" responded Adams. "I think we can take him. In the first race of the season, we took third. Second race, we took second. I see a trend."

"Yeah, me too, but—" Nell stopped short and pointed at the ground a short distance away at Minter, "*Look!*"

Adams looked. "What? Look at what? I don't see anything but Milt."

Nell stepped closer, whispering in Adams ear. "The *shoes!*"

"The what?" Adams asked, studying Nell's face for a clue.

"*Shoes,* dammit! His *shoes!*"

Adams recoiled slightly from Nell before glancing at Minter's shoes. Instead of the lace-up driving shoes he expected, Adams saw something else on his driver's feet—black, scuffed wingtips. Adams blinked hard.

"Our guy—the guy on the *pole*—is wearing *Florsheims!*" whispered Nell loudly.

Adams rubbed the back of his neck slowly. "*Jesus ...*" Adams swallowed hard as he slowly approached his driver. "Milt ..."

"Yeah," the driver said, smiling.

Adams cleared his throat. "Well ... you ... um ..." Adams looked down pit road at the other drivers and their glinting cars. The race announcer began to speak over the loudspeaker system.

"What?" asked Minter. "What you want?"

Adams looked at his driver's scruffy dress shoes and rubbed his forehead. "Well, your shoes—they …"

Minter looked down at his shoes. "Oh, yeah … forgot."

Adams cocked his head quizzically. "Forgot what? To change your shoes?"

"No," answered Minter flatly, "forgot ta bring driving shoes."

"But you had them yesterday."

Minter shrugged. "Yeah, but now they're in … motel room."

Stunned, Adams broke an incredulous glare from his driver's eyes and glanced at his watch. The motel was not particularly close by and they all had plenty of preparation work to do right here. The race began soon. Adams swore under his breath.

"It's okay," said Minter reassuringly. He took a long swig on a big cup of water, lifted a foot and waggled it casually. "I drive before in these babies."

~~~~

Adams, rubbing his forehead hard, slowly circled the low-slung black Trans Am in one last pre-race inspection. The side windows were encircled by a thin red stripe that continued forward down the length of the front quarter panels to the front bumper. Another red stripe punctuated the roof, crossing just above the windshield. A silver, reflective, sideways number "0" adorned each door. Sponsor's decals—five on each front quarter panel and another one on each rear quarter panel—gave the car a commercial yet professional look. More importantly, they helped pay the way.

One sponsor was a rental trailer hauling company. The other sponsors were in the automobile business: oil companies, a spark plug supplier, a tire maker and a wheel manufacturer among them. The rear-facing air scoop jutted menacingly from the shaker hood, a hint of the high-performance powerplant below it. The wires from three hood pins snaked behind the split Pontiac grill. At the rear, another skinny red stripe highlighted the top edge of the car's ample spoiler. Below it were the gaping tailpipes from which the black machine's siren sound would soon sing to Mid-Ohio.

It was a good car.

"We got a problem," said Dutch from beneath the Trans Am.

Adams heart skipped a beat. "What problem?"

Dutch slid out on his back from under the car and slowly sat up. "Diff housing's cracked. Axle."

"Shit." Adams eyes narrowed. "Let me see," he murmured, scrambling under the rear of the car. "Dutch, get Nell over here."

"I'm right here," said Nell. "What's up?"

Adams slid out from under the car. "Cracked differential housing."

"How bad?" asked Nell.

Adams looked at Dutch. Dutch shook his head.

Nell glanced at his watch. "Three hours to race time."

Adams sat up slowly. This was worse than the Florsheims. "We need a welder. Fast."

~~~~

Forty-five minutes later, a pungent blue smoke rose from beneath the black Trans Am. Further down pit road Herb Adams cleared his throat as he approached a competitor, who broke off his conversation with his driver. "Everything okay?" the competitor asked Adams.

"Not quite yet, but thanks to you and your welder, it will be soon."

The competitor wiped his hands with a shop towel and nodded in the direction of the black Trans Am. "That's Peter Brock doing the welding. He's running an under-two liter car for Datsun. You'd do the same for him, Herb. And you'd do the same for me."

"Yeah. Anyway, thanks a lot for putting us in touch with him. I'm not sure many other guys out here would have helped the pole sitter like this. I mean we only got a couple hours to go and then we get a big crack in the diff case." Adams looked around. "Some of these guys probably celebrated on hearing that news. Not you. So, thanks." The men shook hands.

"Well, some car you got there. Sounds like a Ferrari or something. Hate to see all that work go for naught."

"Yeah, well, anything I can ever do for you, just let me know."

"Okay. Good luck."

Milt Minter, watching this conversation, took another long swig of cool water from his big mug. It was hot.

~~~~

A short time later, Adams found himself on his back again, under the rear end of the jacked-up Trans Am examining the axle's differential case. The welder had done a nice job. Adams slid out from beneath. "Beautiful," he said through a wide grin.

"Almost as good as me," said Dutch flatly.

~~~~

"Welcome ladies and gentlemen," boomed the loudspeakers to 30,000 fans in the searing heat, "to the 1972 Mid-Ohio Trans-Am." The announced waited for the cheering to subside. "Our race today will be 180 miles long—75 laps around the newly renovated Mid-Ohio circuit. Milt Minter in the number zero Pontiac Firebird Trans Am is on the pole with a qualifying time of 84.7 miles an hour. This machine was prepared by the same group that campaigned the Gray Ghost here last year." The crowd roared its approval.

"They remember," shouted a familiar voice from behind Adams. He turned to see Bob Tullius' smiling face.

Adams clutched his chest in surprise and heartily shook Tullius' hand. "Glad you could make it," said Adams.

"Wouldn't miss it."

"Feeling better?"

Tullius nodded. "Not enough to be out on the track, but a hell of a lot better than before." The cars rumbled to life in pit road, spewing an audible torrent of power across the green Ohio hills.

Adams gave his former driver the thumbs up.

The pony cars rumbled out of pit road and slowly accelerated around the track in two-by-two formation at 45 miles an hour. The pace lap had begun. Next to Minter in the starting grid, on the outside of the front row, was the number 1 Javelin. Behind them in the grid were the number 24

Mustang and number 63 Javelin. Thirty-three other cars, all late-model
Mustangs, Camaros and Javelins, made up the balance of the field.

The checkered flag furiously waved as the accelerating Pontiac and
Javelin ripped across the starting line. The Javelin screamed into the lead
and passed under the bridge ahead of its black pursuer into the first turn.
The angry black Pontiac tore around the big bend and rocketed down the
straight, pursuing the rabbit-like Javelin with ravenous intensity. The cars
swung into Keyhole Chicane in rapid succession, where Minter downshifted
and swung around the Keyhole, pressing him hard against the interior of
the door. Minter allowed himself a small grin. He calmly eased the stick into
fourth and squeezed the gas pedal as far as it would travel. The Firebird
savagely mashed its driver into the seatback. The big engine's song increased in pitch, ripping along the back straight. Then the rear view mirror
flopped down.

"Shit …" muttered Minter, fumbling to adjust it back up.

On the straightaway, the Javelin held its own against the Pontiac behind it. Minter eased off on the pedal and screeched around the slow right
bend into the next straight, still gaining again on the skittish Javelin.

Minter's mirror sagged again. *Who needs it?*

Minter downshifted, hit the gas easy and tore through the Esses, gaining fast now on his quarry. The low black machine galloped along the short
straight at the top of the track and closely traced it south around the bend,
hugging the apex, closing in on the Javelin's tailpipes, nearly touching them.

Minter meshed the stick into fourth and mashed the pedal. The cars
were neck and neck. Minter downshifted, gassed it through the Carousel
and hit the pedal again. His crouching black machine overtook the Javelin
in a burst of harmonious power.

One of the hood latches popped open. *So what?*

Minter snapped the stick into fourth and sped past the start/finish
line, engine growling in triumph.

In the second lap, Minter extended his lead by three seconds over the
Javelin, which was again being hotly pursued—this time by the number 24
Mustang, which hung on the Javelin's tailpipe for nearly the entire lap. Just
behind the second and third place cars was a group that included the
number 63 Javelin, the number 13 Camaro, the number 3 Mustang, and the

number 31 Mustang. But most concerning to Herb Adams and his crew was the fact that the hotshot driver in the number 2 Javelin had already rocketed from 33rd to 11th.

In the third lap, Minter extended his lead by another second over the Javelin, and the big group was ten seconds behind him. Adams wiped a bead of sweat from his creased brow; the hotshot in his number 2 Javelin was now only three seconds behind the big group.

In the fourth lap, Mid-Ohio claimed its first victim. The number 44 Javelin, which had moved from 34th place to the middle of the pack, blew a valve and dropped out. Meanwhile, the hotshot moved into 6th, just behind the number 31 Javelin. Pounded unrelentingly by the pony cars, small hunks of the new track began to break apart in the blazing Ohio heat. The asphalt chunks—marbles—spewed to both the outside and the inside of the track, leaving a single lane for the skinny-wheeled cars to maintain control. But the Firebird, with its big gumballs on all four corners, confidently ripped over the marbles.

In the tenth lap, the number 24 Mustang left the track's groove, crept too close to the edge, slid into the marbles, and was forced to hit the brakes to regain control. The hotshot in the number 2 Javelin exploited the situation and screamed past into second, but he chronically trailed the loping black Firebird by five seconds and the number 24 Mustang, who quickly regained control, was hot on his trail in third. During the next 14 laps, the real race was for second. Then, in lap 24, the number 24 Mustang's engine began to shudder. Sensing a serious and expensive problem if he pressed the matter, the driver wisely decided to coast into pit road. It proved to be the end of the race for the Ford.

In the 42nd lap, the number 3 Mustang dropped out with a busted timing chain. At the halfway point, the hotshot pitted for gas and left-side tires. Almost immediately upon re-entering the race the car's right front tire blew, forcing it to pit again.

"Too bad," grinned Dutch to himself, exhaling a long stream of cigarette smoke.

The number 13 Camaro easily roared into second, but by lap 50 he was a full minute behind the galloping, howling black Firebird at the head of the pack. The hotshot was five seconds behind the Camaro in third.

Milt Minter began to squirm in his seat. He had to piss.

The hotshot moved into second and began slowly closing on Minter. The Pontiac's lead dwindled to 20 seconds. Then the new asphalt claimed another victim; one of the hotshot's tires blew, sending him off the course, spinning in the grass and damaging the Javelin's steering. The car hobbled a full mile to the pit.

Minter winced. Could he pit to piss?

In lap 60, the second place Camaro blew a tire and the hotshot ripped into second, drawing a bead on Minter's Firebird. Five laps later, with their car in the lead, Adams and his crew experienced the unthinkable: the black Firebird spun out.

Minter's bladder could resist no longer. He urinated in his seat.

"Shit," muttered Adams sharply from the pit. The crowed moaned.

Minter quickly regained control and gassed his car back onto the track, but not before the hotshot, now back in second place, gained nine seconds on him despite the fact that the Javelin was unable to fully turn to the left as a result of its earlier spinout.

Minter groaned a loud sigh of relief. The pressure was off his bladder and he was still in first.

Adams turned to Nell. "Twenty laps left?" he asked nervously.

Nell frowned, glancing at his clipboard. "No—only fifteen."

Adams shook his head, "We're on sixty now."

"Yeah, fifteen left."

"But we got eighty laps total."

Nell shook his head, "No, man—only seventy-five."

Adams' eyes narrowed. "Not eighty?"

"Nope—seventy-five. That's it, man. Seventy-five laps."

Adams took a deep breath and studied his clipboard. "Then we put too much gas in at the last pit stop."

"So what," responded Nell matter-of-factly. "Won't matter. Minter is kicking ass."

"But he just spun out …"

Nell grinned at his boss. "He'll be all right. We got a good lead. Only fifteen more laps."

The Firebird flashed past pit road. "Make that fourteen."

~~~~

With three laps remaining and the Firebird comfortably in first, Adams began to feel his heart creep into his throat. Could Minter keep it on the
track? Would he spin out again? Would the engine blow? Would the weld
on the axle fail? Would he get hit by a car he was lapping? *God ...*

At lap 74, Minter was 54 seconds ahead. Minter stuck his left hand out
the window and waved to the crowd. The pit crew began to congratulate
each other. Adams took a deep breath.

This was really happening. They were going to actually win.

A flood of memories washed over him. Bloody knuckles, bitter coffee,
greasy shirts and cheap beer. Coke bottles full of gas. Sleep deprivation.
And the Gray Ghost.

As the black Pontiac loped toward the finish line, the starter ran onto
the track, checkered flag in hand. The Pontiac pit crew erupted in celebration as the starter furiously waved the checkered flag at the Firebird crossing the finish line. Minter's left arm waved wildly out the window, and 54
seconds later, the hotshot sped across the finish line in second place.

Pontiac had won its first ever Trans-Am race.

Minter coasted into pit road and came to a gentle stop alongside his
jubilant pit crew. Adams' smiling face thrust through the driver's side window at Milt Minter. "Yeah man, you did it!" shouted Adams.

Minter grinned, embarrassed. "Yeah. Bucket of water ..."

"What?" asked Adams. "What'd you say?"

Minter shot a glance to his right and then over his left shoulder.
"Water—throw it at my crotch."

Adams' face crinkled. "Water? Why? We got water if you're thirsty."
Adams thrust a water bottle through the window. "Here. Now get out of
the car, come on."

"No. Not thirsty ..."

The pit crew screamed in celebration, hopping around the car. One of
them pounded his fist excitedly on the black hood. Adams, surrounded by
screaming teammates, leaned into the car. "Milt, we just won the race. What
in hell is the matter with you?"

Minter glanced at his crotch. "Well ... I ..."

Adams, his brow furrowed, shook his head and raised his hands. "What? You got to get out of the car now and get the trophy, because you won the goddamn race."

Minter's eyes widened in mild terror. He had to confess. "Yeah, well … throw water on me when I get out. Throw it on my crotch. Lots of it."

"What the hell, Milt?"

Minter stared out the windshield at the celebrating pit crew and drew a deep sigh. "Because I pissed my pants …"

Adams cocked his head quizzically. "You what? You pissed in your pants?"

"Yep! I PISSED MY PANTS, OKAY? So throw water on me so no one can tell."

Adams straightened up, spun around, pointed at a large water jug and barked an order. After a momentary pause, the pit crew brought the jug to the Trans Am's driver's side door.

"Now," Adams whispered loudly. "Right when he gets out, throw the water at his crotch." The bewildered pit crew fell silent. "Just do it," commanded Adams.

Minter pushed the door open, swung his Florsheims onto pit road and stood. He inhaled sharply as a blast of ice cold water flushed his crotch. He caught his breath, thrust his arms in the air and shouted, "Yeah!"

~~~~

A short time later, a reporter asked a water and champagne-soaked Minter whether he could have won if the hotshot had not encountered mechanical trouble. "I knew after the first lap the car was good," Minter replied. "I said to myself, 'Boy, we've got a winner here. If anyone catches me he's going to have to work.'"

Another reporter asked about the floppy rearview mirror.

"I didn't need the rearview mirror anyway today, so it didn't bother me too much." Minter wiped champagne from his stinging eyes and pointed at Adams. "These guys are really good and they'll do anything for you to get the car to run."

Chapter 42

A FEW MONTHS later, Herb Adams stood in his freshly-mowed backyard with a beer in one hand and barbeque tongs in the other. A cool, early-autumn breeze wafted across the yard as half a dozen children played on the grass while the Trans/Action team members and their wives and girlfriends chatted with each other on the back porch. Herb flipped some burgers on the grill.

"Thanks for the barbeque, Herb," said Tom Nell patting his boss on the back. "It's nice of you and Sandi to have invited us all."

"Sure," said Adams. "One last get-together. It's the least we could do for everything you guys did for the team."

"Hey," said a familiar voice. It was Joe Brady. "Heard you guys did okay without me this season." The men shook hands with beaming smiles.

"Somehow we managed," said Adams. "How's graduate school?"

"Good," said Joe. "Not quite as exciting as racing, but not as many bloody knuckles and sleep-deprived nights, either."

"What's next for you, Joe? After graduation?" asked Tom.

"Call me crazy, but I'd like to stay in the auto business. Got an interview with Ford in a few weeks."

"Once a gearhead, always a gearhead," said Adams.

"More like a pencil-neck," said Dutch Scheppleman through a grin.

"How about you, Dutch?" asked Joe. "Any plans?"

Dutch took a long pull on a cigarette and shrugged. "A guy I know at the GM Technical Center wants to talk to me about transferring out there.

Says I'd make a good technician, whatever that is. He heard I was part of the Gray Ghost and Firebird teams."

"So, you going to talk to him?" asked Adams.

"Why not? Something different, maybe."

Harry Quackenboss approached. "The Tech Center?" he asked Dutch. "You'd be surrounded by engineers! Sounds like heaven to me."

"Shit," Dutch grunted. "Didn't think about that. Anyway, how about you, Harry? You still in Ann Arbor?"

Harry nodded, "For now. But long term, I'd like to get into computers and doing some entrepreneurial stuff."

Jeff Young and Tom Goad joined the conversation. "Sounds good," said Jeff. "I'd like to own my own business, too. Maybe out west, like Colorado."

Tom Goad shook his head, "Not me. At this point, I'm going to stick with GM and retire in a few years. I'll leave all that business stuff to you guys. What about Milt? What's he going to do?"

"Let's find out," said Adams. He called Minter over. "What's the future hold for you, Milt? I mean, that oil company signed you as a spokesman or something after we won at Mid-Ohio, right?" asked Adams.

Milt shrugged his shoulders, took a swig of beer and smiled. "I'm not much of a spokesman." He looked at the children playing in the yard under a deep blue sky. "I think I'll just keep driving."

Epilogue

HERB ADAMS AND his team mounted a brief NASCAR campaign in 1973 but Herb resigned from GM in disgust shortly thereafter (but that's another story…). He then worked for a variety of automotive organizations and people in the Detroit area, including Jack and John Delorean, and American Axle & Manufacturing, where he met the author of this book who was then the company's corporate counsel. Herb authored a book called *Chassis Engineering* and "retired" to Tennessee with his wife Sandi in 2012, where he continues to work on various automotive-related projects.

Tom Nell also left GM in 1973 after the short-lived NASCAR campaign and he and his wife Marilyn bought a retail snowmobile shop in Michigan. They later added bicycles to their retail offerings and bought and managed a second shop before retiring to northern Michigan's beautiful Leelanau County in 1997, where they live today.

Joe Brady earned his MBA and thereafter worked briefly for the Ford Motor Company, but never raced professionally again. He married, had four kids and retired in Oklahoma in 2011 after spending 30 years running several oil and gas equipment suppliers. He is still a "gearhead."

Ted Lambiris (the Greek) left GM in 1977 and performed a variety of engineering contract work. He designed the Inland Shifter, which was used by all major U.S. auto manufacturers and later designed a sunroof, which he sold to American Sunroof Corporation ("ASC"). Ted then worked for a variety of automotive suppliers, including ASC and Hurst. He now owns and operates a small re-work and sorting company in the Detroit area that provides services to automotive suppliers.

Dutch Scheppleman transferred to the GM Technical Center in Warren, Michigan as a technician, where GM recognized his talent and promoted him to the salaried ranks. He passed away in 2002.

Don Haller was also promoted to a salaried employee and retired from GM as group leader of the Pontiac Garage at GM's Proving Grounds in Milford, Michigan. He passed away in 2004.

Harry Quackenboss left Honeywell in 1985 and began a career as a self-described "serial entrepreneur" after working in a number of marketing and executive positions with high technology companies, including Cisco Systems and others. He continues his work in Internet and cloud computing technologies in Silicon Valley, where he uses the lessons he learned in racing on nearly a daily basis.

Jeff Young resigned from GM in the mid-1970s and moved to Colorado, where owned and operated a small regional airport. He retired to New Mexico and passed away in 2012.

Tom Goad stayed with GM, was promoted to chief of special vehicles at the Pontiac Motor Division and retired in 1975. He lives in Birmingham, Michigan in the house he and his wife built in 1964.

Bob Tullius, a well-known and very talented driver, completed his remarkable racing career in 1986 but continued to own and manage his renowned Group 44 racing team very successfully until 1990 when he ceased racing operations. He now lives in Sebring, Florida and cares for countless feral cats a few hundred yards from the race track with a hangar full of his impressive collection of museum-quality classic race cars and aircraft.

Milt Minter continued his colorful and very successful career as a race car driver, particularly in Porsches. He retired to Sanger, California and passed away in 2004. He is widely and fondly remembered as a gifted driver throughout the American racing community.

CPSIA information can be obtained
at www.ICGtesting.com
Printed in the USA
BVOW08s1648230617
487711BV00003B/194/P